D1556143

Doctors' Commons

Doctor Criminale

I. The Court Room, from R. Ackermann, *Microcosm of London*, 1808

Doctors' Commons

A History of the College of
Advocates and Doctors of Law

G. D. SQUIBB

CLARENDON PRESS · OXFORD
1977

Oxford University Press, Walton Street, Oxford OX2 6DP

OXFORD LONDON GLASGOW NEW YORK
TORONTO MELBOURNE WELLINGTON CAPE TOWN
IBADAN NAIROBI DAR ES SALAAM LUSAKA ADDIS ABABA
KUALA LUMPUR SINGAPORE JAKARTA HONG KONG TOKYO
DELHI BOMBAY CALCUTTA MADRAS KARACHI

British Library Cataloguing in Publication Data

Squibb, George Drewry
   Doctors' Commons
   1. Doctors' Commons – History
   I. Title
   340'.06'24212   KD498   77-30061
   ISBN 0-19-825339-7

*Printed in Great Britain by
Cox & Wyman Ltd,
London, Fakenham and Reading*

PREFACE

The revival in recent years of interest in the history of the courts in which the English civilians practised seems to make it opportune to produce a history of the Society, commonly known as Doctors' Commons, which was for most practising civilians the counterpart of the common lawyers' Inns of Court. The name of Doctors' Commons came to be applied also to the various courts in which the members of the Society practised, as in *The last will and testament of Doctors Commons*, published in 1641, which was a satirical attack on the ecclesiastical courts. Finally, it was extended topographically to an indefinite area in the vicinity of Great Knightrider Street in which the officers of the courts and the proctors had their offices. This book is concerned only with the Society and its members.

Hitherto the only work entirely devoted to the subject has been Dr. Charles Coote's *Lives of Eminent English Civilians*, published anonymously in 1804, which contains a list of most of the advocates who joined Doctors' Commons between 1512 and 1803. By ignoring all the other members Coote gave an entirely false impression of the Society in its early days. His work has been frequently cited for want of anything better, but reliance upon it has been the cause of many errors in and omissions from standard biographical works, particularly Foster's *Alumni Oxonienses*, Venn's *Alumni Cantabrigienses*, and the *Dictionary of National Biography*. Coote used only one of the surviving records of the Society and that in a misleading manner, which has given rise to misapprehension both as to the nature of the document itself and as to the light which it throws on the foundation of the Society.

The title of William Senior's *Doctors' Commons and the Old Court of Admiralty*, published in 1922, raises expectations which the book itself does not satisfy. Out of 112 pages only twenty-five are devoted to a chapter entitled 'The Rise of the College of Advocates', and in this chapter only seven pages actually deal with the Society. Since the publication of Senior's work the only substantial contribution towards a history of Doctors' Commons has been a series of papers dealing mainly with the topographical aspect of the matter, published in the *London Topographical Record* in 1931.

Some readers may consider that Appendix III occupies a disproportionate amount of space. Its justification is that no society can be understood without some knowledge of the kind of people who have joined it and the part they have played in its affairs. The particulars set out in the Appendix and its chronological arrangement are intended to show for each member of Doctors' Commons what Andrew Clark described in his *Register of the University of Oxford*[1] as 'the type and mould of the men he was brought into contact with. . . . , the counties they came from, the social stratum in which they had their origin, their average age, and the like', together with the length of his membership and the extent to which he entered into the life of the Society, either as an office-holder or as a benefactor.

The note on p. xiv that county locations are given as they were at the relevant times before the changes made by modern legislation does not reflect an indolent unwillingness to take the trouble to ascertain in which new county an ancient parish is now to be found. To state the present counties would in some cases be to falsify the information about a member to be derived from his county of origin in times when a man would talk of his county as his 'country', and when that county could influence not only his choice of university or college, but also his political and religious allegiances. To describe Dr. William Smythe as a native of the county of Humberside would be both anachronistic and meaningless: he was a Lincolnshireman and ought still to be so regarded. Dr. Harwood was a native of Berkshire and

[1] ii, pt i (O.H.S. x, 1887), p. xiv.

Dr. Loveday of Oxfordshire, but Dr. Harwood's birthplace is now in Oxfordshire and Dr. Loveday's in Berkshire.

In the course of my work I have had reason to be grateful to the owners and custodians of the manuscripts on which it is founded and in particular to the staffs of the Lambeth Palace Library and the Public Record Office. I am also grateful to Mr. C. W. Crawley of Trinity Hall and Mr. J. S. G. Simmons of All Souls College for much kindness and hospitality when working on manuscripts in their respective college libraries, and to Mrs. Margaret Hogan for typing from my often difficult manuscript. Acknowledgements and thanks are due to the following for permission to reproduce illustrations: The Archbishop of Canterbury and the Trustees of the Lambeth Palace Library (plate II); the London Topographical Society (plate III); and the Trustees of the British Library (plates IV and V). Finally, I should like to record that the Delegates of the Clarendon Press have received no subvention for the publication of this work.

G.D.S.

Cerne Abbas
June 1977

CONTENTS

LIST OF PLATES

ABBREVIATIONS

A	subscription as an advocate
Act Books	*Index to the Act Books of the Archbishops of Canterbury, 1663–1859* (British Record Soc. lv, 1929; lxiii, 1938)
adm. Arches	admitted to practise in the Court of Arches as an advocate
admon	letters of administration
Al. Ox.	J. Foster, *Alumni Oxonienses* (London, 1887–8; Oxford, 1888–92)
Anglesey Ped.	J. E. Griffith, *Pedigrees of Angelsey and Carnarvonshire Families* (Horncastle, 1914)
arm. fil.	son of an esquire (in Oxford University matriculation register)
Ashm.	Ashmolean MS.
Ath. Oxon.	A. Wood, *Athenae Oxonienses* (3rd ed.)
B. & C.	Barnewall and Creswell's Reports 1822–30
B.L.	British Library
B.R.U.C.	A. B. Emden, *Biographical Register of the University of Cambridge* (Cambridge, 1963)
B.R.U.O. i–iii	A. B. Emden, *Biographical Register of the University of Oxford to A.D. 1500* (Oxford, 1957–9)
B.R.U.O. iv	A. B. Emden, *Biographical Register of the University of Oxford A.D. 1501 to 1540* (Oxford, 1974)
barr.	barrister
Bodl.	Bodleian Library
Borthwick Inst.	Borthwick Institute of Historical Research, York
Bro. P.C.	J. Brown's Cases in Parliament, 1702–1800
Browne Willis	B. Willis, *Survey of the Cathedrals* (1727)
bur.	buried (unless otherwise stated, at St. Benet Paul's Wharf, London)
C	subscription as a contributor
C. & Y. Soc.	Canterbury and York Society

C.B.	Commons Book (L.P.L., DC 25)
C.P.R.	*Calendar of Patent Rolls*
C.S.P.D.	*Calendar of State Papers, Domestic*
Chambers	D. S. Chambers, *Faculty Office Registers 1534–1549* (Oxford, 1966)
Churchill	I. J. Churchill, *Canterbury Administration*
Coll. Top. & Gen.	*Collectanea Topographica & Genealogica*
Coot.	C. Coote, *Sketches of the . . . English Civilians*
D.N.B.	*Dictionary of National Biography*
D.W.B.	*Dictionary of Welsh Biography*
E.H.R.	*English Historical Review*
East	East's Reports, 1800–12
G.I.	Gray's Inn
gen. fil.	son of a gentleman (in Oxford University matriculation register)
Grantees	*Grantees of Arms* (Harl. Soc. lxvi, 1915)
Harl. Soc.	Harleian Society
Hay	D. Hay, 'Pietro Griffo, An Italian in England 1506–1512', in *Italian Studies*, ii, 1938.
Hemp	W. J. Hemp, 'Coats of Arms from "Doctors' Commons"', in 26 *Antiquaries Journal*
Hist. MSS. Comm.	*Historical Manuscripts Commission*
I.p.m. for London	*Inquisitiones post mortem for the City of London* (British Record Soc. xxxvi, 1908)
I.T.	Inner Temple
Incep. C.L.	Inceptor in Civil Law
Knights	*Le Neve's Pedigrees of Knights* (Harl. Soc. viii, 1873)
L. & P. *Hen. VIII*	*Calendar of Letters and Papers Foreign and Domestic, Henry VIII* (1862–1932)
L.B.	Long Book (P.R.O., PRO 30/26/8)
L.I.	Lincoln's Inn
L.J. Ecc.	Law Journal Reports, Ecclesiastical
L.P.L.	Lambeth Palace Library
L.Q.R.	*Law Quarterly Review*
L.T.R.	*London Topographical Record*
Le Neve	J. Le Neve, *Fasti Ecclesiae Anglicanae 1300–1541* (3rd ed.) (1962–7)
Le Neve 1541–1857	J. Le Neve, *Fasti Ecclesiae Anglicanae 1541–1857* (3rd ed.) (1969–)

Levack	B. P. Levack, *Civil Lawyers in England 1603–1641*
Lic. C.L.	Licentiate in Civil Law
Lincs. Ped.	*Lincolnshire Pedigrees* (Harl. Soc. li, 1903)
London Inhabitants	*London Inhabitants within the Walls, 1695* (London Record Soc. ii, 1966)
M.B.	Minute Book (L.P.L., DC 2)
M.I.	monumental inscription (unless otherwise stated, at St. Benet Paul's Wharf, London)
M.T.	Middle Temple
Marchant	R. A. Marchant, *The Church under the Law* (Cambridge, 1969)
Miege	G. Miege, *Present State of Great Britain*
Misc. Gen. et Her.	*Miscellanea Genealogica et Heraldica*
Newcourt	R. Newcourt, *Repertorium Ecclesiasticum Parochiale Londinense* (London, 1710)
O. Cist.	Cistercian monk
O. Clun.	Cluniac monk
O.F.M.	Order of Friars Minor (Franciscan or Grey Friars)
O.S.A.	Augustinian canon
O.S.B.	Benedictine monk
O.S.J. Jer.	Order of St. John of Jerusalem
Ormerod	G. Ormerod, *History of the County Palatine and City of Chester* (2nd ed., 1875–82)
P.C.C.	Prerogative Court of Canterbury
P.R.O.	Public Record Office
Parks	G. B. Parks, *The English Traveller in Italy* (Rome, 1954)
pleb. fil.	son of a man below the rank of a gentleman (in Oxford University matriculation register)
Regg. Wolsey etc.	*Register of Thomas Wolsey*[etc.] (Somerset Record Soc. lv, 1940)
S.B.	Subscription Book (L.P.L., DC 1)
St. Paul's	W. Dugdale, *History of St. Paul's Cathedral*
stud.	student
V.C.C.	Vice-Chancellor's Court
V.C.H.	*Victoria County History*
Vis. Berks.	*Four Visitations of Berkshire* (Harl. Soc. lvi, 1907)

Vis. Cambs.	*Visitations of Cambridgeshire 1575 and 1619* (Harl. Soc. xli, 1897)
Vis. Dorset	*Visitation of the County of Dorset . . . 1623* (Harl. Soc. xx, 1885)
Vis. Essex	*Visitations of Essex* (Harl. Soc. xiii, xiv, 1878)
Vis. Kent	*Visitation of Kent . . . 1619–1621* (Harl. Soc. clii, 1898)
Vis. Leics.	*Visitation of the County of Leicester . . . 1619* (Harl. Soc. ii, 1870)
Vis. London 1568	*Visitation of London 1568* (Harl. Soc. cix, cx, 1963)
Vis. London 1633	*Visitation of London . . . 1633* (Harl. Soc. xv, 1880; xvii, 1883)
Vis. Norfolk	*Visitation of Norfolk . . . 1664* (Harl. Soc. lxxxv, 1933; lxxxvi, 1934)
Vis. Salop	*Visitation of Shropshire . . . 1623* (Harl. Soc. xxviii, xxix, 1889)
Vis. Somerset	*Visitation of the County of Somerset . . . 1623* (Harl. Soc. xi, 1876)
Vis. Sussex	*Visitations of the County of Sussex . . . 1530 . . . 1633–4* (Harl. Soc. liii, 1905)
Vis. Warwick	*Visitation of the County of Warwick . . . 1619* (Harl. Soc. xii, 1877).
Vis. Wilts.	*Wiltshire Visitation Pedigrees 1623* (Harl. Soc. cv, cvi, 1954)
Weaver	F. W. Weaver, *Somerset Incumbents* (Bristol, 1889)
Wood, *Colleges and Halls*	A. Wood, *History and Antiquities of the Colleges and Halls in the University of Oxford* (ed. J. Gutch Oxford, 1786)
Wotton	T. Wotton, *English Baronetage* (1741 ed.)

NOTE ON DATES AND TOPOGRAPHY

Dates between 1 January and 25 March down to 1752 are given as if the year had begun on 1 January.

County locations are given as they were at the relevant times before the changes made by modern legislation.

TABLE OF STATUTES

I

THE EARLY YEARS

THE common law was not studied in either of the ancient English Universities until William Blackstone delivered his first course of lectures at Oxford in 1758, and it could not be offered as a degree subject until the introduction of the School of Law and Modern History at Oxford in 1850. In earlier times academic lawyers devoted themselves solely to the civil law and, until its study was forbidden in 1535, to the canon law. Usually both studies went together, for it was said: 'Canonista sine legibus parum valet legista sine canonibus nihil.'[1]

Although they had no place in the common-law courts, there was no lack of work for these academic lawyers in the unreformed Church. The ecclesiastical legal system had exclusive jurisdiction over the numerous disputes between churchmen relating to ecclesiastical property and income, and ecclesiastical rights and jurisdiction, and over the affairs of laymen relating to marriage, legitimacy, and wills. Even more important than this large field of litigation was the administrative system of the Church, whose complexities required a sound knowledge of law.

Although at any one time many of the clergy were devoting themselves to legal work either as administrators or as practitioners, these men did not form what would now be regarded as a separate legal profession. They looked for advancement not only in the legal sphere, but in the Church at large. They were not all in holy orders, but all were in the minor orders which were sufficient qualification for the holding of ecclesiastical benefices. Legal training, even without legal practice, could set a man on the path to the

---

[1]P. Hughes, *The Reformation in England* (1950), p. 73.

highest preferment. Of the two archbishops and thirteen diocesan bishops in office in England and Wales in 1500 who are known to have had degrees, ten had degrees in canon law or civil law or both. Of the seven cathedral deans with degrees in office in the same year, four had degrees in law. Of fifty-eight archdeacons, thirty had such degrees.

The clergy who specialized in legal practice fell into two groups. There were the advocates who, like the common-law barristers, conducted cases in court, and there were the proctors, whose functions were similar to those of the attorneys in the common-law courts. The advocates usually held doctors' degrees, while the proctors, if they had degrees at all, did not normally proceed beyond the baccalaureate. In the century before the Reformation, advocates were usually men who had been admitted by mandate of the Archbishop of Canterbury to practise in the Court of Arches, though there were some who practised in other courts, in particular those at York, without being advocates of the Court of Arches.[1]

While there was not a diocese without its complement of clergy learned in the law, the greatest concentration of ecclesiastical lawyers was in the City of London. In addition to those who congregated around St. Paul's in the administrative service of the Bishop of London and of the Dean and Chapter, practitioners were attracted to the same neighbourhood by the Archbishop of Canterbury's Court of Arches, which sat in the Church of St. Mary-le-Bow, and his Prerogative Court for the probate of wills, which had its office in Ivy Lane and which frequently, though not invariably, sat in St. Paul's. With so many men with common interests gathered together in more or less daily contact, it is not surprising that they should form themselves into some sort of a society for their mutual benefit.

It may be that the first step towards the foundation of such

[1]For the York advocates see R. A. Marchant, pp. 247–51. Some of the York advocates were also advocates of the Court of Arches.

a society is to be found in the bequest, by Thomas Kent, D.Cn. and C.L., sometime Clerk of the Council, who died in 1469, of twenty-eight named books of civil and canon law to form a library for the use of the Official, Dean, examiners, advocates, and proctors of the Court of Canterbury and other doctors or bachelors of the canon or civil law. These books were to be kept in a building near to St. Paul's, failing which they were to go to All Souls College, Oxford, to be kept in the college library.[1] While there is no direct evidence that this building was ever provided, the fact that there is no record of the transfer of the books to All Souls indicates that effect was given to Kent's primary wish.[2] Although it may be no more than a coincidence, it is at least worthy of remark that Kent's description of those who were to use his books exactly fitted the membership of Doctors' Commons revealed by the later records. It cannot, however, be claimed that Kent was benefiting an existing society, for Richard Blodwell, the first President of Doctors' Commons, was only a boy when Kent died, but it may well be that Kent's library was a factor in bringing about a closer association of those who used it.

It is tempting to see precedents for such an association in the societies in which the common lawyers practising in London found it convenient to group themselves for board and lodging, but so to do is probably to be unduly influenced by the fact that the society which the ecclesiastical lawyers founded ultimately fulfilled for its members the functions of an Inn of Court. The Inns of Court were societies of professional laymen. The ecclesiastical lawyers, although specially learned in their particular field, were clerics whose careers lay in the broader context of the Church as a whole. If they needed a precedent for the formation of their society, they would be more likely to see it in some other clerical society.

[1]P.C.C. 26 Godyn. The list of books set out in Kent's will is printed in *B.R.U.O.* ii. 1038.

[2]N. R. Ker, *Records of All Souls College Library* (Oxford Bibliographical Soc. N.S. xvi, 1971), p, 123.

There was at least one such society in the City of London. On the west side of Dowgate there was a college of priests which, according to John Stow, the sixteenth-century historian of London, was 'a house well furnished with Brasse, Pewter, Naperie, Plate, etc. besides a faire Librarie well stored with bookes, all which of old time was given to a number of Priestes that should keep commons there'.[1]

This college of priests was called Jesus Commons. It had been dissolved and its house turned into tenements by the time that Stow wrote, but it survived long enough to have been the exemplar of a college of ecclesiastical lawyers, most of whom were doctors of law, and to have provided the inspiration of the colloquial name of Doctors' Commons.

There is no direct evidence as to the foundation of Doctors' Commons. The generally accepted account of the early history of the Society is based upon hearsay. It goes back no farther than 1615, when Sir George Buc's *The Third Vniuersitie of England* was published as an appendix to John Stow's *Annales*.[2] Buc regarded London as one of the English universities and Doctors' Commons, then in Mountjoy House, in Knightrider Street, as one of its colleges. Buc said no more of the early history of Doctors' Commons than that before the civilians took Mountjoy House in 1567, they were lodged in Paternoster Row in a house which had formerly been a house for a prebendary residentiary of St. Paul's.

There was also a tradition that the advocates of the Court of Arches 'united themselves together in a Collegiate manner' in a small house in Paternoster Row in the reign of Henry VII, though the first written account of that tradition seems to be no older than the middle of the eighteenth century, when it appeared in 'A Summary Account of the Society of Doctors' Commons' by Dr. Andrew Coltee

---

[1] J. Stow, *Survey of London* (ed. C. L. Kingsford) (Oxford, 1908), i.231.
[2] J. Stow, *Annales* (1631), p. 1077. Buc's appendix was first published with the 1615 edition of Stow's work.

Ducarel.[1] Historians in the present century have been more precise in their dating. The date generally accepted for the foundation of the Society is 1511,[2] though some have put it as late as the 1560s,[3] while one anonymous author has boldly stated that Doctors' Commons dated from 'a period not long after the Norman Conquest'.[4] The available evidence, however, shows that the Society was established well before 1511.

The general acceptance of 1511 as the date of the foundation has been due to misunderstanding of the Society's oldest surviving record, the Subscription Book, caused by failure to consult the original document, coupled with failure to make use of the external evidence on the subject. The external evidence is the earlier. It consists of some contemporary references to the Society during its early years in the accounts of the proctors of the University of Cambridge. Although these accounts have been available in print for over seventy years, their significance does not seem to have been noticed by previous writers on Doctors' Commons.

Immediately after Christmas 1495, John Dowman, the Vice-Chancellor of Cambridge University, James Denton, the Senior Proctor, and a Master of Arts named Suckling

[1] There are manuscript versions of Ducarel's 'Summary Account' in the libraries of the Law Society, Lambeth Palace (MS. 958), All Souls College, Oxford (MS. 325), and the Guildhall (MS. 1353). The Law Society version was printed in 15 *L.T.R.* 21–31. When repeating the tradition, Dr. Charles Coote in his *Sketches of the . . . English Civilians* (1804), p. ii, erroneously advanced the date to 'about the beginning of the reign of the eighth Henry'.

[2] E. Nys, *Le Droit Romain, le Droit des Gens et le Collège des Docteurs en Droit Civil* (Brussels, 1910), p. 114; W. S. Holdsworth, *History of English Law*, iv (3rd ed., 1945), 235; I. J. Churchill, i.422 n. A.; G. Dickens, *The English Reformation* (1964), p. 250; G. N. Clark, *A History of the Royal College of Physicians* (Oxford, 1964), i.62; G. R. Elton, *The Tudor Constitution* (Cambridge, 1968), p. 152; and Levack, p. 19. J. K. McConica, *English Humanists and Reformation Politics* (Oxford, 1965), p. 52 gives the date as 1509. E. Jeffries Davis, 'Doctors' Commons, its Title and Topography', 15 *L.T.R.* 38 has 'apparently founded before 1509'. W. Senior, *Doctors' Commons and the Old Court of Admiralty* (1923), p. 73 and 'The Rise of the College of Advocates', 26 *L.Q.R.* (1931) 195 has '1511 or a few years earlier', while H. E. Malden, *Trinity Hall* (1902), p. 103 has 'not later than November 1511'.

[3] J. Simon, *Education and Society in Tudor England* (Cambridge, 1966), p. 257 n. (1567); A. E. Sutherland, *The Law at Harvard* (Cambridge, Mass., 1967), p. 9 (1561).

[4] *Thomas Hutchinson Tristram: A Memoir* (1916), p. 13.

went to London on business relating to a controversy between the University and the townsmen of Cambridge. The University party put up at the sign of the George in Fleet Street, but went out for a number of meals. In the record of their expenses on the second Friday of their visit, i.e. 8 January 1496,[1] is the following item:

> In iantaculo apud pater noster row
> cum doctoribus de arcubus   xxijd[2]

This is the earliest specific reference to Doctors' Commons so far discovered, although it may be slightly anachronistic to refer to the Society by that name at so early a date.[3]

In the account of the party's expenses a fortnight later there appears the entry:

> Pro Jantaculo apud pater noster row   xvjd.[4]

Although less explicit, this presumably refers to another breakfast at the Commons. The party definitely went there again on another visit to London later in 1496, when the expense account contains the entry:

> Item pro vino allato doctoribus de
> arcubus in pater noster row   xijd.[5]

Since there is evidence of a somewhat later date that strangers were allowed to take meals in Doctors' Commons,[6] it is not possible to deduce from the fact that the refreshment was paid for on each occasion that at least one of the Cambridge party was a member. Nevertheless, Denton's name is the thirteenth in the earliest list of members,[7] so it is therefore likely that he was the host.

While these entries in the Cambridge accounts provide the earliest unequivocal evidence for the existence of Doctors'

---

[1]Christmas Day in 1495 was a Friday.
[2]M. Bateson (ed.), *Grace Book B* (Cambridge, 1903), i.84.
[3]The name 'Doctors' Commons' was in use by 1532, see p. 56 *post*.
[4]*Grace Book B*, i.85.
[5]Ibid., i.88.
[6]See p. 77 *post*.
[7]See p. 122 *post*.

Commons so far discovered, it is possible that there is evidence in those accounts for an even earlier *terminus a quo* for the foundation of the Society. In 1494 a representative of the University visited London and included among his expenses:

pro cena apud hospicium college mei   vijd. ob.[1]

There does not appear to have been at that time any institution other than Doctors' Commons in London which would answer to the description of 'hospicium college mei' when used by an official of the University of Cambridge.

It is unlikely that the Society had been founded long before the visit in 1494. Unfortunately there is no record of when Richard Blodwell, who is described as the first President and must therefore have been one of the original members, took his doctorate. All that can be said is that he had not proceeded beyond his bachelor's degrees in civil and canon law in the autumn of 1484[2] and that he was a doctor by 1495.[3]

Turning from the external evidence of the Cambridge Grace Book to the Society's own record, it is necessary to describe the document and to establish its true nature before considering what light it can throw on the early days of Doctors' Commons. It is now preserved in the library of Lambeth Palace.[4] It contains 138 parchment folios $16\frac{1}{2}''\times$ $12''$, numbered consecutively in the rop right-hand corner of the recto of each folio. It is bound in wooden boards covered with tooled leather, the spine being modern. It was designed to be kept on a desk or table, each side of the binding having brass corners and a central boss.

Although used by Thomas Oughton in the introduction to his *Ordo Judiciorum*, published in 1728, and by Dr. Ducarel in his 'Summary Account of the Society of Doctors'

[1] *Grace Book B*, i.68. The earlier part of this account containing the name of the accountant is missing.
[2] *Cal. Papal Registers*, xiv. 320.
[3] *B.R.U.O.* i.203.
[4] L.P.L., DC1 (hereafter referred to as S.B.).

Commons', which remained in manuscript until 1931,[1] the Subscription Book seems never to have received the detailed examination which is necessary to ascertain the nature of the book itself, and so to draw from it the evidence which it contains relating to the early history of the Society. Indeed, it was long thought to have disappeared and so was not consulted by the authors of the papers on Doctors' Commons published by the London Topographical Society in 1931.[2] This is pre-eminently a case in which it is necessary to go to the original manuscript to examine what Maitland called 'the anatomy of the book'.[3] It is only by seeing the way in which the scribe set about his work that its purpose and the manner in which it was intended to be used can be appreciated. As will appear, the spaces left blank are as important as those filled with writing.

As recorded in the lengthy laudatory dedication on f.4, the volume was presented to 'the most excellent and most distinguished College of Doctors and Co-Advocates of the Metropolitan See of Canterbury' on 12 November 1511 by a member, Robert Spenser, as a memorial of the generosity and brotherly affection of the annual subscribers and other contributors to the funds of the Society.[4] It remained in use until the last member was admitted in 1855. Although included in the auctioneer's catalogue of the Society's library in April 1861, it was withdrawn from the sale,[5] and the surviving members of the Society resolved that it should

[1] Printed in 15 *L.T.R.* 21–31.

[2] 15 *L.T.R.* 4–86.

[3] F. W. Maitland, *Domesday Book and Beyond* (1897), p. 178.

[4] The Latin text of the dedication is printed in T. Oughton, *Ordo Judiciorum* (1728), i, pp. ii–iii. There is a translation in J. T. Law, *Forms of Ecclesiastical Law* (1831), p. iii. Spenser was described in the dedication as 'the least among the doctors of civil and canon law', and he was described as a doctor in the place allotted for his subscription, but when he came to make his subscription he carefully altered 'doctor' to 'scholar' (S.B., f.11ᵛ). A similar amendment of the dedication indicates that it was not composed by Spenser himself. The dedication has also been amended by the obliteration of the pontifical year. This latter amendment was probably made in 1535, when the name of the Pope was ordered to be erased from service books used in England. (G. R. Elton, *Policy and Police* (Cambridge, 1972), 236–8, 291, 364.)

[5] It was lot no. 2449. There is a transcript of the catalogue entry in E. Jeffries Davis, 'Doctors' Commons, its Title and Topography', 15 *L.T.R.* 38.

be deposited for safe custody in the Lambeth Palace Library.[1] It appears from letters now inserted in the book that it was not delivered until July 1869, when Sir Travers Twiss sent it to Archbishop Tait.[2] The book has been referred to in several ways. In a resolution passed on 2 May 1632 it was called 'the blacke booke'.[3] It was referred to as the 'Subscription Book' in a minute of 13 July 1723.[4] In an inventory of documents made about 1725 it was 'The Large Vellum Leav'd Book',[5] but in 1728 it was called the 'Treasurer's Book' in Thomas Oughton's *Ordo Judiciorum*,[6] and as such it was referred to by Dr. Ducarel in his 'Summary Account'. However, Dr. Coote in his *Sketches of the Lives and Characters of Eminent English Civilians*, published in 1804, described the book as 'the register of the Society'.[7] It was called 'the Original Register' in the 1861 sale catalogue,[8] a description which was adopted by the late Miss Jeffries Davis in her paper on Doctors' Commons. This nomenclature was also adopted by the binder who lettered the modern spine of the volume.

That neither 'Treasurer's Book' nor 'Register' is an appropriate name is made clear by an examination of the book. After writing the dedicatory inscription and a copy of the rules of the Society, the scribe laid out twenty-two pages (ff.4ᵛ.–15ᵛ.) by writing on the left-hand side of each page the names and short descriptions (usually by reference to their

[1]L.P.L., DC2 (hereafter referred as M.B.), 10 July 1865.

[2]It is stated by Jeffries Davis, loc. cit., that the volume was not accessible, but it would seem that its location was not known to the author. C. Sturge, *Cuthbert Tunstall* (1938), p. 17, states that it was 'in private ownership' in January 1938.

[3]S.B., f.79. Since the binding appears to date from the gift of the book in 1511 and is not black, it would seem that the expression 'black book' had become a generic term for any important book of record: cf. the Black Book of the Exchequer, the Black Book of the Admiralty and the Black Book of Lincoln's Inn. Similarly the nickname 'Domesday' was applied to other records of a specially authoritative kind (V. H. Galbraith, *Domesday Book* (Oxford, 1974), p. 122).

[4]L.B., f. 243.

[5]L.P.L., DC13.

[6]Vol. i, p. iii n.

[7]Coote, p. 9. Coote added to the confusion by applying the name of 'the treasurer's book' to the Long Book (ibid., p. 51 n.).

[8]See p. 8, n. 5 *ante*.

degrees) of the members, five to a page, leaving the rest of the page blank for each named person to insert in the appropriate space, his promise to pay his annual contribution to the funds of the Society in some such words as those used by Richard Blodwell in the first entry:

> Ego promitto durante vita mea naturali solvere singulis annis collegio doctorum et advocatorum curie de archubus . . . vj*s* vij*d*.[1]

There was, however, no standard formula, the wording being apparently left to the member concerned. Only about a third of these undertakings were inserted.

The scribe of folios 4ᵛ. to 15ᵛ. of the Subscription Book was probably on the staff of one of the ecclesiastical courts, for laying out the book in this manner was an adaptation of the usual canon-law practice of writing the title of each case in a court act-book in advance of a session, and leaving a space in which to enter the record of the action taken in court.[2] After folio 15ᵛ. he left seventy-eight folios blank for future use and then at the head of folio 93 he wrote 'Quo ordine doctores admittuntur in archubus'. The remaining forty-four folios he left blank, the reason for the inequality between the seventy-eight and forty-four blank folios no doubt being that there was then a substantial proportion of members who were not advocates and that he expected that this would continue to be the case, as it in fact did, for many years.

From 1512 onwards there were inserted in the first group of blank folios the names of all members as they were admitted, with their promises to pay their annual contributions, and in the second group of blank folios the names of the new members who were advocates with a record of the payment of the advocates' entrance fee. As in the case of the promises to pay the annual contributions, there was no

[1]See Plate II.
[2]As to this practice, see R. H. Helmholz, *Marriage Litigation in Medieval England* (Cambridge, 1974), p. 8. The same practice was followed in the civil-law courts, but not in the common-law courts.

II. The Subscription Book, f. 4v

standard formula, but ultimately a common form came to be adopted. For the annual contribution this was:

Ego A.B., e Coll. C.,[1] promitto me soliturum Societati Advocatorum de Arcubus Londini singulis annis quoad vixero sex solidos et octo denarios admissus in numerum Commensalium die   A.D.

A.B.

The additional subscription by the advocates became standardized in the form:

Ego A.B., e Coll. C., admissus fui in commensalem Dominorum Advocatorum de Arcubus Londini et solvi viginti libras[2] pro introitu juxta decretum predictum[3]   die   A.D.

A.B.

Although by copying the names a list of the members can be obtained, the book was not a register, nor was it an account of money received, but a collection of legally enforceable obligations. Thus on 11 October 1560 the book was exhibited in the Court of Chancery in a suit against the executors of John Blythe of Lichfield for contributions due to the Society, whereupon process was obtained by order of the Lord Keeper, Sir Nicholas Bacon.[4] From the Society's point of view, the really important part of each entry was not the name at the beginning, but the signature at the end. In this respect the book is similar to the diocesan subscription registers, which contain the recognition of the Royal Supremacy, the promise to use the Book of Common Prayer, and the adhesion to the Thirty-nine Articles required of ordinands and beneficed clergymen.[5] The book can therefore more appropriately be called the 'Subscription Book'

---

[1]The member's college is not stated before 1750.

[2]The entrance fee was increased from £1 to £6.13s.4d. in 1579, then doubled to £13.6s.8d. in 1590, and finally raised to £20 in 1689; See p. 43 *post*.

[3]This refers to the rules entered at ff.2ᵛ,3: see p. 9 *ante*.

[4]S.B., f.1.

[5]As to subscription registers, see D. M. Owen, *The Records of the Established Church in England* (1970), pp. 25–6.

than either the 'Treasurer's Book' or the 'Register'. The value of each entry was limited to the lifetime of the member who made it. As each in due course ceased to have effect it was marked 'mortuus' or 'obiit' or sometimes merely 'm.' or 'ob.'. It would have been useful to the historian if the date of death had been added, but all that was required for practical purposes was the statement that the member was dead.[1]

It may seem pedantic to seek an accurate way of referring to this ancient volume, but since the previous nomenclature has not only been for the most part misleading, but lacking in consistency, it is worth while, even at this late stage in its history, to follow the apparently unique precedent of 1723 and to refer to it again in a manner which properly describes it.[2]

The mistaken impression that the Subscription Book is a register is assisted by a transcript of the names in the first part of the book made by Dr. Ducarel, which by closing up the names into a continuous list with dates, conceals the true nature of the original record.[3] Later Ducarel made a further copy of his list with copious annotations, many amounting to miniature biographies, which concealed the character of his source even more effectively.[4] Dr. Coote's *Lives of Eminent English Civilians* is equally misleading, for he described the contents of the Subscription Book as two 'lists, one containing the names of mere *commensales* and honorary members, as well as of pleaders and surrogates', the other 'comprehending only professed advocates'.[5]

Although Dr. Coote used the advocates' subscriptions, which he termed 'the second list', as the basis of his work, it

---

[1]The Scriveners' Company kept a book of similar undertakings by its members, which were marked 'mort.' or 'mortuus' as they were discharged by death: see F. W. Steer (ed.), *Scriveners' Company Common Paper 1357–1628* (London Record Soc. iv, 1968), plates I, II, III.

[2]This also avoids the confusion introduced into the nomenclature by Coote and followed by Levack, p. 283, where the book is named 'Register of Doctors' Commons' and the Long Book (as to which see p. 110 *post*) is named 'Treasurer's Book of Doctors' Commons'.

[3]Guildhall MS. 1353.

[4]All Souls Coll., MS. 325.

[5]Coote, p. 9.

is apparent that he did not do this consistently. When dealing with the period from 1557 to 1579 he also used the contributors' subscriptions, picking out the names of those who held doctors' degrees in law. The result of this was that he included in his list of advocates four members (Drs. Lougher, Oxenbregg, Wendon, and Worley) who were not advocates.[1] On the other hand, by using the contributors' subscriptions he accidentally succeeded in including two advocates (Drs. Mowse and Langforde) who did not subscribe as such, and so would have been omitted if he had used only the advocates' subscriptions.

To his list Dr. Coote added an index, which is of limited value, since it includes only the names to which he annexed 'biographical Sketches, characteristic *Memoranda*, or other Notices'. This index thus contains only 235 of the 767 members named in the subscriptions. As a result of its selective character, those not included in the index are not recorded as advocates in Foster's *Alumni Oxonienses*.[2] The names of the advocates admitted after 1803 and those of the subscribers who were not advocates have never before been printed. Not only has Coote's self-imposed limitation given a very unbalanced impression of the composition of the membership in the early days of the Society, but it was the fact that his list of advocates was taken from the part of the record which contains no date earlier than February 1512, which led to the belief that Doctors' Commons was founded in 1511.[3] Even without the external evidence afforded by the fifteenth-century Cambridge proctors' accounts,[4] the internal evidence of the names which were inserted in the first part of the record against the spaces left for the subscriptions

---

[1]Lougher was admitted an advocate several years after subscribing as a contributor: see p. 156 *post*.

[2]The names of the advocates to 1803 were reprinted from Coote's work in Nys, *Le Droit Romain le Droit des Gens et le Collège des Docteurs en Droit Civil*, pp. 140–55. This work has no index and, of course, repeats Coote's errors and omissions. It is of little value as a history of Doctors' Commons, for thirteen of the twenty-one pages in the chapter relating to the topic consist of an account of the courts in which the civilians practised.

[3]See p. 5 *ante*.   [4]See p. 6 *ante*.

would have shown that the foundation was much earlier than the generally accepted date of 1511.

Apart from writing a few notes on f.128 in 1526 and 1528, the officer responsible for the entries in the Subscription Book kept to the original plan until 1560, when he began to enter on blank folios memoranda and copies of documents relating to the Society. These were entered on folios chosen at random. By 1594 this practice had become so well established that it was ordered that the terms on which some building work was to be done should be written in 'our Booke where other our Actes and decrees are usuallie sett downe and descrybed'.[1] The last entry of this nature was made in 1681, after which it became the practice to make entries of this sort in the Long Book, which then ceased to be used for its original purpose as an account book. While the entries in the Subscription Book contain valuable material, they do not form a continuous record, but are a haphazard collection of separate and disparate items.

Some of this additional material was used by Thomas Oughton in the introduction to his *Ordo Judiciorum*, published in 1728, and by Dr. Ducarel in his 'Summary Account', but it has only been known to later writers through Oughton's and Ducarel's work. The remainder has remained unused, because the Subscription Book was incorrectly thought to be either lost or inaccessible.

Although the names on ff.4ᵛ to 15ᵛ of the Subscription Book were set out with spaces for the subscriptions of all the members of Doctors' Commons, both advocates and others, living in November 1511, it is clear that the scribe was not writing from first-hand knowledge, but was taking his material from some already existing document, for he included the names of some men who were already dead. The will of Edward Lane had been proved on 13 December 1510;[2] William Wynslat had died by June 1510;[3] and Henry Mompesson had been dead for two years, his will

---

[1]S.B., f.92.   [2]P.C.C. 37 Bennett.   [3]B.R.U.O. iii. 2059.

having been proved on 29 November 1509.[1] The list of names in the earlier document down to and including Mompesson's must, therefore, have been drawn up no later than Mompesson's death. If 'Nance' on f.10 can be correctly identified as John Nance, D.Cn. and C.L., whose will was proved on 15 November 1508,[2] a still earlier date for the part down to Nance's name is justified.

An examination of the names of the members believed by the scribe to be alive in 1511 affords some indication of the nature of the document from which he copied the names. There are 113 of them. With one exception, which will be mentioned later, the first nineteen are those of doctors of canon law or civil law or both laws.[3] After them come a bachelor of theology and two other men, who have not been identified. Then there is a group of six proctors, making twenty-eight in all. The remaining eighty-five names are those of an assortment of doctors of law, doctors of theology, bishops and other ecclesiastical dignitaries, heads of religious houses, and proctors, entered according to no discernible classification. The contrast between the classification of the first twenty-eight names and the lack of classification of the following eighty-five appears to indicate that the document consisted of a list of the Society drawn up in order of precedence as at a particular time, to which had been added the names of new members as they joined. The one apparent exception to this pattern is William Shragger, whose name stands in the second place, although he was but a master of arts. The most likely explanation of Shragger's high place seems to be that he was a proctor and that as the senior proctor member he was given the rank of vice-president of the Society.

[1]P.C.C. 23 Bennett. Jeffries Davis states (15 *L.T.R.* 36 n.) that William Walter died on 12 July 1509, but that was the date of Walter's admission, the error being taken from a mistranscription from the Subscription Book by Ducarel in Guildhall MS. 1535, f.14ᵛ, owing to the later insertion of the word 'mortuus' near the date. See p. 12 *ante*.

[2]P.C.C. 9 Bennett.

[3]Two (William Haryngton and Richard Rawson) have no degree stated, but both were in fact doctors of law.

The internal evidence is not sufficient to show precisely when the list of members in order of precedence was drawn up, but the few dates attached to some of the added names appear to indicate a date somewhere near 1505 for the original list. The twenty-eight names in the list cannot, however, be regarded as a complete nominal roll of the Society at that date, for the original document may well have also contained the names of some members who were known to the scribe to have died before he began the engrossment of the Subscription Book in 1511. The twenty-eight names would be those of the members whom he believed to be still alive.

Even if allowance is made for some deaths between *c*.1505 and 1511, it is clear that there was a great increase in the membership during this period. It is also clear that the scope of the membership was considerably widened. It could well have been that the increase in the size of the Society made it desirable to place membership on a more formal footing by requiring the undertakings in the subscriptions.

Of the known members in or about 1505, eighteen were doctors of law and seven were proctors, with only three who cannot be identified as falling into either category. In the absence of any record of those admitted as advocates of the Court of Arches at this period, certainty is not possible, but it seems likely that most of the doctors were also advocates, for the first certain reference to the Society, that in the Cambridge University Grace Book, describes its members as 'doctors of the Arches'.[1] If this description of the Society in 1496 was literally true, the original doctor members cannot have exceeded twelve, that being the number of advocates of the Court of Arches then and for some time afterwards[2] and

---

[1]See p. 6 *ante*.

[2]The statute 21 Hen. VIII, c.13, s.28, excluded from its provisions relating to non-residence on benefices as many of 'the twelve advocates of the arches' as should be spiritual men. The statute was slightly out of date, for the number of advocates had been increased to sixteen by Archbishop Warham in 1528 (*Hist. MSS. Comm.*, 9th Rep., Pt. I, App., p. 1218).

may well have been fewer, for it is certain that at later periods there were times when not all the advocates were members of the Society.[1] While it is possible that the original membership was confined to advocates, the better view seems to be that from the first the membership embraced the wider circle of men concerned with canon law and civil law, who were the objects of Thomas Kent's benefaction.[2] It seems highly unlikely that advocates who had been members from the beginning would have been willing to allow to Shragger precedence before themselves if that had not been part of the original constitution of the Society. Be this as it may, the Subscription Book makes it clear that about 1505 the Society was almost entirely composed of practitioners in the Court of Arches, both advocates and proctors.

By the time that the dedicatory inscription in the Subscription Book came to be composed in the autumn of 1511, the description of the Society had become 'the College of Doctors and Co-advocates of the metropolitan see of Canterbury' (*Doctorum et Coadvocatorum Ecclesiae Christi Cantuaricusis Collegium*),[3] but there was a substantial non-practising element among the members, including many who did not hold degrees in law. Robert Spenser, the donor of the Subscription Book, was one of the non-practising members, and it is stated in the dedication that he made his gift hoping that it might be a memorial of the generosity and brotherly affection of the annual subscribers and other contributors towards the funds of the Society, whereby the memory of their good deeds might be perpetually kept alive and handed down for the approval of posterity.[4] Indeed, the 'annual subscribers and other contributors' then out-numbered the advocates in the Society and were to continue to do so for the next half-century.

[1] See p. 204 *post*.
[2] See p. 3 *ante*.
[3] S.B., f.4.
[4] Translation in Law, *Forms of Ecclesiastical Law*, p. iii., Latin text in Oughton, *Ordo Judiciorum*, i.ii.

The membership entered in 1511 was made up in the following manner:

Doctors of Law		60
Proctors		
(a) Bachelors of Law	3	
(b) Others	7	
		10
Bishops		
(a) Diocesan	4	
(b) Suffragan	1	
		5
Heads of Religious Houses		11
Doctors of Theology		7
Bachelors of Theology		2
Bachelors of Law (other than Proctors)		5
Papal Collectors		2
'Priest'		1
Doctor of Medicine		1
Unclassified		9
		113

Even if allowance is made for members whose deaths were unknown to the scribe, a mere list of the 113 men whom he believed to be members in 1511 would give a misleading impression of the Society at that time. That only a minority of the nominal members took any part in the life of the Society is shown by the fact that about two-thirds of the spaces left for the members' subscriptions were never filled. The obvious inference is that those who did not enter their subscriptions never came to the house in Paternoster Row after the Subscription Book was opened. Those who did enter their subscriptions can be classified as follows:

Doctors of Law	31
Doctors of Theology	4
Doctor of Medicine	1
Proctor	1
Papal Collector	1
'Student of Law'	1
	39

It may be that some of this comparatively small number

of subscribers did not appear at all frequently, but it can at least be said of them that they showed some interest in the Society and that the majority of them were doctors of law.

The distribution of the completed subscriptions also seems to be significant. Of the nineteen most senior members of the Society thirteen (68 per cent) were subscribers, all of them being doctors of law. Of the next ninety-four members only twenty-six (27 per cent) were subscribers, eighteen of them being doctors of law. This indicates that most of the active members were engaged in legal work in London, and that the practice of admitting a substantial proportion of non-practising members, most of whom did not take any part in the life of the Society, began shortly after the compilation of the list of members about 1505.

The extension of the membership to men who were not lawyers started with those who were living and working near to Paternoster Row and could therefore have been regular frequenters of the common table. The first was John Smyth, who, despite his medical degree, was a residentiary canon of St. Paul's. Then came William Bolton, the Prior of St. Bartholomew, Smithfield, and John Colet, Dean of St. Paul's. Not long after Colet's admission Geoffrey Blythe, Bishop of Coventry and Lichfield, was admitted. He was the first of a new kind of non-practising member, one who would have occasion to travel to London from time to time and would find in Doctors' Commons a convenient and congenial club. It must have been particularly convenient when Convocation met in St. Paul's before Cardinal Wolsey changed the venue to the Jerusalem Chamber at Westminster. Blythe's example was soon followed by the Bishops of Llandaff, St. David's, and Exeter, the Abbots of Stratford, Talley, and Battle, and the Priors of Merton, Lewes, Bradenstoke, Bruton, and Ely, together with the Treasurer of Salisbury Cathedral, canons of Lichfield and Wells, and the Archdeacons of Lincoln and Richmond. No doubt the influence of John Colet is to be seen in the admissions of the humanist scholars Polydore Vergil and William Grocyn during the autumn of 1508. A number of these non-practising members did not make their subscriptions in the Subscription Book and must therefore have ceased their active membership by 1511. Nevertheless, the membership of the Society was then no longer confined to practising advocates, but had widened to embrace a number of leading churchmen who found the advocates agreeable companions and their house a convenient meeting place. On the other hand, the admission of proctors seems to have led to little use of their privileges.

Coote realized that the men whose names were recorded in 1511 were a mixture of practitioners and non-practitioners, but he found it impossible to separate them with precision, contenting himself with stating in a footnote the names of twelve members who might have been advocates about this time, which he regarded as the time of the instutition of the Society.[1] Although in the absence of any record of the admission of advocates to practise in the Court of Arches at this period, it is indeed impossible to perform this task of identifying the advocates with precision, it seems not to be too wide an assumption to regard the signatories as being primarily practitioners. It can also be assumed that those members who held judicial office in the courts of the Archbishop of Canterbury had been admitted as advocates earlier in their careers, though it would not be safe to make the same assumption about the holders of judicial office under diocesan bishops, with the exception of the Vicar-General of the Bishop of London, who seems always to have been an advocate.

It is remarkable that of the group of six proctors who were members c.1505 only one completed his subscription, and that none of the three other proctors who had joined by 1511 was a subscriber. The one proctor who did subscribe, Robert Portland, differs from his fellows in being described as 'Dominus', which indicates that he was a beneficed priest.

[1]Coote, p. 10.

In fact he was the Rector of St. Nicholas Acon in the City of London.

Several of the subscriptions have dates earlier than the date on which Robert Spenser presented the book to the Society. These dates, which appear in chronological order, are therefore not the dates of the subscriptions, but the dates of joining the Society. That the object of inserting the dates was not to provide an historical record, but to show the date on which each annual contribution would become payable is indicated by the fact that in two cases (John Smyth and William Bond) the years are not stated. The full dates are 30 September 1508 for the sixtieth subscription, 6 December 1508 for the seventy-fourth,[1] 12 July 1509 for the eighty-fifth,[2] 19 December 1509, for the ninetieth, while the last four are respectively dated 18 May, 20 May, 20 October, and 20 October 1511.

A further indication of the length of membership in 1511 is given by the thirtieth subscription, that of William Bolton, Prior of St. Bartholomew, Smithfield. Bolton became Prior on 27 August 1505, so the succeeding names must be those of members joining after this date. It does not, of course, follow that the members whose subscriptions precede Bolton's joined before 27 August 1505. All that can be said is that they joined before Bolton, who joined on or after 27 August 1505. The twenty-eighth subscription, that of John Smyth, 'medicine professor', is dated 12 May without the year, but it seems probable that the year was 1505.

In the absence of a complete list of advocates it is impossible to say what proportion of the advocates belonged to the Society in its early days. The view that the Society included from the outset almost all of the advocates of the Arches[3] is clearly untenable in the light of the Subscription Book. One of the most noticeable features of the names of

---

[1] That of Robert Spenser, the donor of the book.
[2] That of William Walter, referred to at p. 15, n, 1 *ante*.
[3] 15 *L.T.R.* 39.

the members when the book was started, is the absence of the senior civilians then holding the judicial offices of Official Principal of the Court of Canterbury, Dean of the Arches, Master of the Prerogative Court of Canterbury, and Judge of the Court of Admiralty. In addition to these judges, there were other senior civilians whose names do not appear among the members in 1511.[1]

The absence of these senior civilians is emphasized by the fact that the first President of the Society was Richard Blodwell, who took his doctorate sometime between 1484 and 1495. While it is possible that he became president by election and not by virtue of his seniority as a doctor, a junior doctor would be unlikely to be elected president by a membership whose seniority was much greater than his own. Indeed, there is no known member of whom there is positive evidence that he took a doctor's degree before Blodwell, though some members could have been somewhat senior to him. The proper inference seems to be that at the outset the Society must have had a membership of fairly junior doctors drawn from the ranks of those who proceeded to their doctorates in the late 1480s and early 1490s.

[1]For a list of civilian judges and advocates who were not members of Doctors' Commons see Appendix IV, p. 204 *post*.

II

THE MEMBERSHIP

THE passage of time inevitably changed the character of the membership of Doctors' Commons. As the young doctors who founded the Society got older they were joined by younger men, so that the range of ages gradually widened. More importantly, in many cases advancing years brought preferment. The success of the members must have enhanced the standing of the Society and rendered membership of it more attractive. The first half of the second decade saw a considerable increase in the size of the membership and in its quality. By the time that the Subscription Book was started in 1511 the Society had changed considerably, both in numbers and in status from what it had been in the beginning. During the rest of the Society's existence there were further changes, so that at the end it bore very little resemblance to what it had been in 1511.

A comparatively minor change was the early disappearance of the proctors. The first group of six proctors had but few successors. There was none between 1524 and 1552 and only one in each of the years 1560, 1564, and 1569. Some of the entrants with bachelors' degrees in canon law or civil law may have been proctors, but even if all the bachelors of law were proctors, the proctors in Doctors' Commons must always have been a small minority, with an inferior status indicated by an annual contribution at half the rate paid by the advocates.

The admission of non-practising members continued on a much larger scale and for a much longer period. During the second and third decades of the sixteenth century the admissions of non-practitioners greatly exceeded those of advocates and proctors. The non-practitioners, however, probably ate at the common table comparatively infrequently, so that in spite of their numerical superiority they would be a minority of those present on any one day. During the first half of the century the non-practising members were mostly churchmen of middling rank, with a few abbots and bishops, who would use the Society's premises as a club on an equal footing with the advocates.

The admission of four bishops on one day in 1555 seems to indicate the introduction of a new category of non-practising members, comparable to the honorary benchers of the Inns of Court, elected on account of their eminence without expectation of regular or even frequent attendance. Other groups of bishops were admitted in 1600 and 1612, while the last admissions of non-practising members were those of the Archbishop of Canterbury and two bishops on the occasion of the Archbishop's visitation of the Court of Arches in 1634. There were also laymen in the same 'honorary' category, such as the Master of the Rolls in 1604, and the Chancellor of the Duchy of Lancaster in 1608. One of the most eminent of the non-practising members, Thomas More, did not fall into the 'honorary' category, for when he was admitted in 1514 at the age of thirty-six at the outset of his career, he had advanced no farther than the office of Under-Sheriff of the City of London and so would find his membership to be of practical value on days on which he was engaged in performing his official duties.

By the end of the sixteenth century the membership had reverted to its original character. Apart from a few honorary members, the Society consisted exclusively of advocates, for the last proctor had been admitted in 1569 and the practice of admitting ordinary members who were not advocates had ceased by virtue of a resolution passed on 6 May 1570.[1] On the other hand, there continued to be some advocates of the Court of Arches who were not members of Doctors' Commons.[2]

[1] S.B., f.89.
[2] A list of these non-members is contained in App. IV, p. 204 *post*.

By 1600, however, the advocates differed fundamentally from those who had foregathered in Paternoster Row at the end of the fifteenth century, who were churchmen to whom legal practice and judicial office were likely to be but stepping-stones to high ecclesiastical preferment. Their successors were laymen and professional lawyers for whom, like their contemporaries in the common law, the law provided the occupation of a lifetime, with judicial office as the height to which the ambition of a layman could aspire. By 1600 the advocates had become a lay profession of civil lawyers instead of a clerical sub-profession of canon lawyers. Not only were the advocates who can be identified among the members when the Subscription Book was opened in 1511, like their non-practising fellows, in orders, but many of them held ecclesiastical benefices. Although priests were not, with certain exceptions, eligible to be advocates, dispensations from this disability could be obtained.[1] While a layman could qualify for admission as an advocate by studying civil and canon law for five, or at least four years, in the schools of a university or town and attending in the Court of Canterbury for at least a year,[2] there was little to encourage him to do so. Not only could he not hope for the ecclesiastical preferment which so frequently fell to successful advocates, but he was not even qualified to act as a judge in an ecclesiastical court, for the rule of the canon law was that no lay or married man could exercise any ecclesiastical jurisdiction.[3] This meant that the successful lay advocate in the early sixteenth century could look for promotion only to the judgeship of the Court of Admiralty.

Although the laicization of Doctors' Commons was accelerated by the reform of the Church of England, the process began before Henry VIII broke with Rome. It can be assumed that all the members admitted before 3 December 1514 were, if not in holy orders, at least in minor orders,

[1]Churchill, i.451–2.
[2]Ibid. i.451.
[3]Preamble to Statute 37 Hen. VIII, c.17.

which were the minimum but necessary qualification for
holding an ecclesiastical benefice, for when Thomas More
and William Carew were admitted on that day, it was
thought necessary to describe each of them in the Subscription Book as 'laicus'.[1] They were the only members to be so
described. Thereafter lay members ceased to be a matter for
comment.

There was, however, no sudden break with the past. The
complete laicization of the Society was preceded by an
intermediate stage in which advocates in minor orders took
to living as laymen. The first of these 'hybrids' seems to have
been John Fayter, who was admitted to Doctors' Commons
on 31 July 1522. He must have been in orders, for he was for
a short time rector of Midley, co. Kent,[2] yet he was married,
for in his will he mentioned his wife and two sons, one of
them appropriately named Justinian.[3]

A few months after Fayter, John Tregonwell made his
subscription as an advocate. Tregonwell was also in orders.
He had been vicar of St. Issey, co. Cornwall, and later in life
he was rector of Hope All Saints, co. Kent and also a canon
of Westminster. Nevertheless, he had the career of a layman:
he married twice, he was a Member of Parliament, he was
knighted, and on his brass in the church of Milton Abbey he
is shown in armour and an armorial tabard. William Petre,
who subscribed as an advocate in 1533, had a *curriculum vitae*
very similar to that of Tregonwell: he was also twice
married, sat in Parliament, and was knighted, but he was
qualified for a brief tenure of a canonry of Lincoln between
November 1536 and April 1537. Similar 'hybrids' included
Francis Cave (subscribed 14 October 1533), who was rector
of Bingham, co. Nottingham until 1538, but who was
described in the pardon which he obtained at the beginning
of the reign of Mary I as 'late of St Faith in Paternoster Row,
D.C.L. alias late of Wolkenested alias Godstone, Surrey,

[1] S.B., ff.18v, 19.
[2] B.R.U.O. iv. 201.
[3] P.C.C. 15 Thower (1532) (as 'Fewter').

esquire, alias of the late abbey de Pratis in the parish of St Leonard, Leicester, *esquire*',[1] and Richard Lyell (subscribed 7 March 1538), who shortly after he became the precentor and a canon of Wells was described as 'a temporal man'.[2]

The first advocate member of Doctors' Commons not to have been in even minor orders seems to have been Thomas Legh, who made his subscription on 7 October 1531. He had, however, many successors who were in orders, some of them in holy orders, during the next two decades, but as the Court of Arches became more attractive to laymen it became less attractive to the clergy.

The preponderance of laymen among the advocates joining Doctors' Commons during the closing years of the reign of Henry VIII may be fairly attributed to the changes brought about by the monarch's ecclesiastical policy. The breach with the Papacy was given statutory recognition by the statute 24 Hen. VIII, c.12, which abolished appeals from the English ecclesiastical courts to the See of Rome. By the statute 26 Hen. VIII, c.1 Henry was declared to be the Supreme Head on earth of the Church of England. Shortly afterwards Thomas Cromwell was appointed the King's vicegerent in spiritual matters. Cromwell and his master, being laymen and married, appointed other married laymen to be their officials, commissaries, judges, and visitors. Their authority for doing this is stated in the recitals to the statute 37 Hen. VIII, c.17 to have been the abolition by a statute of 25 Hen. VIII of the papal ordinances and constitutions that 'no lay or married man should or might exercise or occupy any jurisdiction ecclesiastical, nor should be any judge or register in any ecclesiastical court'. It is not clear which statute of 25 Hen. VIII was being relied on for this proposition. Possibly 25 Hen. VIII, c.19 was intended, though this does not support the recital in 37 Hen. VIII, c.17 in so many words. Nevertheless, whether the statute 25 Hen. VIII, c.19 authorized it or not, the recital to 37 Hen. VIII, c.17 is of

[1] *C.P.R. 1553-4*, p. 346.
[2] Ibid., p. 76.

importance as showing what was in fact done. Clearly there was more work available for lay ecclesiastical lawyers and less scope for their clerical counterparts. It may be that 37 Hen. VIII, c.17 was passed for the avoidance of doubts, for on 28 February 1546, shortly after it was passed, Dr. William Coke, 'layman and married', was appointed by Cranmer to succeed Dr. John Cockes, priest, as Dean of the Arches under the statute whereby ecclesiastical jurisdiction might be wielded by married laymen.[1]

This increase in the numbers of lay advocates had no doubt been assisted by the statute 24 Hen. VIII, c.12. So long as appeals to Rome were possible, clerical advocates would be essential, and doubtless many clients would instruct a clerical rather than a lay advocate in a court of first instance so that the advocate would be qualified to follow the cause to Rome, should that become necessary.

While the entry of laymen into the ranks of the advocates can be dated with the aid of the Subscription Book, the disappearance of the clerical advocates cannot be traced with equal precision. In the absence of anything corresponding to the *Law List*, it is not possible to determine when any given advocate ceased to practise. Some of the clerical advocates would receive ecclesiastical preferment, such as bishoprics, inconsistent with their continuing in practice; others would go on until they died. All that can be determined with certainty is when clerical advocates last started in practice. The fact that they had no clerical successors indicates that advocacy was ceasing to be attractive to those who wished to make their way in the reformed Church of England. The distinction of being the last ordained man to be admitted to Doctors' Commons as an advocate seems to belong to Oliver Lloyd, who was admitted in 1609 and ended his life in 1625 as Dean of Hereford.

So complete was the elimination of the ecclesiastical advocates that ordination came to be a disqualification for

---

[1]Churchill, i.594–5. The statute is wrongly cited as of 36 Hen. VIII. It was repealed by 1 & 2 Ph.&M., c.8, s.22, but re-enacted by 1 Eliz.I, c.1, s.12.

admission as an advocate. This was decided by the Court of King's Bench in R. v. *Archbishop of Canterbury*.[1] Furthermore, an advocate who took orders ceased to be qualified to practise in the courts at Doctors' Commons.[2]

Having regard to the long period during which the Subscription Book was in use, the standard of the entries is surprisingly high. There were some irregularities, but they were comparatively few. During the sixteenth century there are some advocates' subscriptions for which there are no corresponding commoners' subscriptions. The only other omissions apparent on the face of the document were in the nineteenth century when spaces were left for some subscriptions and never filled, though the names were inserted in pencil. Despite the fact that these subscriptions were never completed, it is clear that the men who should have signed them were regarded as members of the Society, for their arms were put up in the court-room. Furthermore, there are members mentioned in the miscellaneous entries in the Subscription Book who do not appear in either series of subscriptions. Entries for these men have therefore been inserted in the Register in Appendix III.

In addition to these omissions of which there is evidence in the Subscription Book itself, there were other omissions of which there is external evidence. This evidence is in the Long Book,[3] where some of the terminal lists of the members in commons and out of commons contain the names of some who do not appear in the Subscription Book. While the names in these terminal lists are set out in an approximate order of seniority of membership of the Society, the degree of approximation, as indicated by the relative positions of the names of subscribers in the Subscription Book, is not such as to make it possible to insert these additional names with certainty in their correct positions in the register in Appendix III. The best that can be done is to place them as

---

[1](1807), 8 East 213. See p. 42 *post*.

[2]D. Irving, *An Introduction to the Study of the Civil Law* (4th ed., 1837), p. 116, citing the case of Dr. John Taylor, who was ordained in 1747.

[3]P.R.O., PRO 30/26/8 (hereafter referred to as L.B.).

if they had subscribed during the terms in which their names first appear in the lists.

Although some advocates are absent from the Subscription Book on account of faulty record-keeping, there are others whose absence is due to the fact that they were not members. The records of the admission of advocates to the Court of Arches do not cover the whole of the period during which the Subscription Book was in use, but where they can be compared with the entries in the Subscription Book from the beginning of the reign of Elizabeth I it is apparent that there was no necessary connection between admission as an advocate and becoming a member of Doctors' Commons. Some men had been advocates for many years before they appear in the Subscription Book. Such a one was Sir Thomas Crompton, who was admitted as an advocate in 1590 and did not become a member of Doctors' Commons until 1605.[1] Some advocates, on the other hand, never became members of Doctors' Commons at all. A list of advocates whose names do not appear in either the Subscription Book or the other surviving records of the Society are set out in Appendix IV.[2]

Although the educational qualification for admission as an advocate of the Court of Arches was technically nothing more precise than the study of civil and canon law for five, or at least four years, in the schools of a university or town,[3] in practice the advocates admitted during the existence of Doctors' Commons held doctorates in civil law or

[2]In using the biographies in Levack, pp. 205–82 it must be borne in mind that what is there described as 'Warrant Doc. Comm.' was the Archbishop of Canterbury's mandate for admission as an advocate of the Court of Arches, and that what is there called 'full admission' was admission to Doctors' Commons. The Archbishop's warrant did not, as is stated by Mr. Levack at p. 21, secure admission to Doctors' Commons. The distinction there drawn between those who secured admission and those who eventually became 'fellows or full members' is not in accordance with the facts. Admission as an advocate did not carry with it some kind of associate membership of Doctors' Commons. There was only one grade of membership for advocates.

[3]See p. 204 *post*. The Appendix does not contain all the early seventeenth-century non-members who appear in Levack, since Mr. Levack includes in his classification of 'civil lawyers' all doctors of law, irrespective of whether they were legal practitioners.

[3]Churchill, i.451.

canon law or both. That this was a matter of practice and not
a legal necessity is shown by the admission as late as 1618 of
Richard Zouche, while still only a bachelor of civil law.

During the first half-century of Doctors' Commons many
of the advocates had obtained their doctorates at foreign
universities, mostly in Italy. It was a common practice for
those holding foreign doctorates to be incorporated at
Oxford or Cambridge, but a number who are credited with
doctors' degrees in the Subscription Book do not appear in
the published records of either university and so must be
presumed to have had foreign doctorates as their sole
qualifications. The practice of studying law at foreign
universities declined after the Reformation and ultimately
ceased, but it continued until as late as 1586, when Julius
Caesar, who held the degree of D.C.L. at the University of
Paris, was admitted as an advocate.

Of the two English universities, Oxford produced the
majority of advocate members of Doctors' Commons, there
being 259 of them, compared with 194 from Cambridge,
though during the second half of the sixteenth century there
were fifty-three from Cambridge and only forty from Oxford.
The distribution between the colleges in each university was
very uneven. Trinity Hall with seventy-eight and All Souls
with sixty-two took the lead, New College being a poor
third with thirty-seven. The only other colleges to produce
more than ten advocates were Christ Church with twenty-
one, Merton and St. John's, Cambridge with sixteen each,
King's with fifteen, St. John's, Oxford with thirteen,
and Trinity, Cambridge with twelve. This distribution was
not, however, evenly spread over the whole period of the
Society's existence. Forty-five of the seventy-eight members
from Trinity Hall joined between 1601 and 1750, while All
Souls showed an almost unbroken decline from eighteen in
the period before 1551 to sixteen, eleven, eight, five, one,
and three during the succeeding six half-centuries. King's
and Trinity, Cambridge, produced most of their advocates
during the second half of the sixteenth century, while New

College produced only one of its thirty-seven after 1685. Christ Church, on the other hand, came late into the field, with none before 1604, and seven out of its twenty-one in the nineteenth century, that being the highest number from any Oxford college during that period. At the other end of the scale, two Oxford colleges, Worcester and Hertford, never had a representative in Doctors' Commons, a record which was equalled at Cambridge by St. Catharine's and Emmanuel.

Turning from an overall view to the composition of the Society at particular times, the positions at the granting of the Royal Charter in 1768 and at the coming into force of the Probate Act 1857 may be taken as typical. In 1768 there were eight members from Cambridge, seven of them being from Trinity Hall and one from Gonville and Caius College, while the Oxford contingent of seven members consisted of three from St. John's and one each from Oriel, All Souls, Christ Church, and Trinity. In 1857 there were again eight members from Cambridge, five being from Trinity Hall and three from St. John's, Oxford being represented by four members from St. John's, three from Oriel, two each from All Souls, Christ Church, and Magdalen Hall, and one each from University College, Balliol, Lincoln, Trinity, and St. Mary Hall. There was thus a strong representation from Trinity Hall, but it would be wrong to regard Doctors' Commons as merely a 'colony' or 'appanage' of Trinity Hall.[1]

The necessity to obtain a doctor's degree resulted in the average age of admission as an advocate being about thirty. Admission was followed by the 'year of silence', during which it must have been difficult or even impossible for the new advocate to earn an income, unless he happened to be a fellow of his college. The civil-law bar was therefore not a career open to those who had to earn a living at an early age. Its membership was accordingly largely confined to those whose fathers were in a position to support them during the period of acquiring a practice. Beyond this it is difficult to

[1]Both words are used in Malden, p. 106.

generalize about the family backgrounds of advocates. The majority of the fathers were described as 'esquire' or 'gentleman', which could mean almost anything.[1] The pedigrees of many were recorded at the heralds' visitations during the sixteenth and seventeenth centuries, but there was a leaven of non-armigerous fathers, some of whose advocate sons received grants of arms when established as advocates.[2] By the beginning of the eighteenth century it was assumed that advocates would be armigerous, since it was agreed that each advocate should put up his arms in the court-room.[3]

Turning from the heraldic status of the fathers of advocates to their actual occupations, from the beginning of the seventeenth century the majority of clearly classifiable fathers were to be found in the ranks of the clergy, ranging from bishops to those commonly known as the 'inferior clergy'. According to Dr. Coote, during the second half of the eighteenth century Drs. Smalbroke, Harris, and Wynne 'held a private club' as the sons of bishops.[4] Only a few advocates' fathers were tradesmen, and they were probably in a substantial way of business, especially those who were citizens of London. The tradesmen fathers included a Torrington hatter (Budd), a London waterman (Thomas Pynfold), a Petersfield saddler (John Bettesworth I), a Cambridge draper (Fisher), and a Bath watchmaker (Laurence). To them may perhaps be added some who were described as 'plebeian' in the Oxford matriculation registers, though this is an unreliable guide to status, since some described their fathers in this way, in order to avoid the higher fees payable on matriculation and subsequently by the sons of gentlemen.[5]

[1] As to the imprecision of these terms, see G. D. Squibb, *The High Court of Chivalry* (Oxford, 1959), pp. 170–7.

[2] References to grants of arms to members of Doctors' Commons are included in Appendix III.

[3] See p. 73 *post*. [4] Coote, p. 121.

[5] Dr. George Dale's father is described as a 'plebeian' in the Oxford matriculation register, but as a gentleman in the Middle Temple admission register: see p. 165 *post*. As to the variations of fees according to the rank of the father of an Oxford undergraduate, see A. Clark (ed.), *Register of the University of Oxford*, ii (O.H.S. x, 1887), p. xxv.

Not surprisingly, a number of advocates embraced their profession because of family ties. Some were the sons of advocates and some the sons of proctors. There were also a few families in which advocates were followed both by sons and grandsons. There were also interrelationships of a less direct nature. Sir William Bird, Dean of the Arches (d.1624) was followed by his nephew Dr. William Bird (admitted 1627) and by Dr. Tobias Worlich (admitted 1647), who was probably a son of his maternal first cousin.

A complex network of kinship is disclosed in the will of Dr. Ellys, proved in 1596,[1] in which he mentioned as his kinsmen Drs. William Aubrey I, Henry Jones, John Lloyd, and David Yale.[2] This was not the complete extent of this cousinhood of Welshmen, for in his will, proved in 1574, Dr. John Gwynne described Dr. John Lloyd as his cousin.[3] Dr. John Gwynne was an uncle of one John Wynne, who was also the nephew of Dr. Henry Jones and of Dr. Thomas Yale.[4] The ramifications extended even farther, for Dr. David Yale was a nephew of Dr. Thomas Yale and married a daughter of Dr. John Lloyd,[5] and a daughter of Dr. William Aubrey I married Dr. Dun, one of whose daughters married Dr. Richard Trevor. It could well be that there were even more members of this kindred, for there was a strong Welsh element in the membership of Doctors' Commons during the sixteenth century. Of the forty-three advocates admitted before 1550 whose places of origin can be discovered eight (18·6 per cent) were from Wales, and during the latter half of the century the percentage had risen to 24·1 (14 out of 58). During the next two half-centuries the percentage of Welshmen fell to 8·5 and 6·4, and thereafter, only about 4 per cent of the advocates were of Welsh origin.

[1] P.C.C. 28 Drake.
[2] Ibid,
[3] P.C.C. 27 Martyn.
[4] *Calendar of Wynn (of Gwydir) Papers* (Aberystwith, Cardiff, and London, 1926), nos. 38, 46, 80–1.
[5] *Cheshire and Lancashire Funeral Certificates* (Lancashire and Cheshire Rec. Soc. vi, 1882), pp. 135–6.

Another group of civilian kinsmen flourished a century later. Their relationships can be conveniently shown in pedigree form.

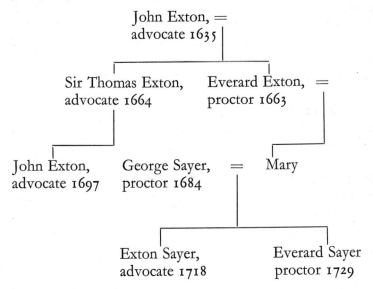

John Exton, =
advocate 1635

Sir Thomas Exton,   Everard Exton, =
advocate 1664   proctor 1663

John Exton,   George Sayer,   =   Mary
advocate 1697   proctor 1684

Exton Sayer,   Everard Sayer
advocate 1718   proctor 1729

There were many other interrelationships, both by kindred and affinity, between the families of advocates and proctors, but advocates and proctors were not the only people who made a living in the ecclesiastcial and civil-law courts. Below them were a variety of holders of minor offices in those courts. For the most part these minor officials are not easy to identify, but the existence of a complicated system of relationships between them and members of Doctors' Commons is revealed in a scarce pamphlet by William Bowdler Wilson. Writing under the pseudonym of 'Lynx', Wilson published in 1874 *A Plea for the Entire Suppression of Patronage, The Bane of Her Majesty's Civil Service*. This was an attack on the nepotism which prevailed in the making of appointments in the Court of Probate, to which the jurisdiction and many of the officers of the Prerogative Court of Canterbury had been transferred in 1858. Wilson gave detailed particulars of many relationships.

Although he was writing in 1874, the dates of some of the appointments which he mentioned show that the situation which he pilloried was not a recent innovation. It will suffice to notice the kindred of three members of Doctors' Commons. Dr. Bayford was the son of a proctor, and he was also the uncle of D. H. Owen, a Registrar of the Court of Probate, H. G. Owen, a Registrar's secretary, Heseltine Augustus Owen, and C. A. E. Wells, both members of the Record Keeper's staff, and W. C. Butler of the Seats Department. Dr. Herbert Jenner, later Sir Herbert Jenner-Fust, was the son of one proctor (Robert) and the brother of another (George). His eldest son, Dr. Herbert Jenner-Fust, was an advocate, and of his younger sons, Edward Francis was a Registrar of the Court of Probate, and Montagu Herbert, was in the Seats Department, later becoming a Registrar. One of Sir Herbert's daughters married Francis Hart Dyke, a proctor, one of his grandsons, H. A. R. Jenner, was the Registrar's Secretary and another, H. A. Jenner, had a place in the Personal Applications Department of the Court of Probate, while Lady Jenner-Fust's nephew, H. F. Lascelles, was in the Seats Department. Dr. Middleton did not come of a civilian family, but he had a brother (Charles John) who was a proctor, another brother, G. Middleton, and an uncle, N. G. Middleton, in the Seats Department, and another uncle, A. G. Middleton, who was a Registrar's secretary, while his wife's cousin, H. L. Strong, was a Registrar.[1] It is unlikely that such a situation was peculiar to the probate jurisdiction. If an equally extensive system of relationships prevailed in the other courts in which the civilians practised, it would seem that Charles Dickens was probably literally correct when he described the hearing of a case in the court-room at Doctors' Commons as 'a cosey, dosey, old-fashioned, time-forgotten, sleepy-headed little family-party.[2]

---

[1]Wilson did not mention the names, but they were added by James Kennerley Hemp, Principal Clerk of Seats in the Principal Probate Registry, to a copy which was given to Sir Anthony Wagner, Garter King of Arms, by the late W. J. Hemp.

[2]*David Copperfield*, ch. xxiii.

III

THE CONSTITUTION

ACCORDING to Dr. Ducarel, about the time or not long after the formation of the Society there was a proposal to found, and perhaps to endow, a College of Civilians, of which Dr. Richard Blodwell was to have been the first President.[1] If there was such a proposal, nothing came of it. Although the Society was sometimes called 'The College', as in Robert Spenser's dedication of the Subscription Book,[2] it remained unincorporated for nearly three centuries. In this it resembled the Inns of Court, but unlike the Inns, with their students, barristers, and benchers, Doctors' Commons had no grades of membership, with the prospect of promotion from one to another.

Until the Society was incorporated by Royal Charter in 1768 there was no formal qualification for membership. Writing in the time of James I, Sir George Buc stated that the following classes were eligible for membership:

The Judge of the High Court of Admiralty, being a doctor of civil law; the Dean of the Arches, being a doctor of civil and canon law; the Commissioners or Judges of the Court of Delegates; the Vicar-General; the Chancellors of the Archbishop of Canterbury and the Bishop of London; the Master of the Prerogative Court of Canterbury; the Judge of the Court of Audience; the Judges of the Court of High Commission, being professed civilians; Doctors of civil and canon law, being advocates in these courts; and the proctors in these courts, being bachelors of civil and canon law.[3]

Buc's description of the classes of members was a

[1] A. C. Ducarel, 'Summary Account', 15 *L.T.R.* 24.
[2] S.B., f.4.
[3] G. Buc, *The Third Vniuersitie of England*, appended to J. Stow, *Annales* (1631), p. 1078).

statement of practice rather than a precise definition of the classes of men who were eligible for membership. It bears internal evidence of having been composed long before it was published and then amended from time to time. The references to degrees in canon law show that it is derived from a version written before those degrees ceased to be conferred about 1535. This original version must have been amended after the evolution of the Court of High Commission between 1535 and 1580.[1] On the other hand, the retention of the proctors indicates that it was not further revised after 1569, when the last proctor was admitted. It is thus not an exact statement of the position when Buc's work was first published in 1615, nor indeed is it a statement of the position at any particular time. It can only be regarded as an amalgam of statements of what had been the practice at various times during the sixteenth century.

The Society's records show that in its early years the majority of the members were advocates of the Court of Arches, with a minority having apparently nothing in common with each other except their liking for the company of the advocates. The latter were a comparatively short-lived category of members. It was decided at a meeting held on 6 May 1570 that thenceforth admissions to the Society should be confined to advocates of the Court of Arches. However, the rights of the existing contributors were saved, and it was also ordered that no advocate or proctor of the Court of Arches should knowingly act against any contributor without the leave of the judge of the Court, as had until then been the custom in the case of the advocates themselves, on pain of losing the benefit of his privilege for ever.[2]

Despite this formal restriction of membership to advocates, there were a few exceptions made. On 6 June 1572 the Society complied with the request of Lord Burghley to

[1] R. G. Usher, *The Rise and Fall of the High Commission* (Oxford, 1913), pp. 64–90.
[2] S.B., f.89. Until about 1810 it was the custom for the advocates and proctors to assemble at an annual dinner (L.P.L., MS. 1560, f.15).

admit William Lewen, the receiver of the revenues of Burghley's son-in-law, the Earl of Oxford, although he was then only a student of civil law.[1] The Society received its reward for compliance with Burghley's wishes on 18 June 1575, when he addressed a warrant to the Officers of the Custom House for discharging the Doctors of the Arches from the payment of the impost on two tuns of wine for their common use.[2] Another request for the waiver of the 1570 rule came from Archbishop Parker, whose request for the admission of John Herbert, M.A. was complied with on 24 November 1573.[3] Nevertheless, the effect of the rule was to change the character of the Society by eliminating the leaven of non-professional members. After the death of the last survivor of the non-advocate members the Society was a purely professional association with a few eminent men as 'honorary' members.[4]

Despite the exclusion of non-advocates, the number of members grew uncomfortably. It was therefore resolved on 25 June 1579 that on account of the limitations of the common table and of the linen, no more members were to be admitted until the number fell to twenty, preference being given to the senior advocates in the order of their admission to the Court of Arches.[5] The position had eased by 20 January 1582, when it was ordered that all advocates might be admitted, the membership having fallen by death and retirement.[6] Eight more were admitted during the next five months.[7]

The membership having been thus filled, Dr. Cosin was admitted on 14 October 1585 at the request of the Archbishop of Canterbury, and a similar request on behalf of the younger Dr. Drury was acceded to on 26 April 1586,[4] while on 20 January 1586 it was resolved that Dr. Julius Caesar,

[1]S.B., f.88ᵛ. Lewen subsequently took his LL.D. at Cambridge and subscribed as an advocate on 7 May 1576.
[2]Ibid., f.127ᵛ. Ducarel mistakenly gave the credit fort his warrant to the Queen (15 L.T.R. 29).
[3]S.B., f.88ᵛ.   [4]See p. 24 ante.
[5]S.B., f.89ᵛ.   [6]Ibid.
[7]Ibid., ff.42ᵛ, 43.   [8]Ibid., f.90.

the Judge of the Court of Admiralty, should be admitted as an extraordinary member, notwithstanding that there was no vacancy, on account of the convenience to the advocates and their clients of his having chambers in the College.[1]

The decision to limit the number of members to twenty was radically altered on 11 May 1593, when it was ordered that the number should be increased by thirteen at the beginning of the following Michaelmas term.[2] This was the last attempt to limit the number of members, but it was many years before the membership of Doctors' Commons became coincident with the whole body of advocates of the Court of Arches.[3]

Since membership of Doctors' Commons was not in itself a qualification for practice as an advocate, there were no doubt always some men who did not join for no other reason than that they preferred not to do so. Perhaps there were others who would have liked to have been members, but were not elected. Nevertheless, many of the advocates who were not members of Doctors' Commons fall into certain broad categories. Some were senior civilians when the Society was formed, and their non-membership supports the inference that in its early days the Society was composed of comparatively young men.[4] Then the majority of those who became advocates in the 1580s would have been unable to join on account of the lack of space, and by the time the number of members was increased in 1590, some of them would have died or retired from practice. This may account for the lengthy periods which sometimes elapsed between admission as an advocate and membership of Doctors' Commons. Thus, Sir Thomas Crompton became an advocate in 1590, but did not join Doctors' Commons until 1605. The five men who were admitted as advocates on 23 October 1637 seem to form another distinct category, though

---

[1] Ibid., f.89ᵛ.   [2] Ibid., f.91ᵛ.

[3] See App. IV, p. 204 *post*. Malden, *Trinity Hall*, p. 105 mistakenly states that the Society 'tried with some success to confine practice in the Ecclesiastical Courts to members of its own body'.

[4] See p. 22 *ante*.

there seems to be no apparent reason why they did not join the Society. Finally, John St. John falls into a category of his own. He had the Lambeth degree of D.C.L. conferred on him by Archbishop Sancroft, but since he had not taken his doctor's degree at Oxford or Cambridge, the two senior members of Doctors' Commons refused to present him according to custom.[1] Notwithstanding this resistance by the advocates, Sancroft issued his fiat for St. John's admission as an advocate. St. John was accordingly admitted on 4 February 1681, though the senior doctors persisted in their refusal to present him to the Dean of the Arches. It was a hollow victory for St. John, since the advocates unanimously declined to practise with him in any cause. Furthermore, no judge appointed him to be a surrogate, neither was he instructed by any of the proctors.[2] After about three years he gave up the profession and was ordained, becoming rector of Yielden, co. Bedford.

Notwithstanding the abortive outcome of the admission of Dr. St. John, the members of the Society were invited to consider three similar cases during the eighteenth century. In Archbishop Potter's time (1737–47) Dr. Bettesworth, the Dean of the Arches, was asked to sound the Society about the admission of James Erskine, the second son of the Earl of Mar, but no further step was taken in the matter. The next to be rejected was John Hawkesworth, upon whom the Lambeth degree of LL.D. was conferred in 1756.[3] Finally, a meeting on 19 June 1759 was informed that an application had been made to Archbishop Secker for the degree of LL.D. to be conferred upon Dr. Bailey, a Scottish LL.D. and late Judge of the Court of Admiralty in Ireland, with a view to his admission at Doctors' Commons. Upon being informed that it had been agreed by the meeting that no doctor of laws could be admitted as an advocate unless he had

---

[1] Letter dated 28 Jan. 1679 from Sir Robert Wyseman, Dean of the Arches, to Archbishop Sancroft (Bodl., MS. Tanner 39, p. 169).

[2] Dr. Ducarel *ex rel.* Sir Nathaniel Lloyd (All Souls Coll., MS. 325, unfoliated).

[3] *Act Books*, i.388; Irving, *An Introduction to the Study of the Civil Law*, p. 115. There is a biography of Hawkesworth in *D.N.B.*

regularly taken his degree at Oxford or Cambridge, the Archbishop told Dr. Ducarel that he would never do any. thing to disoblige the Society.[1]

Thenceforward it became the invariable practice to admit as advocates only those who had regularly taken doctors' degrees in law at Oxford or Cambridge, but in 1767 the Archbishop was faced with a further problem. Dr. Birch, who had taken the degree of D.C.L. regularly at Oxford and had also been ordained deacon, applied to the Archbishop for a fiat to be admitted an advocate. The Archbishop referred the case to the Dean of the Arches and the Society of Doctors for their opinion. It was unanimously agreed that the Archbishop should be informed that it would be more agreeable to the members of the Society that a fiat should not be granted.[2] Dr. Birch accepted the refusal, but Dr. Nathaniel Highmore, who was also a deacon, was more persistent. When his application for a fiat was rejected in 1806, he first of all appealed to the Visitors of the College, but abandoning his appeal, he applied to the Court of King's Bench for a mandamus ordering the Archbishop to issue his fiat.[3] This application was refused, and there was no further similar attempt to gain admission as an advocate. Ordination was not only a bar to admission as an advocate and so to the College, but subsequent ordination terminated member- ship of the College, as in the case of Dr. Herbert, upon whose ordination in 1814 it was resolved that he should be invited to dine in commons whenever he wished to do so.[4]

Each member paid an annual fee. The advocates paid 6s.8d., and most of the others paid the same. Originally there was a special rate of 3s.4d. for proctors,[5] but from the admission of Edward Biggs in 1564 proctors paid at the

---

[1]All Souls Coll., MS. 325; L.P.L., DC23. There is no record that Bailey ever received his Lambeth degree.

[2]L.B., f.295ᵛ. There is no entry relating to Dr. Birch in *Al. Ox.*

[3]R. v. *Archbishop of Canterbury* (1807), 8 East 213; L.B., f.351.

[4]L.B., f.356.

[5]One proctor (Richard Watkyns) undertook to pay 3s.8d. (S.B., f.29ᵛ), but this may have been a slip.

general rate of 6s.8d. The only unusual fees were those of
two nobles paid by aliens.[1] Although their annual fees were
mostly the same as those of the advocates, the other contributors had different rights and obligations in respect of the
common table.[2]

Unlike the other members, the advocates paid an admission fee. In 1512 this was 20s. and it remained at this figure
until it was sharply increased to £6.13s.4d. on 20 January
1582.[3] On 11 May 1590 it was doubled at £13.6s.8d.,[4] and
finally it went up to £20 on 23 October 1689, the last increase being stated to be on account of the expense incurred
by the Society in rebuilding and furnishing the public rooms
after the Great Fire of 1666.[5]

Usually membership was only terminated by death,
though retirement from practice often also terminated
attendance at the common table. The incidence of retirement seems to have been high, though it is rarely possible to
determine with precision which advocates were in practice
at any given time. There is, however, a list drawn up in 1576
which shows that out of a total of thirty-eight advocates of
the Court of Arches living in London, only fifteen were then
in practice.[6] Expulsion, on the other hand, was rare. Dr.
John Veysey (admitted 1530) was expelled for accusing one
of his fellow commoners about words spoken at the common table.[7]

On 2 May 1632 it was ordered that Dr. Hart should be
removed out of commons for publicly professing himself to
be a popish recusant, but he was readmitted on 6 May 1633,

---

[1]Pietro Griffo in 1511 (S.B., f.15) Silvester Darius and Felix Massagrogen in 1518
(ibid., f.21ᵛ). Amereus Brethanus, however, undertook to pay only 6s.8d. in 1559
(ibid., f.38).
[2]See p. 78 *post*.
[3]S.B., f.89ᵛ. Ducarel in his 'Summary Account' dated this increase 25 June 1579,
but on that day only the admission fee of the Master of Trinity Hall was raised to
£6.13s.4d.
[4]Ibid., f.91ᵛ.
[5]Ibid., f.115ᵛ.
[6]P.R.O., SP 12/109/39. There were others (not named) beyond the seas or living
in the country.
[7]S.B., f.33ᵛ.

he having received the sacrament and attended divine service and it being proved that he embraced the religion of the Established Church.[1]

The members of the Society usually held their business meetings in the dining-room immediately after dinner. The meetings were usually held on the Arches day, i.e., the first day on which the Court of Arches sat in each term.[2] This day was usually known as the day of propositions, but it could be postponed by consent.[3] On 6 May 1570 it was decided that petitions could be made, and grants and favours conferred, only on the appointed days. No act was to be considered binding or made conclusive without the express sanction of the Dean of the Arches (if in the City of London) and the Treasurer.[4] Although the meetings were primarily concerned with domestic affairs relating to board and lodging, matters of professional importance were occasionally discussed. Thus, about 1615 a complaint was sent to James I about bishops and archdeacons who had appointed to be chancellors and officials divines unlearned in civil and canon law.[5] Then in 1625 a similar complaint was sent to Charles I about the appointment by Francis Godwin, Bishop of Hereford, of his son, who was 'altogether ignorant of the said laws', to be his chancellor.[6] Indeed, after the membership of the Society was confined to advocates, little care was taken to keep the affairs of the Society separate from those of

[1] Ibid., f.79.
[2] For a table of the court days in the Court of Arches see Law, *Forms of Ecclesiastical Law*, pp. 365–6.
[3] S.B., f.79.
[4] Ibid., f.89.
[5] Ibid., f.78ᵛ. The King signified to the Archbishop of Canterbury that it was his pleasure that such divines should be displaced, whereupon Robert Robotham, son-in-law of Francis Godwin, the Bishop of Llandaff, was removed from the chancellorship of that diocese.
[6] Ibid. The King referred the matter to the Archbishop of Canterbury for inquiry. If he found the complaint proved the Archbishop was to remove the chancellor and confer the place on a professor of the civil law. He was also to advise with the Lord Keeper, the Lord Treasurer, the Earl Marshal, and the Lord Chamberlain as to a fitting course for confining all offices of ecclesiastical jurisdiction to the professors of the civil law. Malden, *Trinity Hall*, p. 105 mistakenly states that the King refused to comply with the petition, 'probably prompted by Laud'.

the profession at large. Thus, the Subscription Book was used to record a Royal Warrant of 20 December 1681 confirming the exemption granted on 16 December 1632 of the advocates, proctors, registers, and other officers of the Court of Arches and of other ecclesiastical courts and of the Court of Admiralty from serving the office of constable and other inferior offices in the same manner as barristers, attorneys, registers, and other officers of the temporal courts at Westminster.[1]

There were, however, privileges which concerned the Society as such, and not the members in their personal capacities. On 18 March 1634 there was an order of the Privy Council exempting Doctors' Commons from the ship money, since the civilians dwelt and were assessed in other places.[2] On the other hand, the Society was only partially successful in its petition from exemption from taxes, burdens, and impositions in the same manner as the Serjeants' Inns.[3] It received a Royal Warrant dated 12 November 1673 confirming a report of the Lord Treasurer that the Society ought to pay taxes proportionate to its ground-rent, but that the doctors ought not to be taxed on their lodgings, they being there for the judging of cases and the practice of their profession.[4]

Whether or not Dr. Blodwell was to have been the first President of an incorporated college, as Dr. Ducarel surmised, he was the first President of the unincorporated Society.[5] It is not certain how long his term of office continued. If the description of him in 1511 as 'huius Collegij primus presidens' was literally correct, he had by then been succeeded by the second President, but in the absence of any description of a member as 'secundus presidens', it seems

---

[1] S.B., f.135ᵛ. Advocates residing in the City and paying scot and lot or taxed by the Common Council were to be entitled to vote at the elections of Common Councilmen.

[2] Ibid., f.79ᵛ.

[3] There were two Serjeants' Inns, one in Fleet Street and the other in Chancery Lane.

[4] Ibid., ff.129ᵛ–130ᵛ.

[5] Ibid., fᵛ.–4ᵛ.

more likely that Blodwell remained in office until his death early in 1513.

There is no evidence as to who succeeded Blodwell in the presidency or as to the holder of this office during the next half century, but during the greater part of the Society's existence, it was the invariable practice for the Dean of the Arches to be the President. It is not certain how early this practice originated. It is unlikely to have been before the offices of Official Principal of the Court of Canterbury and Dean of the Arches became in effect combined by being conferred upon the same man as of course, for when the two offices were held separately the Dean only presided in the Court of Canterbury in the absence of the Official as his commissary-general.[1] It was the Official who was the leading ecclesiastical lawyer of his day, and it would be he, rather than the Dean of the Arches, who would be President of Doctors' Commons when it became the practice for professional precedence to be the qualification for the office.

After it became the practice to appoint the same man to be both Official and Dean, the man so appointed was colloquially referred to as the Dean of the Arches, although in formal documents he was styled 'Almae Curiae Cantuariensis de Arcubus London Officialis Principalis'.[2] Accordingly, it cannot be said with certainty whether a man described as Dean of the Arches in the early years of the sixteenth century was Dean only, or whether he was Official as well, unless there is direct evidence as to the identity of the Official at the time in question.

The first Official to be Dean of the Arches concurrently was Humphrey Hawardyn, who was appointed to both offices on 5 February 1504.[3] Hawardyn's name does not appear in the Subscription Book, so he is unlikely to have been a member of Doctors' Commons. Thomas Wodyngton, who was Official in 1520-2,[4] was a member of the Society,

---

[1] As to the confusion between the Official and the Dean of the Arches, see Churchill i.458-9.
[2] e.g. Oughton, *Ordo Judiciorum*, ii. 33, 347.
[3] Churchill, ii. 238, 240.   [4] Ibid., ii. 238.

but he seems to have taken no interest in it after 1511, for he never entered his subscription in the place left for it in the Subscription Book, so he is unlikely to have been President. All the subsequent Officials and Deans were members of the Society, but the position as to the tenure of the two offices is far from clear until David Pole was appointed Dean on 17 March 1556 and Official ten days later.[1] His successor, Henry Cole, was appointed to both offices on the same day, 1 October 1557.[2] Cole was followed in rapid succession by Nicholas Harpisfield on 28 October 1558[3] and by William Mowse, who was appointed official on 30 May, and Dean on 13 June 1559.[4]

Any or all of these Officials could have been President of Doctors' Commons, but there is no certainty until 25 October 1560, when Robert Weston, who had succeeded Mowse as Official and Dean the previous January, presided at a meeting of the Society.[5] Thereafter every Official appears in the records of the Society as President. That he did so as Official and not as Dean, is shown by the appointment of John Cooke B.D., who was not a member of Doctors' Commons, to be Dean of the Arches on 8 July 1572, at which time the Official was Thomas Yale.[6]

There was a technical hiatus in the succession during the Interregnum, when there was no Dean of the Arches owing to the abolition of archiepiscopal jurisdiction from 5 September 1646 by the Ordinance for the Abolition of Archbishops and Bishops.[7] During this enforced vacancy in the office of Dean of the Arches the acting President of the

---

[1] L.P.L., MS. 1351, f.88.
[2] Ibid.
[3] Ibid., f.88ᵛ.
[4] J. Strype, *Life and Acts of Matthew Parker* (Oxford, 1821), p. 87.
[5] S.B., f.2.
[6] *Registrum Matthei Parker*, iii (C. & Y. Soc. xxxix, 1933), 1058.
[7] C. H. Firth and R. S. Rait, *Acts and Ordinances of the Interregnum 1642–1660* (1911), i. 879–93. The abolition of the Court of Arches led to a temporary change in the style of the Society. In 1647 members were admitted 'in contubernio Advocatorum Lond. et ex novissimo decreto', but in 1648 there was a reversion to earlier usage, and members were admitted 'in commensalem Advocatorum de Archubus', in spite of there being no Court of Arches.

Society was the senior Judge of the Court of Admiralty, there being during this period more than one Judge of the Court.[1]

The Judge of the Court of Admiralty and the King's Advocate had precedence in the Society next after the Dean of the Arches from the seventeenth century onwards, though it is not clear when they were first accorded in the Society the precedence which they enjoyed in the profession. This precedence in the Society, however, carried with it no duties. Otherwise precedence in the Society was according to priority of admission to membership and not professional precedence.[2] This rule extended to the holders of the various offices tenable by members, who had no precedence *virtute officicii*.

The senior office-holder was the Treasurer. The Treasurer is first mentioned in the Constitutions of 6 May 1570, which provided that the senior advocate of those in commons at the common table should undertake the office of Treasurer. His duty was to direct, govern, reprimand, or correct, as he saw fit, all persons (advocates excepted), whether servants of the Society or of the commoners, in matters relating to provisions, repairs, or other things which appeared to him to be to the advantage of the Society. He was also entrusted with the care and custody of the goods and possessions of the Society. The express sanction of the Treasurer (with that of the Dean, if in London) was required to every act of the Society.[3] The Treasurer was also charged with the safe-keeping of the Society's plate, which he had to hand over to his successor in office.

The Constitutions of 1570 provided that the Treasurer was to hold office for a year from 24 June, but by the beginning of the seventeenth century it had become common for Treasurers to remain in office for several years. Thus, Dr. (later Sir William) Byrde and Sir Henry Marten each served

---

[1] e.g. Dr. William Clerke presided at a meeting on 3 February 1649 (S.B., f.79^v.).
[2] Ibid., f.89.
[3] Ibid.

for four years from 1608 to 1611 and 1617 to 1620 respectively. It does not appear how it came about that Dr. Bramston was able to remain in office for eight years from 1699 to 1706, but it must have caused some dissatisfaction among his brethren, for on 20 March 1707 it was resolved that no Treasurer should continue longer in office than two years unless chosen again.[1] In contrast to this eagerness to be Treasurer, Sir George Newman had paid 40s. in 1620 as a composition for not undertaking the office.[2]

Next to the Treasurer came the Librarian. There was no library until about 1697 and no Librarian until 1706, when Dr. Charles Pinfold, the elder, was appointed.[3] Pinfold continued to be Librarian until 1728, but thereafter the Librarian normally held office for two years and then succeeded to the Treasureship.

The first appearance in the records of the junior office tenable by a member of the Society is the appointment on 21 April 1730 of Dr. Kinaston as Register in place of Dr. Audley, who was appointed Librarian.[4] The title of this office might appear to indicate that the holder was entrusted with the keeping of some record, perhaps the Subscription Book. However, the Commons Book for the period 1738–79[5] shows that the Register was responsible for the expenses connected with the dinners in Hall, which he paid out of money collected from the members by the Porter. This duty was ultimately reflected in a change in the title of the office. The title continued to be Register (subject to a change to 'Registrar' from 1771) until 29 July 1791, when Dr. Battine was appointed Steward in succession to Dr. Arnold, who had been appointed Registrar in the previous year.[6] During Dr. Battine's tenure of this office he was known indifferently

[1] L.B., f.233.
[2] Ibid., f.116. This is the only mention of such a composition, but the amount of detail in the accounts varies greatly from year to year.
[3] See p. 89 *post*.
[4] L.B., f. 250.
[5] L.P.L., DC25 (hereafter referred to as C.B). There are no earlier or later Commons Books.
[6] L.B., ff.340, 341.

as Registrar and Steward, being reappointed as Registrar in 1793, as Steward in 1796, and as Registrar in 1798.[1] His immediate successors were appointed as Stewards until 1806, when there was a reversion to the title of Registrar until 1812.[2] There is no record of any further appointment until 1820, when Dr. Dodson was appointed Steward.[3] Thereafter there was no further change.

The usual course was for the members to serve each of the offices of Register (or Steward), Librarian, and Treasurer for two years. There were some variations, such as Dr. Dale's refusal to proceed from Register to Librarian in 1750 on account of his 'necessary absence'[4] and Dr. Francis Simpson's death in 1781 while Librarian. There were also a few occasions on which the officers were continued beyond the usual two years, but the only substantial departure from the normal *cursus honorum* occurred in the case of Dr. Battine. This was brought about by the appointment in 1785 of Dr. Fisher as Librarian, without vacating the office of Registrar, which he had held since 1783. When Dr. Fisher moved on to be Treasurer in 1787, Dr. Battine was appointed Librarian without ever having been Registrar. He then served for two years as Librarian and two years as Treasurer, but in 1791 he was appointed Steward, in which office he continued (sometimes being styled Registrar) for a record period of nine years. During this period each of the junior members who would in the ordinary course have been appointed Registrar (or Steward) proceeded to the Librarianship *per saltem* and then served as Treasurer.[5]

In the early days of the Society the Steward was an employee, for the rules entered at the beginning of the Subscription Book refer to the Steward and the 'other servants' of the Society.[6] The names of the earliest Stewards

[1] Ibid., ff.342ᵛ., 343ᵛ., 345.
[2] Ibid., ff.346ᵛ., 347ᵛ., 348, 349, 350, 352, 353, 355ᵛ.
[3] Ibid., f.365ᵛ.
[4] Ibid., f.268ᵛ.
[5] Ibid., ff.334-346ᵛ., *passim*.
[6] S.B., f.3.

are not in the records, but 'William the Stuarde of the Comens' was named as a legatee in the will of Dr. Towneshend, dated 7 October 1538.[1] The first Steward named in the records was David Mathew, who occurs on 29 April 1568,[2] and there is a regular succession for nearly a century thereafter until Edward Sommers was buried at St. Benet Paul's Wharf on 27 April 1662.[3]

The Steward was in charge of the servants serving and bringing dishes from the kitchen to the advocates' table, and he decided when and in what quantity wine, cheese, pears, apples, and other things necessary for the advocate should be supplied.[4] Among his duties was the keeping of the Subscription Book.[5] He also had an account book, which has not survived.[6] There is no evidence that a successor to Sommers was appointed after his death in 1662. It may well be that he had no successor, because during the eighteenth century there were different arrangements with regard to the service of meals,[7] and these arrangements may have originated in the preceding century.

While the Treasurer may have had some clerical assistance, there is no mention of an Under-Treasurer until Philip Moore, described as of Doctors' Commons, was appointed to that office with a stipend of ten guineas a year from Michaelmas 1770.[8] Moore retired on 1 December 1802,

---

[1] P.C.C. 21 Dyngeley.

[2] L.B., f.5.

[3] Sommers is identifiable as the Steward by an entry of the payment of a debt to Mrs. Sommers, administratrix of 'the late Steward' (L.B., f.196ᵛ.). The intervening recorded Stewards were Thomas Byfeld, occurs 13 Dec. 1569 (S.B., f.103); Henry Scott, occurs 1579 to 6 Nov. 1588 (L.B., ff.27ᵛ., 41); Richard Evans, apptd. 7 Nov. 1588 (ibid., f.41), retired before 17 Jan. 1597 (will as 'late Stewarde to the righte worshipfull Societye of the doctors' (P.C.C. 36 Wallopp)); Thomas Moze, occurs 1597 (L.B., f.66ᵛ.); John Coveney, occurs 1603 (ibid., f.80v.); William Owen, apptd. 1630, on the death of Coveney (ibid., f.143ᵛ.), bur. St. Benet Paul's Wharf 2 Aug. 1637; Francis Bennet, occurs June 1638 (L.B., f.167ᵛ.). Richard Lyon petitioned for the place of Steward after the death of Owen, but was apparently unsuccessful *C.S.P.D. 1644–5*, p. 217).

[4] S.B., f.3.

[5] Order for the expulsion of Dr. Hart (see p. 43 *ante*) entered by the Steward by order of the Society (ibid., f.79).

[6] L.B., f.44.   [7] See p. 79 *post.*

[8] L.B., f.309.

when William Gwinnell was appointed in his place.[1]
Gwinnell retired on account of his advancing years and ill
health, and was succeeded by Henry Watts, who was
appointed 25 March 1843.[2] Watts's name appears in the
Law List until 1886, although the office must have become a
sinecure after the sale of the Society's property. The duties
were presumably similar to those of the Sub-Treasurer or
Under-Treasurer of one of the Inns of Court.

Again like an Inn of Court, there was a Porter. The first
Porter whose name is known was William Adison, who was
a legatee in the will of Dr. Mowse, dated 30 May 1586.[3]
Nothing is known of Adison beyond his name, but there are
many references to Porters in the Society's records down to
James Maskell, whose employment was terminated by his
appointment as Usher of the new Court of Probate in
January 1858.[4]

There must always have been a Cook. The first one whose
name is known was William Hickman, who was a legatee in
the will of Dr. Mowse in 1586.[5] The only other Cook whose
name has survived was Mrs. Clare Wright. Mrs. Wright was
living in the College with her two daughters in 1695.[6] She
left the Society's service in the autumn of 1710. Apparently
she was not dismissed, since her debts to the poulterer and

---

[1] Ibid., f.347ᵛ. Gwinnell had probably been Moore's clerk, since he appears with
Moore as a witness to several leases of chambers from 1786 (L.P.L., D.C.9).

[2] M.B., s.d.

[3] P.C.C. 6 Leicester.

[4] The intervening Porters on record were: William Hicman, occurs 17 Jan. 1597
(Will of Richard Evans, P.C.C. 36 Wallopp); —— Norwood, occurs 3 July 1623
(L.B., f.121); Anthony Edmonds, retired by reason of age and infirmity 5 Nov. 1681
(ibid., f.207ᵛ.); Simon Gentry, apptd. 5 Nov. 1681 (ibid.); Thomas Booker, apptd.
26 Jan. 1698 (ibid., f.228ᵛ.), bur. St. Benet Paul's Wharf 3 May 1704; Joseph Lamp-
son, bur. 4 Apr. 1728; William Waters, bur. 18 Apr. 1729; Peter Powell, occurs 1
Apr. 1732 (Library Account Book), bur. 21 Mar. 1752; John Joplin, resigned 13
Nov. 1770 (L.B., f.308); Richard Wheadon, apptd. 13 Nov. 1770 (ibid.); Henry
Rutter, apptd. shortly before 25 Mar. 1811, but probably irregularly, the duties being
performed by deputies, Thomas Baker from 1811 to c.1830, and William Barnard
from c.1830 (M.B. 20 Jan. 1843); William Barnard, apptd. 20 Jan. 1843 (ibid.), d. by
4 Nov. 1851, when Maskell apptd. (M.B. 4 Nov. 1851).

[5] See n. 3 *supra*. It may be that Hicman was the William Hickman who was Porter
in 1597; see n. 4 *supra*.

[6] *London Inhabitants*, pp. xxxi, 329.

the baker were paid as a gift from the Society, and she was given a pension of £3 a term out of the wine money, but it was resolved that she should not be replaced, and a cook employed only from term to term.[1]

The Society also employed a Gardener on what appears from the vouchers to have been a part-time basis.[2] On 11 November 1795 it was ordered that a Watchman should be stationed at some convenient place within the College. A watch-box was to be erected for him, and he was to be furnished with a watch-coat, a staff, a lantern, candles, a tinder-box, and a rattle. He was to be on duty from 11 p.m. until 6 a.m. between Lady Day and Michaelmas, and until 7 a.m. between Michaelmas and Lady Day. He was to go all round the inside of the College, crying the time of the night or morning every half-hour. For this he was to be paid 12s. a week from Lady Day to Michaelmas, and 15s. a week from Michaelmas to Lady Day.[3]. From 1836 there were also an Assistant Porter and a Sub-Librarian, the Porter having previously acted as Sub-Librarian.[4]

The legal constitution of the Society was fundamentally changed on 24 June 1768 by the granting of a Royal Charter, whereby it was incorporated by the name of 'The College of Doctors of Law exercent in the Ecclesiastical and Admiralty Courts'.[5] The persons named in the Charter were Dr. Hay, Dean of the Arches, Sir Thomas Salusbury, Judge of the Court of Admiralty, Dr. Marriott, King's Advocate, and thirteen other advocates.

The charter was a straightforward incorporation of the previously unincorporated Society. The late Miss Jeffries Davis's statement that after the charter 'the two bodies, the College of Advocates and the Society of Doctors, became

[1]L.B., f.236ᵛ. Mrs. Wright went on living near the scene of her former labours and was buried in St. Benet's churchyard on 14 September 1715. As to the later Cooks, see p. 79 *post*.

[2]L.P.L., DC26, *passim*.

[3]L.B., f.348ᵛ.

[4]Report on the Office of Porter, M.B., 20 Jan. 1843

[5]For the necessity to obtain a charter, see p. 75 *post*. For the text of the charter, see Appendix V, p. 210 *post*.

identical'[1] is meaningless: there never were two bodies to become identical. Although in law the new College was distinct from the old Society, the change was of a technical character. For the first time the membership was formally limited to those who had regularly taken the degree of doctor of law at Oxford or Cambridge and had also been duly admitted as advocates of the Court of Arches, but this had then been the practice for over a century. Existing practice was probably also given formal statement by the provision that a candidate should not be admitted a fellow of the College unless a majority of the whole College was present and a majority of those present concurred in the election. Indeed, the incorporation would make little, if any, change in the day-to-day life of the members, as is indicated by the fact that the records continued to be kept in the same form in the same books. The charter provided that when any doctor was admitted into the College, his name should be registered in a register book to be kept for the purpose, but all that happened was that the subscriptions continued to be entered in the old Subscription Book in the same way as before. As in the case of the unincorporated Society, the affairs of the College were governed by all the members. In this respect it was rather like an Inn of Court composed solely of benchers. The members were, however, made subject to the visitation of the Archbishop of Canterbury, the Lord Chancellor or Lord Keeper of the Great Seal, the Lord Privy Seal, and the two principal Secretaries of State, who were to compose and redress any differences or abuses which might arise or happen concerning the government or affairs of the College. This again was little more than giving legal form to existing practice, for the Archbishop had exercised a general supervision over the affairs of the unincorporated Society.

The only apparent change in the management of the members' affairs was the starting of the Term Book containing lists of the names of all the members term by term and

---

[1] 15 *L.T.R.* 39.

showing the amounts paid and in arrears. The series of Term Books runs from 1768 to 1864. Until Michaelmas Term 1847 there were two lists for each term, one for wine and commons and the other for general dues, but thereafter there was only one list, since the terminal charge for wine and commons was abolished.[1] It is possible with the aid of the Term Books to discover when an advocate's membership ceased, for it was provided by the charter that a doctor once admitted should remain a fellow so long as he should continue to be rated to the commons and other annual dues of the College. This was the only material change in the pre-existing practice made by the Charter.

The grant of the charter made it necessary to have a common seal. At first the seal of the Official of the Court of Arches was used,[2] but no time was lost in having a seal engraved. It was a pointed oval with the marginal inscription THE SEAL OF THE COLL. OF DRS EXERCENT IN ECCL. AND ADMTY COURTS MDCCLXVIII. In the centre was a bogus coat-of-arms displaying the pall of the Archbishop of Canterbury debruised by a fouled anchor with a royal crown in chief.[3]

[1] L.P.L., DC16–19.
[2] e.g. mortgage dated 24 June 1768 (L.P.L., DC8).
[3] There are several leases bearing this seal in L.P.L., DC9.

IV

THE BUILDINGS

I PATERNOSTER ROW

THE position in Paternoster Row of the first Doctors' Commons can be identified from the parcels of a lease of an adjacent house granted by the Dean and Chapter of St. Paul's to Andrew Smythe, one of the proctors of the Court of Arches, on 1 December 1532. Smythe's house is described as adjoining the 'great canonical house' of the Dean and Chapter in Paternoster Row against the gate of the 'postron' of St. Faith's church, 'now named the Doctors' Commons'. Both properties were on the north side of Paternoster Row, for Smythe's house was stated to be bounded on the west by the entry going into Doctors' Commons, and their hall, and an entry leading from the hall to their kitchen, and on the north by the kitchen and well-house.[1] The 'great canonical house' may have been the house opposite the postern gate of St. Paul's which was delivered to William Morland, canon of St. Paul's, on 14 February 1477.[2] This house would have become available for the doctors on Morland's death before 10 May 1492,[3] which is consistent with the existence of the Society in 1496, or possibly 1494, indicated by the Cambridge proctors' accounts.[4] Since the doctors' house later became a tavern known by the sign of the Queen's Head,[5] the entry from the street was presumably what later became Queen's Head Alley, shown on street maps of the locality until the Second World War.

The description of the boundaries in Smythe's lease shows that the hall of Doctors' Commons was approached from the

---

[1]*Hist. MSS. Comm.*, Rep. ix (1883), App., p. 11a.
[2]*Cal. Close Rolls 1476–85*, p. 38.
[3]Le Neve, v. 34.
[4]See pp. 5–7 *ante*.
[5]Buc, *The Third Vniuersitie*, p. 1077.

street by an entry, and that there was another entry from the north side of the hall leading to the kitchen and well-house lying to the east of the entry behind Smythe's house. Apart from this meagre description, all that is known of the house in Paternoster Row is that it was not very attractive. Buc described it as a 'meaner and lesser, and less convenient house' than Mountjoy House to which the Society moved in 1568.[1] According to Ducarel's 'Summary Account', it was small, and the advocates were greatly straitened for want of room.[2] This tradition finds support in the unflattering eye-witness account by Andrea Ammonius, Henry VIII's Latin Secretary, in a letter to Erasmus, dated 18 November 1511. Erasmus had been inquiring about a place in which he could lodge in London, and Ammonius told him that there was near St. Paul's a college of doctors, who were said to live comfortably, though Ammonius thought it no better than a privy (*cloaca*).[3]

Erasmus did not become a member of Doctors' Commons (or if he did, he was one of the very few members who did not sign the Subscription Book), but he may have lodged there for a time, for he visited London during the following Christmas vacation. However, it is equally likely that during this visit he stayed in Knightrider Street with his friend William, Lord Mountjoy, at Mountjoy House, which was later to become the second home of Doctors' Commons. That Erasmus was a guest at Mountjoy House during one of his visits to London is proved by the fact that a set of chambers there let to Dr. Stanhope in 1580 included an upper room called 'Erasmus Bower'.[3] Whether Erasmus actually lived in the Paternoster Row house or not, he would almost certainly have taken meals there from time to time, for he had many friends among the members of the Society.

---

[1]Buc, loc. cit.

[2]15 *L.T.R.* 25.

[3]P. S. Allen, *Erasmi Epistolae*, i (1906), 488. Ammonius was difficult to please, for in a letter to Erasmus written a few weeks earlier he had complained about the deficiencies in English houses in general.

[4]B. L., Add. Charter 15,009, cited in 15 *L.T.R.* 42.

Among those whom he knew were John Colet, Dean of St. Paul's, William Grocyn, Polydore Vergil, Cuthbert Tunstall, and Peter Gryphus, the papal collector. Ammonius, on the other hand, despite the unattractiveness of the premises, thought it worth his while to become a member four years later.[1]

Inconvenient though the house was, it continued to be the Society's home for another half-century after Erasmus thought of lodging there. It was not until 1568 that a move was made to the site in Knightrider Street, to which the name of Doctors' Commons was attached for nearly three centuries.

After the migration to Knightrider Street the Dean and Chapter of St. Paul's let the house in Paternoster Row to George Harryson, a notary public and proctor, who had been a member of Doctors' Commons since 1560. When he died in 1579 Harryson left to his wife Anne his lease of 'the mansion house in Paternoster Row called the old Comons where the Doctors sometyme dyd dwell or remayne'.[2] It had become the Queen's Head Tavern by 1612,[3] but later in the seventeenth century it was divided into several houses known as 'Old Doctors' Commons', which were destroyed in the Great Fire in 1666.[4] The site is now included in some new development, and there are no remaining physical features by which it can be identified.

II KNIGHTRIDER STREET

According to Sir Robert Cotton, Cardinal Wolsey intended to provide the members of Doctors' Commons with 'a much more beautiful and magnificent college' to be built of stone, and he had a 'plan and model' for it prepared.[5] Cotton's evidence is but hearsay, for he was not born until 1570. Nevertheless, Wolsey may have taken an interest in

---

[1]See p. 134 *post*.
[2]P.C.C. 35 Bakon.
[3]Buc, *The Third Vniuersitie*, p. 1077.
[4]P. E. Jones (ed.), *The Fire Court* (1966), i. 135.
[5]Buc, op. cit., p. 1078.

Doctors' Commons, since Thomas Larke, the brother of his mistress, became a member in 1515, and a few months before his death in 1530 his bastard son, Thomas White, joined the Society. That Wolsey got so far as having a plan and model prepared before the project foundered, seems to indicate that his intentions were frustrated by his fall from power in 1529. When many years later the Society was eventually rehoused it was not through any benefactor's bounty, but at the expense of the members.

The move to Knightrider Street in 1568 was brought about by the negotiating ability of one of the members of the Society, Dr. Henry Hervey. Hervey had joined Doctors' Commons in 1550 and had been Master of Trinity Hall, Cambridge since 1559. Although commonly credited with having also been Dean of the Arches, he did not in fact hold that office and so was not the President of Doctors' Commons.[1] In 1568 he was the senior of five Trinity Hall members of Doctors' Commons, the others being Drs. Mitche, Drury, Forthe, and Oxenbridge.

Trinity Hall had from its foundation in 1350 been devoted to the study of civil law and canon law and had already furnished Doctors' Commons with a number of members, so it is not surprising that the two societies were willing to enter into a more formal relationship. By his method of engineering the move of Doctors' Commons from Paternoster Row, Hervey forged a link with Trinity Hall which was to continue for almost exactly two centuries, though at least two of the members, Dr. Jones and Dr. Aubrey, both All Souls men, regretted that the link was not with All Souls.[2] However, although the link which Hervey forged was a strong one, it is going too far to describe Doctors' Commons as a 'colony' and an 'appanage' of Trinity Hall.[3]

---

[1]The error had originated by 1612 (Buc, op. cit., p. 1077) and has been perpetuated by numerous authors down to the present century. It may have been due to the fact that Harvey was Vicar-General of the Archbishop of Canterbury.

[2]Deposition of Thomas Wheeler, Register of Court of the Audience, in *Styward* v. *Binge* (1599) (Trinity Hall MS., Cupboard No. 5, Parcel No. 2).

[3]Malden, *Trinity Hall*, p. 106.

The new home of Doctors' Commons was a large house with a garden belonging to the Dean and Chapter of St. Paul's, situated at the corner of the western part of Knightrider Street (later known as Great Knightrider Street, the eastern part being known as Little Knightrider Street) and St. Benet's Hill (since re-named Godliman Street).[1] The house had had a succession of distinguished occupants, including Thomas, Lord Stanley (d. 1459), Sir John Saye, Speaker of the House of Commons (d. 1478), Margaret, Countess of Richmond (d. 1509), and lastly Charles, Lord Mountjoy. Mountjoy probably had to leave because he was in financial difficulties in 1567.[2]

The house was at this time subject to a lease for fifty years from Michaelmas 1567 at a rent of £5 a year granted by the Dean and Chapter to Sir Thomas Pope, the founder of Trinity College, Oxford, on 8 April 1555. Pope had died in 1559, but at some time before or after his death his interest must have been acquired by Trinity Hall, for on 2 February 1568 the Dean and Chapter executed a further lease of Mountjoy House to the Master, Fellows and Scholars of Trinity Hall for ninety-nine years from the expiration of the 1555 lease at a rent of £5.8s.0d. a year, together with an additional rent of 8s. a year during the currency of the earlier lease. The lease was expressed to be in consideration of the rebuilding of the 'divers apartments in the house' by Trinity Hall, so that 'the Advocates and Doctors of the Arches in London and others of that Company and Commons learned men graduates of the Universities' should therein inhabit. The premises were in the first place to be occupied by the unmarried advocates, but should they not suffice to fill the rooms or should they refuse to inhabit them, by married advocates, failing whom other doctors of law first and then other graduate members of the Society, but no wives were to lodge or abide there. The link with Trinity

---

[1] Great Knightrider Street has disappeared in redevelopment since the Second World War, but the site of Doctors' Commons can be identified by reference to Little Knightrider Street, which survives.

[2] C. Cross, *The Puritan Earl* (1966), p. 88.

Hall was reinforced by a provision that the Master should have one chamber above and another beneath 'the west end of the garden upon the stone building'. Finally, it was provided that the advocates should freely give the best advice and counsel concerning the ecclesiastical laws of the realm, should the Dean and Chapter need it.[1]

The Society later testified its gratitude to Dr. Hervey for his part in securing the grant of the lease by adopting as its arms *Gules, on a bend argent 3 trefoils slipped within a bordure vert*. This was supposed to be Hervey's coat with the bordure added for a difference.[2] It cannot, however, have been adopted in his lifetime, for he bore an entirely different coat—*Or, a chevron and in chief 3 leopard's faces gules*,[3] but the trefoil coat had come to be regarded as the Society's arms as early as 1612.[4] Doctors' Commons was credited with this coat by heraldic authors later in the seventeenth century. One of them, Sylvanus Morgan, in *The Sphere of Gentry*, provided the following fanciful explanation:

. . . and the Coat is thus blazoned, Gules on a Bend Argent, three Trefoiles within a Bordure vert, the Law of Nations being like the Trefoile, *Noctis non deficit humor*, and where the Law is not bordered, *In tuo languore languescimus*; and therefore how much do these men deserve to be blazoned by *Heraldry*, who to their perpetual honour have made a Hedge about our Laws, and provided *Seminaries*.[5]

There is no surviving representation of the arms from before the Fire of London, but the armorial panel which was formerly in the rebuilt court-room, with the inscription: 'HEN. HERVIE LL.D. Anl: Trin: Cantab: Custos hujus

---

[1]Copy lease in S.B., ff.74–8. The lease granted by the Dean and Chapter to the College of Physicians provided for free medical advice (G. N. Clark, *A History of the Royal College of Physicians* (Oxford, 1964), i. 328 n.).

[2]Buc, *The Third Vniuersitie*, p. 1078.

[3]*Warren's Book* (Cambridge, 1911), pp. 15, 73. The coat used by Doctors' Commons was based on that of Hervey of Ickworth, co. Suffolk, but Dr. Hervey was of the family of Stradbroke in that county.

[4]Buc's dedication to Sir Edward Coke is dated 24 August 1612 (op. cit., p. 1061).

[5](1661), Third Book, p. 62.

Societatis STATOR 1549', painted in 1709, survived the nine-teenth-century destruction.[1]

Although it is convenient for the purposes of this work to refer to the second home of the Society as Mountjoy House in order to distinguish it from the house in Paternoster Row, the name of Doctors' Commons was transferred to it after the Society went into possession, and by 1588 it was referred to as 'the house formerly called Mountjoye Place and now anglice the Doctors Commons'.[2] The name Doctors' Commons later came to be applied to the courts in which the advocates practised and also to the neighbour-hood where the officers of the courts were housed, but in this work it is confined to its original meaning of the Society and its premises.[3]

The parcels of the 1568 lease define the western boundary of the demised premises as 'a tenement called St. Arken-wald's Rent'. This property, also known as St. Erkenwald's Tenements, was a row of eight houses, also in the ownership of the Dean and Chapter, fronting on to Great Knightrider Street. These houses were let by the Dean and Chapter on 6 February 1571 to John Incent, a proctor and a member of Doctors' Commons.[4] At some uncertain date the eastern-most six of them were let to advocates and came to be regarded as part of the College premises, though they re-mained tenurially separate until the Society acquired the freehold in 1783.

There is but little evidence about the fabric of Mountjoy House. Although Trinity Hall was required by the 1568 lease to reconstruct part of the premises, this did not involve any major alteration of the existing building. According to Thomas Wheeler, the Register of the Court of Audience, when he gave evidence in *Styward* v. *Binge* in 1599, at the time of the move the doctors chose their chambers and lodgings according to their seniority and dignity and built

[1]See p. 74 *post*. Hervey joined the Society on 27 Jan. 1550.
[2]*I.p.m. for London*, p. 106.
[3]For the wider uses of the name, see 15 L.T.R. 43–50.
[4]*C. S.P.D. 1547–80*, p. 263.

them and altered them as they wished. Some of them laid out quite substantial sums: Dr. Lewes spent £200 and Drs. Huick, Mowse and Jones £100 each, while John Lewis, a proctor, spent £300.[1] Dr. Hervey reserved for himself and his successors as Masters of Trinity Hall a lodging at the west end of the dining chamber and built a brick wall in the garden. The Society had the use of the dining chamber, gardens, courts, kitchen, buttery, pantry, porter's lodge, steward's chamber, cellar, coal-house, wood-house, larder, and other common rooms and houses of office and service, paying a small rent to Trinity Hall, but without a lease. Various benefactors paid for wainscotting and painting the hall, dining chamber, and common rooms. Dr. Yale, glazed a window at the east end of the dining chamber, and Drs. Martin and Lewes glazed other windows. There was a proposal by Trinity Hall to build over the hall and in 'the green back court', but this was resisted by the advocates. The rents of the chambers and lodgings were fixed by Dr. Hervey with the assent of the fellows of Trinity Hall.[2]

John Stow, writing in 1598, described Mountjoy House as a 'great house builded of stone'.[3] It was said to have been built 'in the forme of a Colledge'.[4] The terms of a licence to build over the hall granted to Dr. Whetcroft on 3 June 1594 show that the main axis of the hall lay from east to west and that it had two large windows on the south side and three smaller ones on the north.[5] A consent given to Dr. John Exton on 3 February 1648 for the enlargement of his chambers reveals that the hall was on the first floor of a building adjoining a covered entry or passage into the garden.[6]

The only comprehensive description of Mountjoy House during its occupation by Doctors' Commons is contained in

[1]Trinity Hall MS., Cupboard No. 5, Parcel No. 2.
[2]Depositions of Thomas Creake, LL.D. and Thomas Wheeler (ibid.).
[3]Stow, *Survey of London* (ed. C. L. Kingsford), ii. 17.
[4]Pleading in the Fire Court, 1670, cited in 15 *L.T.R.* 64.
[5]S.B., f.92.
[6]Ibid., f.79ᵛ.

a deed dated 28 May 1650, whereby Sir John Wollaston and the other trustees appointed by an Act of 30 April 1649[3] conveyed for £234 the freehold of the premises to Roger Clavell and Robert Thomas of Doctors' Commons for sixty-six and a half years, six weeks, and five days and then to Trinity Hall.[2] This transaction became, of course, invalid at the Restoration.[3] The over-all dimensions of the property described in the deed correspond exactly with those shown on the nineteenth-century Ordnance Survey map, except that the frontage to Great Knightrider Street was only 115 ft from the street corner, the frontage farther west being that of St. Erkenwald's Tenements. The entrance from Benet Hill led into the first court, around which were the lodgings late in the tenure of Drs. Heath, Mason, Turner, and Allen. This court was the forerunner of the later Little College Square. Then came the little courtyard in which stood the hall with a cellar on its west side and a room over the cellar late in the tenure of Dr. Wiseman. At the east end of the hall was the buttery with several rooms over it late in the tenure of Dr. Zouch. There were also several rooms over the hall late in the tenure of Dr. Walker. Although it is not expressly so stated in the indenture, the north side of the hall seems to have fronted on to Great Knightrider Street. To the south was a yard with the rooms late in the tenure of Drs. Forth and Clarke on the east and the rooms late in the tenure of Dr. Dorislaus on the south. Adjoining this yard was 'the fair dining room'. Then came a 'green court or yard' with rooms late in the tenure of Drs. King and Sweit, Sir Nathaniel Brent, and Dr. Worlich on the south, and rooms late in the tenure of Drs. Bond and Pepys on the west.[4] Then came the garden with several lodgings late in

---

[1] Act for abolishing of Deans, Deans and Chapters, etc. (Firth and Rait, *Acts and Ordinances of the Interregnum*, ii. 81–104).

[2] The enrolment on the Close Roll (P.R.O., C.54/3547) supplies some words illegible in the original indenture at Trinity Hall.

[3] It was excluded from the savings in the statute 12 Car. II, c.11, s.50.

[4] Dr. Pepys's name is spelt 'Peapes', which seems to indicate that the common pronunciation of the diarist's name is the correct one and 'Peppis' a modern affectation.

the tenure of Sir George Parry at the east end and another little yard at the west end.

There is a glimpse of the interior of 'the fair dining room' in an account of the heraldry in it, made in 1617.[1] The heraldry in the dining chamber included the shields of arms of Dr. Thomas Yale and Dr. Thomas Martin. These shields were presumably in the windows which Yale and Martin glazed shortly after the Society took over Mountjoy House[2] In addition, there were the shields of Dr. Matthew Carew, Dr. John Herbert,——Denny, and——Saye, 'Curiae Prerogativae Judex'.[3] There were also three other unnamed shields bearing the arms of Trinity Hall and New College and an unidentified coat, *Argent, on a cross sable, 4 lions, 2 in fess passant gardant and 1 in chief and 1 in base rampant, or,* which may have been in the window glazed by Dr. Lewes.[4]

The chambers in Mountjoy House were let to advocates by Trinity Hall, some on repairing leases, usually for terms of twenty-one years, and some on yearly tenancies.[5] In the mid-seventeenth century there were eleven sets of chambers let on leases and eight were let on yearly tenancies.[6] Those who had leases had to repair the common rooms as well as their own chambers.[7]

---

[1]Coll. Arm., MS. Hutton's Church Notes, p. 41a. In addition to church notes, this manuscript contains notes taken in some secular buildings.

[2]See p. 63 *ante*. The arms in Yale's window were *Azure, on a cross argent, a saltire sable*, which are entirely different from those subsequently used by the Yale family. The Martin shield was not named, but that bearing *Argent, an eagle displayed gules* must have been his: see *Vis. Cambs.*, p. 47.

[3]The Troutbeck quartering in the Denny arms indicates one of the numerous descendants of Edmund Denny, Baron of the Exchequer (d. 1520) (see *Visitation of Norfolk, 1563, 1589 and 1613* (Harl. Soc. xxxii, 1891), p. 101), though none of them seems to have had any apparent connection with Doctors' Commons. The Saye shield had a quartering for Colbrooke (shown in a marginal drawing as an impalement) and seems to have been that of William Saye, a proctor of the Court of Arches (see *Vis. London 1568*, p. 81). It is unlikely that a proctor would have been the Judge of the Prerogative Court of Canterbury, so the note-taker may have written 'Judex' instead of 'Registrarius'.

[4]See p. 63 *ante*.

[5]Petition to Fire Court in 1670 reciting the practice before the Great Fire, cited in 15 L.T.R. 59–61.

[6]15 L.T.R. 59–60, where the names of the tenants are given. One of the lessees was a proctor.

[7]Ibid., pp. 61, 64.

Although each advocate was a sub-lessee of Trinity Hall, the practice was for the members to decide which of them should be permitted to apply to Trinity Hall for a lease of a vacant chamber.[1] This was called in question in 1634, when, after the death of Sir William Byrde, Dean of the Arches, Dr. Duck obtained a lease of his chamber from Trinity Hall before submitting the matter to a meeting. On 3 December 1634 it was formally decided that when a chamber fell vacant by death or surrender, the petition for a new lease should first be made to the Dean of the Arches and all the doctors of the Arches admitted into commons, and whichever doctor actually in commons they should nominate could then apply to Trinity Hall for a lease on the usual terms.[2] This procedure was bypassed in 1648. On 16 December Dr. Duck died, and two days later Oliver Cromwell, then M.P. for Cambridge, wrote to the Fellows of Trinity Hall to ask that Dr. Dorislaus should be preferred before any other in the letting of Duck's chamber in Doctor's Commons.[3] That Cromwell's letter had the desired effect is shown by the deed of 1650 in which certain rooms are described as having been late in the tenure of Dr. Dorislaus.[4]

Although Mountjoy House itself was primarily reserved for the occupation of unmarried advocates, it became the focus of the married ones as well. Many of the married advocates had their homes in the immediate neighbourhood. At some time before 1587 Dr. Matthew Carew and Dr. Thomas Skevington had houses in Addle Hill to the west.[5] About 1589 there were seven advocates, Drs. Martin, Clerk, Stanhope, Jones, Aubrey, Dunn, and Caesar, living in the parish of St. Benet Paul's Wharf, in which Mountjoy House was situated, and eight others, Drs. Dale, Forthe, Creake,

---

[1] S.B., f.79. Dr. Wood on the death of Dr. Edmund Pope.
[2] Ibid., f.78.
[3] Trinity Hall, MS. Miscell. Papers, vol. iv, transcribed in Malden, *Trinity Hall*, p. 148.
[4] See p. 64 *ante*.
[5] *I.p.m. for London*, p. 105.

Farrand, Hudson, Gardiner, Chippendale, and Amye, lived in the nearby parish of St. Gregory.[1]

By the middle of the seventeenth century doubts had arisen regarding the legal relationship between Doctors' Commons and Trinity Hall, the latter claiming that it held the lease of 1568 in its own right and not in trust for the Society. In order to settle the matter the Society exhibited a bill in Chancery in May 1656.[2] The suit dragged on until by orders dated 13 July 1663 and 17 May 1664 the matter was referred to Serjeant Glynne and Sir Jefferey Palmer, who on 14 January 1665 decided that the doctors who had leases of their chambers could renew them on demand for twenty-one years at the same rent without fine, and that those who were in possession without leases could take leases for twenty-one years without fine, and that when the lease of 1568 expired Trinity Hall should pay the fine and hold the renewed lease on the same trust.[3]

The end of Mountjoy House came in the Great Fire of London in 1666. On 3 September the fire reached the College of Arms on the east and St. Benet's Church and the houses in Thames Street on the south. On the following day it consumed Mountjoy House.[4] Someone carried away the Subscription Book and the Long Book. If any of the Society's other possessions were saved, they have since disappeared.

The Society was temporarily rehoused in Exeter House, on the north side of the Strand opposite the Savoy, by an Order in Council made on 5 October 1666.[5] Since the church of St. Mary-le-Bow was also burnt, it was necessary to find temporary accommodation for the Court of Arches. It must

[1]Subsidy Roll, printed in *Vis. London 1568*, p. 154.

[2]Sub nom. *Mason* v. *Trinity Hall*. The documents in the matter are L.P.L., DC3.

[3]*Bettesworth* v. *Dean and Chapter of St. Paul's* (1728), 1 Bro. P.C. 240, 242. Malden, *Trinity Hall*, p. 106 states that the proceedings which began under the Commonwealth went on for three-quarters of a century, but the proceedings in the early part of the eighteenth century were entirely separate: see p. 75 *post*.

[4]W. G. Bell, *The Great Fire of London* (3rd ed., 1922), map facing p. 24.

[5]*Bettesworth* v. *Dean and Chapter of St Paul's* (1728), 1 Bro. P.C. 240.

have been a convenience for the advocates when the Court was also given quarters in Exeter House.[1]

When Sir Christopher Wren prepared his first plan for the rebuilding of the City on an entirely new lay-out he made provision for placing Doctors' Commons on an island site immediately to the east of St. Paul's.[2] When this plan was abandoned, it was proposed that Mountjoy House should be rebuilt on its old site. The advocates, however, were in no hurry to leave Exeter House, which they found was 'more conveniently situated' for them.[3] In order to persuade them to return to Castle Baynard Ward they were promised that if the 'professors of the civil law' and the ecclesiastical courts would return, such professors should be free from bearing any office in the Ward. Furthermore, the King made an order exempting them from bearing any office in the City of London.[4]

The first definite step towards a return to the old site in Great Knightrider Street was not taken until June 1669, and then the initiative came from the City. The Sheriffs presented to the King a petition for the rebuilding of Doctors' Commons. This petition was referred to the Privy Council and set in train a series of negotiations, which culminated in the presentation of petitions to the Fire Court by Trinity Hall and the Dean and Chapter of St. Paul's. The powers of the Court were limited: under the original Act 19 Car. II, c.2, s.2 it could not order new leases for terms exceeding forty years, and by the amending Act 22 Car. II, c.11, s.23 forty years could not be added to an existing lease to make the whole term more than sixty years. The petitions were heard on 15 December 1670, when the Court exercised its power to the full by decreeing that the term of the lease of

---

[1] T. F. Reddaway, *The Rebuilding of London after the Great Fire* (1940), p. 30, and see p. 69 *post*.

[2] C. Wren, *Parentalia* (1750), pl. facing p. 268.

[3] E. A. Pickard and E. Jeffries Davis, 'The Rebuilding of Doctors' Commons, 1666–72', 15 *L.T.R.* 55.

[4] S.B., f.136. On 22 December 1679 Ravis Benson, one of the clerks of the Prerogative Office, was held to be within this order and was accordingly discharged from being a vestrymen in the parish of St. Benet Paul's Wharf (ibid.).

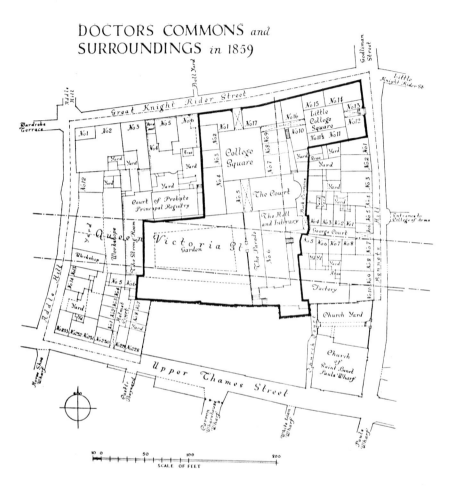

III. Plan of Doctors' Commons and surroundings in 1859

1568 should be made up to sixty years from Michaelmas 1670 at the old rent of £5.8s.od.[1]

Since there had been nineteen sets of 'chambers or lodgings' in Mountjoy House, it was arranged that nineteen advocates were to rebuild the chambers and the hall, dining-room, kitchen, cellar, buttery, and porter's lodge; Trinity Hall was to grant to each of the rebuilders a lease of his set of chambers for forty years from Michaelmas 1670 with a covenant for a new lease for forty years after the expiration of sixteen years;[2] the total rent of the nineteen sets of chambers was to be £63.13s.4d., which had been the rental before the Fire; and Trinity Hall was to grant a general lease in trust for all the rebuilders, their executors, administrators and assigns, of the common rooms, gardens, court-yards, and vacant places for forty years from Michaelmas 1670 at a pepper-corn rent, with a similar covenant for a new lease for forty years after the expiration of sixteen years.[3] It was agreed that the public and common rooms and places were to be repaired solely by the Society, and that Trinity Hall should not be liable for any part of the burden.[4]

The work of building the hall must have been put in hand at once and proceeded with astonishing rapidity, for by an Order in Council, of which notice, dated 14 February 1672, was published in the *London Gazette*, the judges of the ecclesiastical and civil-law courts sitting at Exeter House were authorized and required to adjourn the courts to Doctors' Commons, the King being satisfied that the place was then fit for the reception of the courts.

Of the nineteen sets of chambers, two were built on the east side of the garden to the south of the hall. [5] The others

[1]For a detailed account of the proceedings in the Fire Court see Pickard and Jeffries Davis, op. cit., 15 *L.T.R.* 51–77.

[2]The object of this arrangement was to avoid infringing the provisions of the Act 14 Eliz. I, c.11, as to which see p. 74 *post*.

[3]15 *L.T.R.* 62, 68, 69, 71.

[4]Resolution of 9 December 1676 (S.B., f.136ᵛ.).

[5]All Souls Coll., MS.325. This manuscript contains lists of all the members who contributed to the rebuilding, of their successors in possession when their leases expired at Michaelmas 1726, and of the locations of their chambers taken from the book called 'Thesaury', as to which see p. 114 *post*.

were built round two quadrangles—College Square, entered from Great Knightrider Street, and Little College Square, entered from St. Benet's Hill, with a covered passage connecting them.[1]

There are two views of College Square—one a drawing made in 1854[2] and the other in the *Illustrated London News* of 4 May 1867.[3] While the buildings were of uniform height and of similar design, variations in the doorways and the fenestration reflected the fact that they consisted of separate houses built by different builders. Each house had three floors, with attics and cellars. Their outward appearance was similar to that of a quadrangle or court at Oxford or Cambridge or in one of the Inns of Court, but their construction was fundamentally different. Instead of giving access to a staircase serving sets of chambers on each floor, each doorway was the entrance to a separate house.[4]

All the houses in the College were numbered in one series from one to seventeen at some time during the eighteenth century.[5] The discrepancy between the number of houses and the number of members who undertook the rebuilding was due to several causes. No. 12 was the Porter's lodge. The decree of the Fire Court had provided that it should be built by the nineteen rebuilders with the other common parts, but its site was included in a lease granted on 23 June

[1] The entrance from St. Benet's Hill (known as 'the fore gate') is shown in a drawing made in 1854, reproduced in plate IV. The house to the left of and above the entrance was built by Dr. (later Sir Thomas) Exton (seven hearths). The porter's lodge was on the right of the entrance, and the house on the corner of Great Knightrider Street was built by Sir Walter Walker (seven hearths).

[2] Reproduced in Plate V. The first house on the left was built by Dr. Briggs (four hearths). The next house was built by Dr. (later Sir Richard) Raines (nine hearths). The entrance from Great Knightrider Street in the centre of the north side (known as 'the back gate') was flanked on the left by the house built by Dr. Edward Master (six hearths) and on the right by that built by Sir Robert Wyseman (nine hearths), which was entered from the passage from St. Benet's Hill in the right-hand corner. Next to the passage was the house built by Dr. Lowe (five hearths). To the right of this were the houses built by Dr. John Clark (four hearths) and Dr. Alworth (five hearths).

[3] Reproduced in 15 *L.T.R.*, opp. p. 84.

[4] Four of the houses were built in pairs, each with a common staircase.

[5] Dr. Marriott's address is given as 9 College Square in the 1777 edition of *Browne's General Law List*, p. 147. The numbers are shown on the plan opposite p. 68.

IV. Exterior of Doctors' Commons from the north-east, 1854, from a tinted drawing by T. Hosmer Shepherd

1671 to Sir Walter Walker, who built it.[1] No. 4 was one of the two houses which had been built in two parts, but it had been turned into a single house by 1726. No. 11 had also been built in two parts. It must have been occupied as one, when the houses were numbered, but it was later divided again, the western part being numbered $11\frac{1}{2}$. On the other hand, No. 6 was originally two houses.

The sets of chambers varied greatly in size, as appears from the Hearth Tax return of 1675, which shows Sir Leoline Jenkins as assessed for thirteen hearths, while Dr. Thompson was assessed for only one.[2] The houses were not only designed for residential occupation: they were in fact so occupied. This appears from a list of the households in Doctors' Commons drawn up in 1696.[3] By this time five of the nineteen houses were occupied by proctors, who, like the advocates, lived there with their families. The two largest households each consisted of ten persons—Dr. Newton, his wife, three children, and five servants, and Robert Bargrave, a proctor, his wife, child, and seven servants.

There were not enough houses in the College for all the practising advocates, but in 1696 the occupiers of all the houses lived as well as worked in them. The parish registers of St. Benet Paul's Wharf show that the residential use of the houses continued through the eighteenth century. It is not, however, possible to ascertain how many houses were occupied residentially at any one time until the *Post Office Directory* began to contain a list of private residents in London. In 1843 five advocates were listed in the 'Court Directory' as residents in Doctors' Commons, but the other fifteen advocates with addresses there either had residential

[1]Trinity Hall, MS. Lease of 7 Jan. 1708 to Dr. Lane (recital).
[2]P.R.O., E.179/252/23, printed in 15 *L.T.R.* 74. There was one set of chambers with thirteen hearths, two with nine hearths, one with eight, three with seven, two with six, six with five, four with four, and one with one, there being also five hearths in the common rooms.
[3]B.L., MS. Add. 32, 645, ff.7ᵛ.–8, printed in *London Inhabitants*, p. xxxi. There are twenty-one households listed, of which one consisted of the Porter (a bachelor) and another of the Cook and her two daughters.

addresses elsewhere in London or no address in the 'Court Directory', the latter presumably living in the suburbs. By this time six of the houses were each occupied by two advocates, so the College had by then largely ceased to be a residential area. Furthermore, some of the advocates who were recorded as being resident may have used their houses merely as *pieds à terre*.

Although held on separate leases, the six easternmost houses in St. Erkenwald's Rents had long been occupied by advocates, so advantage was taken of the rebuilding to incorporate them in the College. The sites of these houses formed the western half of the northern range of College Square.

The main entrance to the College was from Great Knightrider Street into College Square. The court-room was in the south-east corner of College Square and was entered by way of a covered passage opposite the main entrance, on the left of which were two doors opening into the court. Beyond the doors into the court the passage led on to the garden.[1] To the east of the garden there was a terrace, called The Parade, in front of the hall and the large house built by Sir Leoline Jenkins.

After the rebuilding the advocates were more conveniently situated than they had been in the old Mountjoy House, for not only did they continue to have the Court of Arches held on their premises, as they had done in Exeter House, but thenceforth the new court-room was also used for the sittings of the Court of Admiralty and of the Prerogative Court of Canterbury and the Bishop of London's Consistory Court. Although the old hall was occasionally used as a court-room,[2] it must have been a great convenience to have a separate court-room available for judicial business at all times.

The plate entitled 'Doctors' Commons', published in 1808

[1] G. J. Foster, *Doctors' Commons: Its Courts and Registries* (1871), p. 5.
[2] e.g. by the Court of Delegates in 1663 (R. G. Marsden (ed.), *Reports of Cases determined by the High Court of Admiralty* (London, 1885), p. 246) and the Court of Admiralty in 1648 (ibid., pp. 235–6).

V. College Square from the south, 1854, from a tinted drawing by T. Hosmer Shepherd

in Ackermann's *Microcosm of London*,[1] shows the interior of the court with a court in session, as described by Charles Dickens in *Sketches by Boz* and *David Copperfield*. The panelled room was divided into two parts by a wooden screen of three arches. The eastern part contained a U-shaped dais, with steps leading down to the northern and southern arches of the screen. The judge's seat was in the apsidal east end of the room, and the advocates sat on the dais on each side. In the well of the court was a large table covered in green baize, at which the proctors sat. At the western end of the table was a low bar, beyond which only the proctors could pass. The western half of the room had a stone floor and was unfurnished, apart from seats along the walls. Here the advocates and proctors could confer with their clients.

The plate shows three rows of oval objects on the wall above the panelling. These bore the arms of the members of Doctors' Commons. It was the custom in the Inns of Court to display the arms of those who had served the office of Reader. This custom was adopted by Doctors' Commons with a difference. Instead of waiting until he had achieved office by seniority, each advocate was required to put up his arms as soon as he was admitted. The series began with the arms of those who were members in 1709, it being agreed on 2 March 1709 that the then Doctors should send in their shields of arms and that all future Doctors should be obliged so to do.[2] However, a list of the arms made after they were removed to be distributed among the last advocates and the representatives of those who had predeceased them shows that some of the arms were those of advocates who were already dead in 1709.[3] It is not clear on what principle these pre-1709 arms had been selected: some were the arms of former Deans of the Arches,[4] some those of ancestors of advocates living in 1709,[5] but for others there is

[1] *Frontispiece.*
[2] L.B., f.235.   [3] Hemp, p. 74.
[4] Sir Richard Lloyd (d. 1686); Sir Thomas Exton (d. 1688); Dr. Oxenden (d. 1703).
[5] Dr. J. Exton (d. 1668); Sir Thomas Pinfold (d. 1701).

no obvious explanation. The arms were painted on panels in oval frames. Three of them, those of Drs. Hervey, Ducarel, and Pratt (without its frame), are now not far from their original home in the chambers of Sir Anthony Wagner, Garter King of Arms, in the College of Arms.[1]

On the wall opposite the judge's seat was a clock, flanked on the one side by a portrait of Sir John Cooke and on the other by one of Sir Edward Simpson, and under the clock were the arms of Dr. William Wynne, dated 9 November 1757.[2] Next to the court on its south side was the dining-room, approached by way of a glazed door, over which hung a bell. A glimpse of the dining-room through the open door can be seen in Ackermann's plate. The only picture in the dining-room was a portrait of Sir George Lee.[2] When the library was formed it was housed in the room over the dining-room.

After the rebuilding there was no substantial further change in the physical state of the premises, but the tenurial situation changed fundamentally during the eighteenth century. The lease held by Trinity Hall, as extended by the decree of the Fire Court, was due to expire at Michaelmas 1730, but it was subject to a covenant for constant renewal at the same rent. However, when negotiations for a new lease were started in 1725 the Dean and Chapter refused a renewal on the ground that as an ecclesiastical corporation they were forbidden by statutes of 1571 (13 Eliz. I, c.10) and 1572 (14 Eliz. I, c.11) to grant a lease of premises in a city or corporate town for more than forty years, so that the covenant for renewal for ninety-nine years with a clause for

---

[1]The account book of Thomas Sharp, herald painter, in the author's possession shows that he painted the arms of Dr. Creswell on 9 July 1810 and Dr. Meyrick on 4 July 1811. These paintings were presumably panels for the court-room.

[2]L.P.L., MS. 1560, f.22. The portrait of Cooke came from Lambeth Palace and was deposited by the Archbishop of Canterbury on 18 Nov. 1771 (*Act Books*, i. 182; L.B., f.314ᵛ.). The portrait of Simpson was presented by Nathaniel Bishop, Deputy Register of the Court of Admiralty on 1 Jan. 1772 (L.B., f.315). The clock was presented by Dr. Harris on 2 Dec. 1771 (ibid., f.314ᵛ.); it was embellished with the bogus arms adopted by the College (Guildhall Library, Drawing P. 1925). The date on Dr. Wynne's arms was that of his admission to the Society.

[3]L.P.L., MS. 1560, f.22.

further renewal contained in the 1568 lease had been rendered invalid, and they were therefore not obliged to renew for forty years. This refusal led to proceedings in the Court of Chancery, in which the contention of the Dean and Chapter was upheld. On appeal to the House of Lords it was decided that, although the covenant for renewal could not be wholly performed, it must be performed in so far as it remained lawful. It was accordingly decreed that a new lease should be granted for a term of forty years from Michaelmas 1730, but without any covenant for renewal.[1]

In 1765, faced with the prospect of becoming homeless at Michaelmas 1770, the advocates filed a bill in Chancery against the Dean and Chapter, praying for an order for the grant of a new lease on the old terms. These proceedings were heard in 1767, when Lord Chancellor Camden dismissed the bill.[2] It was this reverse which caused the advocates to petition for the grant of a Royal Charter. Having obtained the Charter, they were, as a body corporate, in a position to negotiate with the Dean and Chapter for the grant of a direct lease without the interposition of Trinity Hall. This they obtained for a term of forty years, but the fine and expenses amounting to £4,200 were beyond their means and had to be raised by mortgaging the lease.

Although this secured the position until 1810, the long-term prospect was precarious. For security it was necessary to acquire the freehold reversion. This was achieved by a grant from the Crown of £3,000 out of the *droits* of the Admiralty in 1782, followed in the next year by a private Act of Parliament (23 Geo. III, c.xxx), which authorized the carrying into effect of an agreement between the Dean and Chapter and the College for vesting the property in the College in fee simple, reserving a perpetual yearly rent to the Dean and Chapter.

[1] *Bettesworth* v. *Dean and Chapter of St. Paul's* (1728), 1 Bro. P.C. 240. The documents in the case are in L.P.L., DC4.

[2] Memorandum by Dr. John Lee in a Parliamentary Paper of 1859, reprinted in 15 L.T.R. 83. The documents in the case are in L.P.L., DC5.

V

THE COMMON TABLE

THE *raison d'être* of the Society was the meeting together at meal-times, and the hall was the focus of the communal life of the members. There were at first two meals a day—breakfast and supper. Except on court days in the Court of Arches and the Court of Audience,[1] breakfast began immediately after the third stroke of the bell after High Mass in St. Paul's and dinner at the stroke of 5 pm on the bell in the clock tower of St. Paul's.[2]

There were two tables—one for the advocates and one for their servants. The advocates' servants coming into meals and the common servants were required to behave properly to the Steward and the other servants of the Society; they were not to stir up quarrels and disputes between themselves or between their masters; and they were not to use offensive or scandalous words to the Steward, but were quickly and readily to carry out his bidding in the serving and bringing of dishes from the kitchen to the advocates' table and to serve the wine, cheese, pears, or apples, and other things necessary for the advocates when and in the quantity required by him. Each servant in his turn was to do his duty at the Steward's bidding diligently and quickly on pain of losing the meal. After the meal the servants had to remove the dishes, scraps of food, napkins, and other things belonging to the table and then bring water to the advocates for washing their hands. Finally they had to join with the advocates in returning thanks to God for the meal.[3] A rule

---

[1] The Court of Audience had the same jurisdiction as the Court of Arches and was by some called its 'twin sister': Law, *Forms of Ecclesiastical Law*, p. xix. The court days in each of the four terms were governed by festivals of the Church. For tables of court days in the Court of Arches, see ibid., pp. 365–8.

[2] S.B., f.2.ᵛ.

[3] S.B., ff.2ᵛ.–3.

made on 6 May 1570 required that on every day in full term the Dean of the Arches or the senior advocate present should direct a certain portion of the Bible to be read in Latin to the advocates during dinner, the reader being paid 4*d*. each week.[1]

An advocate could bring a stranger to breakfast or dinner at the advocates' table on paying 3*d*. for his meal. It seems also that open house was kept for strangers, for it was provided by the rules of the Society that lay guests at breakfast or dinner at the advocates' table should pay 8*d*. for each meal, doctors and students in either University excepted.[2]

The rules regarding payment for meals were somewhat complicated. The week for this purpose ran from breakfast on Saturday until breakfast on the following Friday, and it was divided into two parts, the first ending with breakfast on Tuesday and the second beginning with dinner on that day. An advocate having a house or chamber in the City of London and practising in the Court of Arches or the Court of Audience, if in the City or the suburbs at the time of six meals, either continuously or at intervals, in one week was a full commoner, and if for three meals in one week he was a half-commoner, paying a half contribution.[3] During Lent the numbers of meals for this purpose were three for a full commoner and two for a half-commoner, and during the two weeks of Christmas the numbers were three for a full commoner and one for a half-commoner. A full commoner or a half-commoner was entitled to an allowance for himself and his servant in respect of each meal from which he was absent, but no allowance was to be made during the two weeks of Christmas or the weeks of Easter and Whitsun. A practising advocate living in London who was absent from the City

---

[1]Ibid., f.89.
[2]Ibid., f.3.
[3]This rule was later varied so that in counting the meals of a whole commoner Friday dinner was reckoned as two (ibid., f.2). In 1560 it was ordered that a servant in commons for four meals should be in half-commons and if for seven meals in whole commons (ibid.).

and suburbs for the whole of the two weeks of Christmas had to pay 12*d.* in relief of the common expenses incurred in his absence. If absent at Easter or Whitsun he had to pay 6*d.*

A contributor was required to pay 3*d.* for his own meal and 2*d.* for each of his servants each time he came.[1] Presumably an advocate who was not chargeable as a full commoner or a half-commoner also paid for his meals as he took them. Those contributors who were members in 1570, when it was decided to limit further admissions to advocates, were given the right to have one meal or the other at the common table without payment.[2]

The contributions to the charges for the year were agreed on 23 June, but it was ordered on 14 October 1611 that an addition or further contribution could be required if it was found after 23 June to be necessary.[3]

Under an order of 14 October 1585 failure to pay commons within six days after the end of a week led to public denunciation at the table and, on failure to pay within another three days, exclusion from the table until payment was made in full. After three denunciations the defaulter was to be excluded in perpetuity.[4]

Advocates who were in London were expected to have their meals in hall, but licences to be absent could be obtained. The most usual ground for granting a licence was that an advocate's wife was in London, the fee for such a licence being 20*s.*[5] On 22 November 1630 Dr. Steward, who had been a member for nearly sixty years, was given leave to be out of commons at his pleasure by reason of his age and want of teeth.[6] On 29 November 1690 Dr Philip Foster was excused from payment by reason of his poverty and sickness.[7]

---

[1] S.B., f.2^v.
[2] Ibid., f.89.
[3] Ibid., f.2.
[4] S.B., f.90. There is no record of this ever happening.
[5] e.g. Dr. James Hussey 10 Jan. 1607 (L.B., f.89^v.).
[6] Ibid., f.143^v.
[7] Ibid., f.221. On 16 December £5 was ordered to be paid out of the common stock towards his burial (ibid., f.221^v.).

The catering procedure was changed in 1710. When Mrs. Wright, the Cook, retired it was decided not to replace her, but to employ a cook from term to term.[1] Who supervised these temporary cooks does not appear, for there are no records relating to the catering earlier than the Commons Book,[2] which begins with Trinity Term, 1738 and ends with Trinity Term 1779. During the period covered by this book the Register made termly payments for food and wine to a succession of persons who are not identified beyond their names. They begin with Thomas Cooke, who was succeeded by William Sparrow at the end of 1738. Sparrow then continued until 1746, when he was succeeded by Mary Sparrow, presumably his widow, who was winding up his affairs. After six months Richard Hughes took over and continued to 1751. Then came William Jones and Mary Jones, one or the other signing the receipts until 1762. They were succeeded by Thomas Willis, who was in his turn succeeded in 1773 by James Griffiths, who signed all the receipts until the close of the book in 1779.

The Register made these payments out of the money collected by the Porter from the members, each of whom paid a term fee and wine money, also on a termly basis, and a charge for commons on a daily basis. In addition, some members treated the others with wine, the usual practice being for each new member to treat for two dinners shortly after his admission, being in return exempted from the payment of commons in respect of the days on which he treated.

It would appear that the persons who were paid for the food and wine were tavern-keepers in the neighbourhood, for in every Hilary Term until 1747 the Register gave half-a guinea to the cook at the Sun Tavern, and from 1747 onwards a similar gift was made to the cook at the Horn Tavern. This Horn Tavern is not to be identified with the present Horn Tavern at the corner of Little Knightrider

[1] See p. 53 *ante*.
[2] L.P.L., DC25.

Street and Sermon Lane. In the period covered by the Commons Book the Horn Tavern was on the east side of Godliman Street, which is much nearer than Sermon Lane to the site of Doctors' Commons.[1]

The money collected from the members by the Porter sometimes turned out to be insufficient to enable the Register to pay the catering bills in full. Instead of making supplementary charges for dinners already eaten, the Register obtained money to make up the deficiency from the Librarian. This practice began in 1771, and similar payments appear in the Commons Book frequently during the remainder of the 1770s.[2] The Librarian's account book shows that a number of payments were made for wine out of the Library funds between 1799 and 1802.

There are no catering accounts after 1779, but the general accounts of the College make it appear that the catering continued to be done by outside contractors. The last such contractor first appears in a resolution passed on 26 February 1856, that Mr. Rich should provide the Hall dinners.[3] This was presumably George Rich, who carried on business as a venison dealer and pastry cook at 2 Ludgate Hill. The accounts contain payments to Rich to the end of 1859, when dining in commons ceased.[4]

Since the advocates' table was the centre of the Society's activities, it is not surprising that some of the benefactions which it received from its members were directed to the common table, such as the legacy of Dr. Glyn, who died in 1557, leaving 20s. to make a 'repast' at his burial.[5]

Of more permanent value were the gifts and legacies of

[1]B. Lillywhite, *London Signs* (1972), p. 288. The Sun Tavern was in Carter Lane (ibid., p. 530). Both are shown on Rocque's *Plan of the Cities of London and Westminster*, published in 1748. The Horn was less than half the distance of the Sun from the back gate of Doctors' Commons.

[2]There are corresponding entries in the Librarian's account book (P.R.O., PRO 30/28/9) and L.B., ff.314, 323.

[3]M.B., s.d.

[4]The last payment of £45.14s.6d. for 1859 was made on 2 March 1860 (L.P.L., DC15).

[5]P.C.C. 25 Wrastley.

plate or of money directed to be laid out on the purchase of plate. The earliest recorded donor of plate was Dr. Honywood, who on the day of his admission, 11 March 1519, gave to the society a gilt spoon with the effigy of an apostle with a little ship in his left hand and a book in his right hand.[1] At the time when Honywood made his entrance gift the Society was about to receive a parting gift from one of its most senior members. By his will proved in April 1519 Dr. Stone left to 'the Honourable Company of the Doctors of tharches in London' a 'swagyd' (i.e. ornamented) cup of silver parcel gilt with a cover.[2] In the next year an advocate member, Dr. Potkyn, died. He did not mention Doctors' Commons in his will proved 25 May 1520,[3] but on 15 April 1522 his brother William, a proctor of the Court of Arches, delivered to the Society a gilt salt with a cover, weighing 14 oz. and suitably inscribed.[4]

There is a gap of over forty years before the next recorded gift of plate. On 6 May 1565 Dr. Thomas Martyn gave six silver spoons with the letters M.M. engraved on the ends of the handles in memory of Mary, his wife.[5] Two days later Walter Jones, Archdeacon of Brecon, gave another six silver spoons with the letters W.I. engraved on the ends of the handles.[6] Both these sets of spoons were probably of the type with seal-top knops, since this is the only type of the period on which initials could be easily engraved.[7]

However, no systematic record of gifts of plate has survived. Probably none was kept, for the inventories of the Society's plate include the names of a number of otherwise unrecorded donors.

There are extant three inventories of plate made when it

[1]S.B., f.23. The ship was the attribute of St. Jude (R. P. L. Milburn, *Saints and their Emblems* (Oxford, 1961), p. 149).
[2]P.C.C. 28 Ayloffe.
[3]P.C.C. 2 Maynwaryng.
[4]See p. 130 *post*, where the inscription is transcribed.
[5]S.B., f. 119
[6]Ibid.
[7]Spoons of this type are illustrated in C. Oman, *English Domestic Silver* (1947), pl. III. 12 and pl. IV. 19.

was handed over by one Treasurer to another. The first is dated 24 June 1573. It contains only four items:

1. The great salt $18\frac{1}{2}$ oz.
2. The other salt $8\frac{1}{2}$ oz.
3. 2 dozen spoons $36\frac{1}{4}$ oz.
4. A basin and ewer the gift of
   the Archbishop of Canterbury 46 oz. and 24 oz.[1]

Although there is a discrepancy between the weight of the 'great salt' in 1573 and that of the Potkyn salt recorded in 1522, they were probably the same object. Twelve of the spoons would be the Martyn and Jones gifts. The other twelve spoons and the other salt could have been otherwise unrecorded gifts or could have been purchased as means of investing the Society's surplus funds, a common practice among colleges and other bodies.[2] Presumably Honywood's Apostle spoon and Stone's 'swagyd' cup had been sold. Archbishop Parker's gift was probably a recent one, for he had presented plate to three Cambridge colleges, Gonville and Caius, Trinity Hall, and Corpus Christi in 1569 and 1570.[3] His gift to Corpus Christi College consisted of a basin and ewer, each having his arms on it. It appears from a later inventory that the Doctors' Commons basin and ewer also bore the Archbishop's arms, so they may have resembled the surviving pieces at Corpus Christi, though these have the arms enamelled, while the inventory describes the arms on the Doctors' Commons pieces as being engraved.[4]

Before the next inventory there were several more gifts. In 1575 Dr. Huycke left to 'the Doctour Commons and to the Companye there my dozen of silver spoones and my twoe Double gilt Cupps with a cover'.[5] Geoffrey Morley left by his will £5 to 'the Company of the Doctors

[1] L.B., f.17.
[2] C. Oman, *Caroline Silver* (1970), p. 2.
[3] E. Alfred Jones, *The Old Plate of the Cambridge Colleges* (Cambridge, 1910), pp. 28, 33, 42.
[4] For an illustration of the basin and ewer at Corpus Christi College, see Jones, op. cit., pl. XLIX.
[5] P.C.C. 36 Pyckering.

and Advocates of the Arches to buye a piece of plate withall
to remaine in theire howse of commons for a memory'.[1]
Instead of the money, however, the Society received from
Morley's executor on 11 December 1580 a silver cup
weighing 18½ oz.[2] In 1584 Dr. Lewes left his basin and ewer
of silver parcel gilt as a memorial.[3] In the following year Dr.
Hervey left £6.13s.4d. to 'the Company of the Arches
keepinge Commons in the Doctors Commons in the Arches
for a piece of plate.[4]

The next inventory was made on 23 June 1589 by Dr.
Standish when he delivered the plate to his successor as
Treasurer, Dr. Skevington. This inventory is of special
interest because it records damage and losses. It contains the
following items:

1. 14 silver spoons with knops engraved
   A.D.C., two of the seals being broken
   from the bowls.
2. There should have been 12 silver spoons
   without letters having gilt knops,
   whereof 9 were delivered to Dr. Standish by Dr. Stanhope and the other 3 be
   wanting: 2 were lost in Mr. Scott's time
   and 1 in Richard Evans's time.[5]
3. There should have been 5 silver spoons
   with gilt knops engraved W.I., whereof
   4 were delivered by Dr. Stanhope (sic)
   to Dr. Skevington, of which one wanted
   the knop, and the fifth was lost either by
   Scott or Evans.
4. There were 3 silver spoons with gilt
   knops engraved M.M., which Dr.
   Stanhope also delivered to Dr. Skevington.

[1]P.C.C. 29 Langley.
[2]S.B., f.119.
[3]P.C.C. 10 Watson.
[4]P.C.C. 14 Brudenell.
[5]Scott and Evans were stewards: see p. 51 ante.

5. 3 bell salts silver and gilt, all engraved,
with their covers all gilt, weighing
together $44\frac{1}{4}$ oz.

6. 1 bell trencher salt with a pepper-box
cover all gilt, weighing $16\frac{3}{4}$ oz.

7. 3 gilt bowls engraved within, without
covers, weighing $32\frac{3}{4}$ oz. less
                                               4 dwt.

8. 1 deep white silver bowl without a
cover of Mr. Geoffrey Morley's gift,
weighing $8\frac{1}{4}$ oz.

9. 1 basin and ewer silver and gilt, engraved with Archbishop Parker's arms,
the ewer $23\frac{1}{2}$ oz.
the basin   45 oz.

10. 1 basin and ewer parcel gilt of Dr.
Lewes's gift, having D.L. on the top of
the ewer and the bottom of the basin,
weighing together   94 oz.

11. A toasting fork of 'brasell',[1] garnished
with silver and gilt at both ends and the
middle[2]

This inventory shows that the Society's spoons were
subject both to hard wear and some measure of either care-
lessness or dishonesty. Of the six spoons given by Archdeacon Jones in 1565 only five were still 'on charge', of
which one had lost its knop and one had been lost by a
Steward, while of the six given in the same year by Dr.
Martyn only three survived. The fourteen spoons with the
knops engraved A.D.C., although newer than the other
spoons, seem to have had some rough usage.

The only other items in the 1573 inventory which are
identifiable in the 1589 inventory are Archbishop Parker's
basin and ewer, though one of the salts mentioned must
have been that given by Dr. Potkyn. Geoffrey Morley's bowl

---

[1] i.e. made of brazil-wood.   [2] L.B., f.42.

weighing 8¼ oz. cannot have been the cup weighing 18½ oz. received from his executor in 1580. Presumably the cup was sold and part of the money received was laid out in the purchase of the less heavy bowl. No doubt the position in Doctors' Commons was no different from that at Trinity Hall, where the plate was treated with 'something more than freedom' and was sold or converted by the college officers at their discretion.[1]

In 1592 Dr. Johns (or Jones) left £10, partly to 'amende' the commons on the day of his burial and partly for a piece of plate for the use of the Society.[2] In the same year Dr. Skeffington directed his executors to cause to be made a 'white bowl of silver' worth £3 with his name and arms engraved on it to be given to the Society.[3] Dr. Aubrey, who died 23 June 1595, left to the Society 'a peece of plate all doble gilte with a cover weyenge 26¾ oz and by me for them specyally appointed'.[4] Dr. Lewen, who died on 15 April 1598, left a legacy to the advocates and proctors of the Arches for a dinner and a piece of plate.[5]

The piece of plate purchased out of Dr. Johns's legacy duly appears in the inventory made on 13 July 1598. This inventory, the last to be entered in the Long Book, contained the following items:

1. A basin and ewer all gilt which Archbishop Parker gave.
2. A basin and ewer parcel gilt which Dr. Lewes gave, being in a case, with D.L. on the bottom of the basin and the cover of the ewer.
3. 3 bell salts with covers gilt.
4. A little bell salt with a cover gilt, being a trencher salt.

[1] *Warren's Book*, p. 95.
[2] P.C.C. 9 Harrington.
[3] P.C.C. 75 Harrington.
[4] P.C.C. 46 Scott.
[5] P.C.C. 1 Lewyn.

5. A gilt bowl with a cover, Dr. Aubrey's
   arms thereon, which he gave.   26¼ oz.
6. 3 flat silver bowls gilt.
7. 3 French bowls gilt which Dr. Jones gave.
8. 2 little (*illegible*) bowls gilt which Dr.
   Forth gave.
9. A great French white bowl which Mr.
   Morley gave.
10. A little white French bowl with Dr.
   Skevington's arms on it which he
   gave.
11. 3 dozen silver spoons with gilt knops
   with A.O.D. on them.
12. A (*illegible*) bowl with a cover, chased
   work, which Dr. Cosin gave at his
   death,[1] weighing   17¾ oz.
13. A toasting fork of 'brasell',[2] the tines of
   silver gilt, and a middle knob and an
   end knob of the same, which Archbishop Sands gave.[3]

The names of the donors of all the pieces which are not in
the 1589 inventory are given in the entries relating to those
pieces in the 1598 inventory, so Dr. Lewen's legacy had not
been laid out in plate before the latter inventory was made.

After this there is no detailed information about the plate.
Some of it survived the hazards of the Civil War and the
Fire of London, for on 10 February 1670 £17.3s.6d. was
received for the sale of old plate.[4] This was plate no longer
required. There was other plate, for on 5 November 1681 it
was ordered that Simon Gentry on his appointment as
Porter should cause an inventory to be made of plate,
pewter, linen, and other utensils of the dining-room and
kitchen, and that at the end of every term the plate, pewter,

---

[1] Cosin died 30 Nov. 1597.
[2] See p. 84, n. 1, *ante*.
[3] L.B., f.70. Archbishop Sandys of York d. 1588.
[4] Ibid., f.203.

and linen should be locked in a box and the key delivered to the Treasurer until the beginning of the next term.[1] The last recorded addition to the Society's plate was the purchase in Michaelmas Term 1739 from Mr. Hart of four silver labels for wine bottles.[2]

What happened to the plate when the Society's property was sold in the 1860s does not appear. There is no mention of it in the records of the period.

[1]Ibid., f.207^v.
[2]C.B., s.d.

VI

THE LIBRARY

WHILE it is possible that the books which were bequeathed by Dr. Thomas Kent for the use of the Official, Dean, Examiners, Advocates, and Proctors of the Court of Arches in 1469 formed the nucleus of a library for the Society in Paternoster Row, there is no direct evidence that effect was given to Kent's wishes,[1] nor is there anything to indicate that the Society had any library in its early days. Indeed, such evidence as there is on the matter is to the contrary. A number of members had sufficient regard for the Society to remember it in their wills, but no bequests of books to the Society have been found, and pecuniary legacies, if earmarked at all, were to be applied to the provision of commemorative dinners or the purchase of plate. Books, on the other hand, even books on canon or civil law, were left to the testators' colleges at Oxford or Cambridge or in some cases to other members of Doctors' Commons personally. If the Kent library was still available for the ecclesiastical lawyers at the end of the fifteenth century, it probably continued under its former management and was not transferred to the newly formed Society.

If the Society had a library in the old Mountjoy House, which is unlikely,[2] the books cannot have survived the Fire of London, for Sir Leoline Jenkins by his will, proved 9 November 1685, left to the Society forty volumes in folio or quarto of law or other books 'to begin their library', the

---

[1] For Kent's bequest, see p. 3 *ante*.

[2] *Pace* J. D. M. Derrett, *Henry Swinburne* (York, 1973), pp. 18, 32, where it is suggested that Swinburne, who died in 1624, may have consulted books in Doctors' Commons, and A. G. Dickens, *The English Reformation* (1964), p. 250, where it is implied that the study of ecclesiastical law survived the Reformation partly because of the library built up by the gifts of bishops at Doctors' Commons. As to the bishops' gifts, see p. 91 *post*.

volumes to be chosen by Sir Richard Lloyd, Dean of the Arches, he first choosing two volumes for himself: the rest of the testator's books were to go to Jesus College, Oxford.[1] Jenkins also left to the Society the manuscript Abstract of the laws of Oleron dedicated to him by his clerk, Thomas Bedford.[2] The manuscript was not received until 2 March 1708.[3]

Jenkins's forty books were kept by the successive Deans of the Arches, 'there being no place set apart for a Library'. Sir Richard Lloyd, who was Dean of the Arches when Jenkins's bequest was received, promised £10 to buy books for the Library 'when there should be a place for it'. Lloyd died in June 1686. Sometime after 1690 his son Nathaniel proposed to pay the £10 if the Society would fix a place for the Library, but it was not until 1697 that the room over the dining-room was 'parted off' and made 'tolerably conveni-ent', the rest of the room being let to the officers of the Prerogative and Admiralty Courts.[4] Dr. Owen Wynne gave two presses for the Jenkins books and Dr. Nathaniel Lloyd another for the books bought with his father's £10. Then Sir John Cooke sent in some books, and Sir Charles Hedges sent some which had been taken in a French prize.[5]

During the early years of the eighteenth century there were two substantial accretions to the Library, each of them collected by a former member of the Society. James Gibson, Town Clerk of London, (d. 1717), presented the library of his ancestor, Sir John Gibson, sometime Judge of the Prerogative Court of Canterbury.[6] Sir John Gibson had died in 1613, so the purchase of all the books of common, canon, and civil law in the library of Dr. Oldys shortly after his death in 1708 must have provided a useful supplement of

---

[1]P.C.C. 136 Cann.

[2]See p. 94 *post*.

[3]L.B., f.235. The late date at which the library was formed would account for its lack of completeness in the works of sixteenth- and seventeenth-century English civilians remarked upon in Derrett, *Henry Swinburne*, p. 18 n.

[4]All Souls Coll., MS. 325, App. G, p. 1; L.B., f.228.

[5]All Souls Coll., MS. 325, App. G, p. 1.

[6]Stow, *A Survey of London* (ed. J. Strype), i. 153.

more modern works. Oldys's library, which filled three large rooms in his chambers, was estimated to be over 1,000 printed books, which with some manuscripts were ranged in a large room next the hall and were then 'methodized' by Dr. Pinfold.[1] Shortly after these valuable accessions Dr. Harwood was able to tell John Strype, then gathering material for his edition of Stow's *Survey of London*, that the Library 'is and will be in a continually growing condition'.[2]

The 'continually growing condition' of the Library was reflected in the continual need for new catalogues. Shortly after Sir Leoline Jenkins's legacy had been received there were enough books to justify the making of a catalogue, and about 1690 there was a separate catalogue of law books.[3] By 1714 it had become necessary to have a new catalogue in two volumes.[4] In 1736 a Mr. Moors was paid 25 guineas for 'methodizing' the library and making another new catalogue.[5] This seems to have been in a form to which additions could be made, for in 1738 a Mr. Garnier was paid 2 guineas for cataloguing books. Presumably these were the books for which 'wainscott' presses were made earlier in the year.

In 1742 the Library received a major benefaction under the will of Sir Nathaniel Lloyd, who left to 'that Honourable and Useful Profession of Civilians The Advocates of Drs. Commons a College of Gentlemen regularly Bred too little Esteemed and too industriously Depressed' books to the value of 100 guineas such as Dr. Strahan should direct to be bought for their library.[6] Effect was given to this bequest by paying 100 guineas to the library fund, from which payment was made to Strahan for the books. Two years later £4.10s.0d. was paid for a bookcase for Lloyd's books.

---

[1] *Notes and Queries*, 2 S.ii (1861), p. 404.
[2] Stow, loc. cit.
[3] *Catalogue of Sale of Library of College of Advocates . . . 22 April 1861 and seven following days*, lots 2422, 2423, purchased by Dr. John Lee (W. H. McAlpine, *Catalogue of the Law Library at Hartwell House* (1865), pp. 71–2).
[4] Ibid., lot 2424, purchased by Dr. John Lee (W. H. McAlpine, op, cit.). This catalogue was made by John Kersey. There is a biography of Kersey in *D.N.B.*
[5] P.R.O., PRO30/26/9.
[6] *Warren's Brok*, p. 321.

The growth of the Library by the bringing together of several collections of books resulted in some duplication. This made it necessary to pass a resolution on 5 February 1765 authorizing Dr. Ducarel to catalogue all the duplicates and such other books as he looked upon as useless to the Library.[1] Presumably these books were sold, but no copy of Ducarel's catalogue appears to have survived.

Work on cataloguing the books in the Library continued to be carried out, the last manuscript version being a catalogue 'in one general alphabet' and another 'classed and in sizes'.[2] Finally there was a printed catalogue, published in 1818.[3]

The Dr. Pinfold who 'methodized' Dr. Oldys's books was the second of three successive generations of advocates. He was appointed Librarian in 1706 and continued to serve in that capacity until 1728. It is perhaps no coincidence that shortly after Pinfold's appointment a new source of revenue for the Library was found. It had been the practice for each bishop on his consecration to pay for a dinner for the members of Doctors' Commons. On 20 March 1706 it was decided that in future the money should be received by Dr. Pinfold towards the Library.[4] On 7 February 1707 two newly appointed bishops, Blackall of Exeter and Trimnell of Norwich, each paid £25 to the Library fund.[5] From then onwards most new archbishops and bishops in the Province of Canterbury made similar gifts. The sums given varied. The usual tariff was £50 from an archbishop and £20 from a bishop, but some gave more and some nothing at all. At first similar payments came from the Province of York. On 11 March 1707 Sir William Dawes, Bt. paid £20 on appointment as Bishop of Chester, and he paid 50 guineas when he was translated to York in 1713, but there were only three

[1] L.B., f.294.
[2] *Catalogue of Sale*. Lots 2425, 2426.
[3] *Catalogue of the Books in the Library of the College of Advocates in Doctors' Commons* (1818). There is a copy in the Guildhall Library.
[4] L.B., f.233.
[5] P.R.O., PRO30/26/9.

other payments from the northern province. No doubt this apparent lack of generosity was due to the fact that the jurisdiction of the Court of Arches was confined to the Province of Canterbury. The last payment from the Province of York was made by Bishop Osbaldeston of Carlisle in 1747. It then came to be accepted that such payments were no longer to be expected.

The collection of the episcopal bounty was placed in the hands of the Porter, who received a commission of 10*s.* out of each payment. A typical entry in the Library accounts is £3.10*s.*0*d.* 'paid to Mr Powell for 7 bishops'. This system continued until 7 June 1762, when it was:

Ordered That upon any future confirmation of every Bishop within the Province of Canterbury the Librarian ... do attend such Bishop in the Dining Room when he signs his Assent & Consent, and do claim the usual fees due to the Library.

The receipts from the bishops exceeded the Library expenses to such an extent that on 4 July 1769 £308.17*s.*6*d.* was invested in the purchase of £350 Bank Reduced 3 per cent Annuities. There was a further investment of £43 on 8 June 1770, but shortly after this there was initiated a new practice of using money in the Library fund for the general expenses of the Society. This began with the sale on 27 November 1770 of £250 of the Bank Annuities to pay the fine to the Dean and Chapter of St. Paul's on the renewal of the lease of the College premises. In the following years there were various payments to the Steward. It may be that these payments were for wine, for in 1799 it began to be stated that payments for wine were made on the requisition of the Steward. In 1801 no less than £47.0*s.*9*d.* was paid for wine out of the Library fund. Perhaps this was regarded as but a reversion to the old custom of applying the bishops' contributions to the provision of dinners. Furthermore, there may have been less reluctance to such an application of the Library fund after 1779, when the £20 admission fee from each new member began to be paid into that fund.

As well as additions to, there were losses from, the Library. The losses are not so well documented as the accessions, but the Library accounts record two of them. On 29 January 1812 £1.10s.od. was paid to Butterworth, the bookseller, for three volumes of Rymer's *Foedera*, which belonged to the Library and which he had purchased at the sale of Dr. Battine's books. This was part of the set which Archbishop Wake had presented to the Library. Six years later Butterworth discovered another book belonging to the Library which he had purchased at the Battine sale. This was a copy of the *editio princeps* of Justinian's *Institutes*. On 3 June 1818 £2.2s.od. was paid for its recovery. The strange feature of these transactions with Butterworth was that Dr. Battine was still alive (he did not die until 1836), yet it does not appear that he ever reimbursed the Society for the money which had to be paid for the recovery of its own property. Perhaps the order of 30 March 1706 that keys of the Library be bought for each Doctor was a mistake.[1]

The Library was by no means confined to canon- and civil-law books. Indeed, such books did not even form the bulk of the Library. There was a comprehensive collection of common-law books, consisting of textbooks and reports, which was similar to that to be found in the library of one of the Inns of Court at the time. Also like an Inn of Court library, the Doctors' Commons Library contained a wide selection of non-legal works. The scope of the printed books in the Library is described in the sale catalogue of 1861 as follows:

The works of the most celebrated English and foreign writers on civil, canon, and ecclesiastical law from the earliest times; a large collection of councils, synods, and decrees; works on church polity and discipline, monastic history and rule; scarce and valuable treatises on the laws of marriage; the works of the Fathers and Doctors of the Church, ecclesiastical historians and more recent divines; antiquities, heraldry, numismatics, county

[1] L.B., f.233.

history and topography, early voyages and travels; rare and curious tracts on various subjects; standard authors in history and biography, both ancient and modern; modern practical law books; valuable works of reference, glossaries, dictionaries, etc.

There was also a small collection of manuscripts. This consisted of:

1. Abstract of the Laws of Oleron and of the laws in the Black Book of the Admiralty and of the maritime laws amongst the Acts of Parliament, etc., with translations of the Laws of Oleron and those in the Black Book, dedicated to Sir Leoline Jenkins by Thomas Bedford. A legacy from Jenkins.[1]

2. Admiralty Papers. Upwards of 200 letters and papers addressed to Sir Charles Hedges, Judge of the Court of Admiralty, 1691–8. Bookplate of Townsend Andrews, LL.B. (Trinity Hall 1756).[2]

3. Letter signed by John Bradshaw as President of the Council of State 1 July 1651. Presented by Dr. Lloyd.[3]

4. Case of *East India Company* v. *Thomas Sands* (1683).[4]

5. Catalogue of processes in the Registry of the Court of Delegates.[5]

6. Papers relating to ecclesiastical jurisdiction, Henry VIII–James I. Mainly copies from B.L., MS. Cotton Cleo. F.1.[6]

7. Common Place Book. Forms of oath, Orders in Council, petitions, etc., mainly relating to the City of London.[7]

8. Notes by Sir Charles Hedges of cases decided by him in the Court of Admiralty 23 Oct. 1690–28 June 1694.[8]

---

[1] Lot 2418. Purchased by Dr. Spinks. Now Inner Temple, Misc. MS. 56. For a full description, see J. Conway Davies, *Catalogue of Manuscripts in the Library . . . of the Inner Temple* (Oxford, 1972), iii. 1225–7.
[2] Lot 2419. Now B.L., Add. MS. 25,098.
[3] Lot 2420.
[4] Lot 2421.
[5] Lot 2427.
[6] Lot 2429. Now B.L., Add. MS. 28, 843.
[7] Lot 2430. Now Guildhall Lib., MS. 213.
[8] Lot 2431. Now B.L., Add. MSS. 24, 102–3.

9. Precedents in Ecclesiastical Causes and notes, etc., by Sir Charles Hedges. Petition of the Advocates of the Arches, drawn up by Dr. Trumbull 1683, but not presented to the King. Petitions of the Advocates drawn up by Drs. Oldys and Hedges.[1]

10. Common Place Book of Civil, Ecclesiastical and Admiralty Laws; List of Sir William Trumbull's books, with catalogue of the writer's own library.[2]

11. Common Place Book on Legal Matters. *c.* 1684.[3]

12. Common Place Book on Matters of Ecclesiastical and Admiralty Law. Partly written by Sir Charles Hedges, 1652–1702.[4]

13. A. C. Ducarel's 'Summary Account'. Presented to Edward Rowe Mores 1754 and at the sale of his library in 1779 claimed and returned.[5]

14. Index to Oughton's *Ordo Judiciorum*, procured for the Library by Dr. Salusbury 1828.[6]

15. Sir Charles Hedges's account of fees and charges received 1691–1702, and Mr. Bedford's accounts 1693–9.[7]

16. Sir Charles Hedges's Letter Book, 1694–1702.[8]

17. G. Heinecci, *Dictata ad Institutiones Juris Civilis*. Written by Alexander Hume Campbell. 2 vv. 1726.[9]

18. Index to 253 Admiralty cases, 1758–66.[10]

19. Nathaniel Pigott, *Analogie of the Common Law of England and of the Civill Law.* 3vv. *c.* 1680.[11]

20. Precedents, Cases, and Opinions.[12]

---

[1]Lot 2432. Now B.L. Add. MS. 24,104.

[2]Lot 2433. This book formerly belonged to Dr. Andrew (d. 1747) and was purchased by Dr. John Lee (McAlpine, op. cit., p. 49).

[3]Lot 2434. This book also belonged to Dr. Andrew and was purchased by Dr. John Lee (ibid.).

[4]Lot 2435.

[5]Lot 2436. Purchased for £10 by Reeves and Turner, booksellers, of Temple Bar (McAlpine, op. cit., p. 73). Now in Law Society's Library.

[6]Lot 2437.

[7]Lot 2438. Now B.L., Add. MS. 24, 105–6.

[8]Lot 2439. Now B.L., Add. MS. 24, 107.

[9]Lot 2440. Campbell was Treasurer of the Inner Temple in 1751.

[10]Lot 2441.   [11]Lot 2442.   [12]Lot 2443.

21. *Processus in Curia Marescalli.* 2 vv.[1]
22. Collection of Cases of Prize Appeals, 1744–60, with MS. notes by Lord Chief Baron Parker and others. Presented by George Parker to Thomas Lister and by him to Dr. J. H. Arnold and by him to the Library.[2]
23. The Consularie Lawes of the Sea, translated out of the Italian, 1678, and other Admiralty items.[3]
24. Copies of documents relating to Ship Money, 1638–9.[4]
25. Statutes of the Order of the Garter, presented to William Cavendish, 1st Duke of Devonshire on his installation [14 May 1689], with his arms emblazoned.[5]

The Library continued to be maintained for a time after the coming into operation of the legislation of 1857 which sealed the fate of Doctors' Commons. The Sub-Librarian resigned on 15 January 1858, having been transferred to the new Court of Probate, but he offered to attend in the Library for three hours a day after the hours of his official duties.[6] This arrangement was short-lived. On 26 January 1859 Dr. Lee proposed that the books and £6,000 should be offered to the Middle Temple for the benefit of its new library and, if not accepted, to be offered to the Inner Temple, Lincoln's Inn, or Gray's Inn. This proposal was not seconded, and on 9 March 1860 it was resolved that the further purchase of books and the salary to the Librarian should be discontinued on the following 1 August.[7]

In the following year the books were sold. About a third of them were bought by the Government for £645.3s.6d. On 22 April 1861 and the seven following days the rest were sold at Hodgson's auction rooms.[8] The auction sale

---

[1] Lot 2444. Now in the College of Arms. Note on fly-leaf of vol. I: 'P. Le Neve 26 May 1704. Belonged to Sjt. Goddard of Lynn, Norf.' Peter Le Neve was appointed Norroy King of Arms 25 May 1704. His books were sold in 1731.

[2] Lot 2445.   [3] Lot 2446.

[4] Lot 2447. Now B.L., MS. Add. 25,040.

[5] Lot 2448.

[6] M.B., s.d.

[7] Ibid.

[8] The auctioneer's annotated copy of the catalogue is in the British Library. It gives the prices, but not the names of the purchasers.

produced £1128.4*s*.10*d*., which with the money received from the Government produced a dividend of £68.4*s*.2*d*. for each of the twenty-six members.[1]

It is apparent from the stamps on them that the books bought by the Government were acquired for the Court of Admiralty and the Court of Probate.[2] They were moved from Westminster to the new Royal Courts of Justice, where some, or possibly all, of them now form part of the Supreme Court Library.

[1] L.P.L., MS. 1560. f.67.
[2] I am grateful to Mr. C. L. Fisher, M.B.E., the Librarian of the Supreme Court, for producing some of these books for my inspection.

VII

THE COLLEGE CHURCH

THE original home of Doctors' Commons in Paternoster Row lay in the parish of St. Faith-under-St. Paul's. The parish church was an undercroft beneath part of the choir of the Cathedral. Being but a short distance from their house, it could be expected that the doctors would use that church for their corporate worship. It is, therefore, at first sight somewhat surprising to find that the only relevant entry in the early records of the Society is of a gift by Dr. Edwards on 28 June 1610 of 40s. towards the building of the seats in 'Paules church'.[1] This would seem to indicate that the doctors worshipped in the Cathedral and not in St. Faith's. However, it was not unknown for St. Faith's to be referred to as being within the Cathedral of which it was structurally part. An earlier example is to be found in the will of Sir Humphrey Talbot, dated 18 February 1492. Talbot's mother, Margaret, Countess of Shrewsbury, had been buried in St. Faith's,[2] and in his will he provided for a stone to be put on the pillar before 'the grave of the lady my moder in Powlis'.[3] It therefore appears that the seats built in 1610 could have been in St. Faith's and that the doctors continued to worship there after they had moved to Mountjoy House.

There is no further evidence about the doctors' corporate worship before the Great Fire. After that there is ample evidence that they used the church of St. Benet Paul's Wharf in which parish Mountjoy House was situate. The back entrance to Mountjoy House from Thames Street by way of Church Court passed along the western boundary of

[1] L.B., f.96ᵛ.
[2] *St. Paul's*, p. 120.
[3] P.C.C. 20 Vox.

the church and churchyard. Being in such close proximity, it is not surprising that St. Benet's church came to fill for Doctors' Commons the role of a college chapel, as it did for the College of Arms on the other side of St. Benet's Hill. Indeed, it was known to the members of Doctors' Commons as 'the College Church'.[1]

It was the custom for the members to attend church as a corporate body in robes. This custom lapsed about 1790, but at a meeting on 25 June 1803 it was decided to revive it and to request the members to attend on all the Sundays during term-time.[2]

When the church was rebuilt after the Fire, a gallery was built in the north aisle for the use of the members of Doctors' Commons. At a meeting on 1 July 1682 it was agreed that each lodging in the Commons should pay £5 towards the charges of this gallery.[3] On 3 November 1693 it was resolved that a cushion should be made for the Doctors' seat in the Church.[4] On 1 October 1712 it was decided to enlarge the seat for the Doctors in the gallery by throwing in the back seats and making double rows. The gallery was also to be 'beautified' in the front by carpeting 'or other ornamental stuff'.[5]

The work was carried out during the following Hilary Term. The gallery was provided with a red valence and cushion, apparently on the desk, long green cushions, apparently on the seats, long hassocks, and the arms of Great Britain, the See of Canterbury, and the Lord High Admiral on the front.[6]

The Doctors' wives sat apart from their husbands. The resolution of 3 November 1693 provided for the enlargement and lining of the 'women's pew' and the wainscotting of the window at the charge of the married men.[7] It would

[1]L.P.L., MS. 1560, f.14.
[2]Ibid.
[3]L.B., f.208ᵛ.
[4]Ibid., f.226.
[5]Ibid., f.239ᵛ.
[6]All Souls Coll., MS. 325   [7]L.B., f.226.

appear that this 'pew' was part of the gallery, for on 25 June 1765 it was resolved that the 'Doctors' Gallery' be new lined and the carpet in the 'Lady's Gallery' cleaned.[1]

In 1837 the seats in the gallery were re-upholstered by Allnut and Company. Their bill for £126.0s.7½d. was regarded as exorbitant, but they refused to abate it, so it was paid under protest, coupled with a statement that Allnut and Company would never again be employed by the College.[2]

The suggestion of the late W. H. Godfrey that the easternmost third of the gallery was appropriated to the College of Arms and that the arms on the front had been re-arranged so as to place the Royal Arms in the centre 'in compliment to the College of Arms'[3] is not borne out by the entries in the Long Book. Not only is there no indication that the gallery was shared with the College of Arms, but it is unlikely that the Doctors would have paid for a set of Royal Arms to be placed on a part of the gallery appropriated to the College of Arms. Furthermore, there are monuments to Sir William Wynne, Dean of the Arches, and Catherine, wife of Sir Christopher Robinson, Judge of the Court of Admiralty, on the walls of the part of the gallery supposedly appropriated to the College of Arms and no monument to an Officer of Arms in any part of the gallery.[4] It was decided on 21 November 1836 that the monuments in the Church to the memory of late members of the College should be 'blackened' and re-gilt and the arms freshly coloured.[5]

The advocates did not confine their expenditure at St. Benet's to their own gallery. The altar, bells, pulpit, most of the ornaments, and a silver bason were given by Sir Leoline Jenkins, Sir Robert Wyseman, Sir Thomas Pinfold, and Mrs. Cottle, the widow of a proctor.[6] The Society also contributed to the general church expenses. They paid

[1]Ibid., f.294ᵛ.
[2]M.B., 14 June 1837.
[3]15 L.T.R. 35, repeated in W. H. Godfrey, *The College of Arms* (1963), p. 38.
[4]F. W. Steer, *Guide to the Church of St. Benet Paul's Wharf* (Chichester, 1970), p. 9.
[5]M.B., s.d.
[6]All Souls Coll., MS. 325, App. G, p. 3.

£2.11s.6d. a year to the clerk and sexton. On 3 July 1832 they resolved to contribute £25 towards £150 to be spent on an organ. On 20 January 1843 they resolved to subscribe £20 towards what has been described as 'about the worst instance of wholesale vandalism in the City'. This was the recasting of the communion plate of St. Benet's. The plate had been given by Eleanor James in 1712, and it was remade into two flagons, two cups, three patens, and five plates.[1]

On 11 November 1843 it was resolved that £20 should be paid to the Afternoon Lecturer at St. Benet's for the year beginning 1 January 1844. This was stated to be on the express understanding that the Lecturer was not to send round to the members of the Society for individual subscriptions, as had apparently been his custom. The payment was continued from year to year, and the Lecturer came to be regarded as the College Chaplain, being so described in a resolution of 15 January 1858 to continue paying his salary. The last payment was made on 7 January 1861.[2]

[1]E. Freshfield, *Communion Plate of the Churches in the City of London* (1894), p. 24; M.B.

[2]L.P.L., DC15; M.B. The Lecturer is named as the Revd. C. Dickens from 1854.

VIII

THE CLOSING YEARS

ALTHOUGH the common-law judges closely confined the jurisdiction of the courts in which the civilians practised by the issue of writs of prohibition against any excess of jurisdiction, there was no real threat to the existence of those courts until the early years of the nineteenth century. The genesis of that threat can be seen in the appointment on 28 January 1830 of a Royal Commission to inquire into the ecclesiastical courts. Owing to the King's death on the following 26 June it was necessary to renew the Commission on 5 July. The Commissioners reported on 15 February 1832, but no further action was then taken.

The first overt act on the part of Parliament appeared in 1836 in s.20 of the Act (6 & 7 Will. IV, c.77) for carrying into effect the reports of two Royal Commissions appointed in 1835 to consider the state of the dioceses in England and Wales. The section began with the preamble 'And whereas it may be expedient to consider the State and Jurisdiction of all the Ecclesiastical Courts in England and Wales' and went on to enact that nothing in the Act should affect the jurisdiction of the ecclesiastical courts for a period of one year after 13 August 1836. This temporary provision was continued by a series of annual Acts until the Act 15 & 16 Vict., c.17 continued it until 1 August 1853.

If these annual extensions induced a feeling of security, it was dispelled on 5 July 1853, when George Hadfield, the Radical member for Sheffield, was granted leave to bring into the House of Commons a bill to transfer the testamentary jurisdiction of the ecclesiastical courts to the courts of common law and the county courts.[1] This bill did not proceed, and on 20 August yet another extension of the

[1]*Hansard's Parliamentary Debates*, cxxviii. 124.

temporary provisions until 1 August 1854 was secured by the Act 16 & 17 Vict., c.108.

In the next session a new bill came before the House of Lords. Instead of a transfer of testamentary jurisdiction to the common-law courts, this bill provided for its transfer to the judges of the Court of Chancery. The terms of this bill alarmed the members of Doctors' Commons, who on 23 February 1854 appointed a committee of six members to report on the course to be adopted to protect their interests when the bill came to be printed. It seems to have been thought that there was no prospect of opposing the bill *in toto*, for on 9 March 1854 it was resolved that proper measures should be taken to obtain the insertion of a clause enabling the College to dispose of its property. A petition was presented to the House of Lords in which it was stated that the information and learning which had until then existed among the petitioners as a bar of ecclesiastical and international lawyers had been mainly fostered by their practising as an associated body; that by the proposed transfer any distinct object in their pursuits would be lost; that such total dispersion would involve the necessity of their applying themselves to fresh branches of law; and that the distribution of the jurisdiction among the four judges of the Court of Chancery would render it impracticable for them to pursue their vocations in a distinct court. The petitioners therefore prayed for a single judge to be appointed for a distinct court, but since they would be compelled to move nearer to the future court, they put forward a draft clause permitting the letting, sale, or exchange of their real and personal property.[1] This bill also failed to become law and the legislative standstill was continued by the Act 17 & 18 Vict., c.65 and then by the Act 18 & 19 Vict., c.75.

Meanwhile, the members became apprehensive that they might have to share the advantage which would accrue to each of them on a realization of the College property with

[1] Copies of petition in M.B., s.d. 14 Mar. 1854 and L.P.L., MS. 1560, ff.38-49.

new members who might be tempted to join by such a prospect. On 3 August 1854 it was resolved that in future every election as a fellow should be conducted in accordance with the precise form prescribed in the charter. No candidate came forward until November 1855, when Dr. Tristram's election was proposed by Dr. Twiss and seconded by Dr. Harding, and an amendment proposed by Dr. Curteis and seconded by Dr. Waddilove that the election should be stood over for consideration until the first day of Michaelmas Term 1856 was rejected. Dr. Spinks then gave notice of motion that no meeting for the election of a new fellow should be held before the expiration of twelve months from his admission as an advocate. This was carried on 26 February 1856.

Dr. Tristram's desire for membership may have appeared to those who opposed it to have been inspired more by enlightened self-interest than by a desire to share the professional and social advantages enjoyed by the members. Any such suspicion, however, turned out to be unfounded. The election of Dr. Tristram was indeed inimical to the interests of those who desired to share in the proceeds of the sale of the property, but not in the way which may have been feared, for in the event he was a supporter of Dr. Lee, who was strongly opposed to the sale. As it turned out, Dr. Tristram's payment of the entrance fee of £20, the amount fixed in 1689, proved to be an exceedingly good investment, for within ten years it brought him about £4,000 as his share of the proceeds of the sale.

The petition of 1854 was successful in that the proposal to transfer the testamentary jurisdiction to the Court of Chancery was dropped and replaced by one for the setting up of a new Court of Probate. The end of Doctors' Commons became inevitable on 25 August 1857, when the Court of Probate Act 1857 received the Royal Assent. S.3 of this Act abolished the testamentary jurisdiction of the ecclesiastical and other courts, and s.4 provided that such jurisdiction should be exercised by a new Court of Probate. By s.40

serjeants and barristers were authorized to practise in the new Court in contentious matters. By way of compensation, s.41 gave to the advocates the right to practise in any court in England, with the same eligibility to appointmntes as if they had been called to the Bar on the days on which they had been admitted as advocates.[1] Finally, s.117 made it lawful for the College, after a resolution to that effect had been come to at a meeting by a majority of the members present, to surrender the charter to the Crown, whereupon the corporation would be dissolved and all the real and personal estate of the College would belong to the members in equal shares as tenants in common for their own use and benefit.

Three days later the Royal Assent was given to the Matrimonial Causes Act 1857. This set up the Court of Divorce and Matrimonial Causes and by s.15 provided that all advocates and barristers should be entitled to practise in the new Court. This left the advocates with their monopolies in the Court of Admiralty and the Court of Arches, but they were soon to lose the former. On 8 August 1859 'An Act to enable Serjeants, Barristers-at-Law, Attorneys and Solicitors to practise in the High Court of Admiralty' (22 & 23 Vict. c.6) received the Royal Assent. The advocates' monopoly in the Court of Arches was never formally abolished, but the common lawyers quietly ousted the civilians, a process which was accepted wheri it was decided that a barrister was competent to sign articles required by s.7 of the Church Discipline Act 1840 to be signed by an advocate practising in Doctors' Commons.[2]

The first step towards putting s.117 of the Court of Probate Act 1857 into operation was taken on 13 January 1858, when notice was given of a meeting to be held two

[1] The advocates' monopoly of non-contentious business was short-lived, for the Court of Probate Act 1858, s.2 entitled serjeants and barristers to practise in all causes and matters in the Court of Probate.

[2] *Mouncey* v. *Robinson* (1867), 37 L.J. Ecc. 8. Malden, *Trinity Hall*, p. 107 states: 'The year 1856 [*sic*] saw the abolition of the rules of the Civil Law in any English Court and the end of the *raison d'être* of Doctors' Commons', but the civil law was not abolished: it was the jurisdiction which was transferred.

days later at which motions for surrendering the charter and vesting the corporate property in trustees and the division of £18,000 Consols between the members would be proposed. The next day Dr. Lee wrote to Dr. Waddilove, the Treasurer, protesting against the proposed dissolution. At the meeting Lee said that the vesting of the property in the members would constitute 'a palpable breach of trust', for the property was held by them in their corporate capacity upon a public trust. Despite Lee's opposition, it was decided upon the proposal of Dr. Waddilove to vest the College property in the members and to appoint a committee to carry the resolution into effect. On 13 March it was resolved to affix the seal to a deed vesting the property in trustees for sale, and this was done on 18 March.[1] On 23 April Lee appealed to the Visitors,[2] but they declined to exercise their visitatorial powers. He then applied to the Court of Queen's Bench for a writ of mandamus to compel them to do so. The application was heard on 12 June 1858 by Lord Campbell C.J., and Coleridge, Erle, and Crompton JJ., who dismissed it.[3] Meanwhile, Lee had also presented a petition to the House of Commons, but this was unsuccessful, so the advocates were then able to proceed to exercise the powers conferred on them by s.117 of the Act of 1857.[4]

It would have been impracticable to have surrendered the charter until arrangements had been made for disposing of the corporate property. As it turned out, those arrangements had to be spread over several years. It was first proposed to sell the buildings to the Government. The purchase was authorized by the Probate and other Courts and Registries Sites Act 1859, s.2 of which empowered the Commissioners of Public Buildings and Works to acquire the College and

---

[1] Copy deed (L.P.L., MS. 2976, ff. 242–56).
[2] Lee's copies of the documents are in L.P.L., MS. 2976, ff. 147–211.
[3] Transcript of the proceedings ibid., ff. 232–41.
[4] Lee's parliamentary agent's bills were £169.13s. and £22.13s., and his solicitor's bill in the Queen's Bench £115.5s. He also had to pay other solicitor's bills of £96.14s.4d. and £21.1s.10d., a total of £425.7s.2d. (L.P.L., MSS. 1560, ff.57–69; 2976, ff.212–23).

other premises in Great Knightrider Street, to remove the buildings, and to appropriate the site for the erection of buildings for the Court of Probate and its registries.[1] Despite the blessing of Parliament, this project was short-lived, for on 22 December 1859 the members of the College considered a proposal for the purchase of the property by the Metropolitan Board of Works.[2]

The Metropolitan Board of Works was at this time planning to construct the Thames Embankment and to make a new road to the east of it which would go straight through the College garden and some of the buildings. Nothing came of the negotiations at this stage. On 28 November 1862 the buildings were offered for sale by auction, but this also proved to be abortive.[3] This is hardly surprising, for it had by then become clear that the Thames Embankment was going to be constructed, the Thames Embankment Act 1862 having received the Royal Assent on 7 August 1862, and this made it highly likely that the ancillary road to the east would also be built. The Board did not, however, obtain power to build the road until the passing of the Metropolis Improvement Act 1863. The negotiations were then resumed and continued for another two years until it was agreed on 19 May 1865 that the Board should purchase the property for £83,950.

The conveyance was completed on 24 June 1865.[4] Thereafter there was nothing left to do but to wind up the affairs of the College and to distribute the proceeds of sale among the members.

The last meeting of the fellows of the College was held on 10 July 1865. It was not then known that that was to be the

---

[1] The property authorized to be acquired is described in the Schedule to the Act. The substance of the part of the Schedule relating to the College of Advocates is in 15 *L.T.R.* 16.

[2] M.B., s.d.

[3] 15 *L.T.R.* 44. The copy of the detailed sale catalogue in the Guildhall Library there referred to was destroyed by enemy action in the Second World War.

[4] L.P.L., MS. 1560, f.73. On 15 June an inventory of the tenant's fixtures and furniture was made (ibid., f.75). This included the Sovereign's Arms, the Admiralty Arms, and the Archiepiscopal Arms in the Court Room (see plate I).

last meeting, for it was resolved that a letter from Dr. Lee should be stood over for future consideration.[1] It was decided at this meeting that the flags of the Civilian Volunteer Corps should be presented to the Inner Temple.[2] By then £78,000 had been distributed among the members on account, and there only remained for distribution £1770. 14s.9d. from the sale of stock and £633.3s.9d. the balance of the Treasurer's Fund. The last cheque was drawn on 13 November 1865.[3]

The Metropolitan Board of Works sold the materials of the buildings by auction on 12 April 1867.[4] The only surviving relics are some panels of wainscotting now in Fulham Palace[5] and three armorial paintings from the court-room.[6]

There was no reason of practical importance why the power conferred by s.117 of the Act of 1857 to surrender the charter and so dissolve the corporation should not then have been exercised, but it was not.[7] The corporation continued to exist as a matter of law, its numbers being gradually reduced by death until by the death of Dr. Jenner-Fust on 30 July 1904, Dr. Tristram became the sole survivor. The College still kept its place in the *Law List* with its one member until the death of Dr. Tristram on 8 March 1912. Tristram retained the charter to the end. Shortly after his death it was sent by his son to Sir William Anson, the Warden of All Souls, for preservation in the Codrington Library.[8] The death of Dr. Tristram brought the legal existence of the

---

[1]M.B., s.d. The minutes of this meeting were never signed.

[2]On 12 July 1798 the Society resolved to pay £100 towards the expenses of the Military Association for the Defence of the Public Offices and Houses in Doctors' Commons (L.B., f.345).

[3]All Souls Coll., MS. 353. Each of the twenty-six members had already received £68.4s.2d. as his share of the proceeds of the sale of the library books.

[4]There is a copy of the sale catalogue in the Guildhall Library (A 199/1 T.1867). For a drawing of College Court with a sale notice posted on Dr. Deane's chambers, see 15 L.T.R., pl. ix, facing p. 84. There is a picture of the interior of the court-room in the course of demolition in the *Illustrated London News* of 4 May 1867.

[5]Illustrated in A. Oswald, 'Fulham Palace' in 75 *Country Life* (1939), p. 193.

[6]See p. 74 *ante*.

[7]*Pace* Malden, *Trinity Hall*, p. 107, where it is stated that the charter was surrendered.

[8]Now All Souls Coll., MS. 353.

College of Advocates to an end.[1] The advocates' barrister successors continued to have some sort of coherence as specialists in the Probate, Divorce, and Admiralty Division of the High Court of Justice until the jurisdiction of that Division was fragmented by the provisions of the Administration of Justice Act 1970. Under that Act the Probate, Divorce and Admiralty Division was re-named the Family Division and left with only the jurisdiction in matrimonial causes and non-contentious and common-form probate business, all other probate business being assigned to the Chancery Division and the admiralty and prize jurisdiction to the Queen's Bench Division. So ended the last vestige of continuity with the Society which first gathered in Paternoster Row under the presidency of Richard Blodwell in the closing years of the fifteenth century.

[1]R. v. *Hughes* (1828), 7 B. & C. 708, 717.

APPENDIX I

THE SOCIETY'S RECORDS

THOSE of the Society's records which are known to have survived are dispersed among several repositories, the bulk of them being in the Lambeth Palace Library. In addition to the known survivors, there is evidence of the former existence of other records, most if not all of which have probably been destroyed, either in the Fire of London or subsequently. The existing records may be classified as follows:

The Subscription Book (L.P.L., DC1).

This can fairly be described as the Society's most important record, for it contains the autographs of most of the members living between 1511 and 1855. It also provides evidence relating to the earliest years of the Society.[1] It was also used to record copies of important documents relating to the Society and some of the proceedings at meetings of members before any regular record of such proceedings was kept. Its contents include the Society's rules and a copy of the lease of Mountjoy House in 1568.

The Long Book (P.R.O., PRO 30/26/8)

This is the second-oldest surviving record, having been purchased for 3s.6d. on 26 June 1563, though the first dated entry is a list of the contributors in 1567.[2] It derived its name from its shape, the pages being tall and narrow. It was also sometimes called 'the Treasurer's Book'. Dr. Coote so described it,[3] and it is so named on the modern binding, but this gives an imperfect idea of the contents of the book. It was started as a termly record of payments by the members in commons and those out of commons. It was soon also used for the Steward's accounts and those of the Treasurer. These accounts vary greatly in quality: some are mere summaries, while others contain a considerable amount of informative detail. Finally, from 1679 until 1828 it was used for the

---

[1]For an evaluation of such evidence, see pp. 7-22 *ante*.
[2]L.B., f.5.
[3]Coote, preface, pp. 51 n., 110 n.

minutes of meetings of members. Like the accounts, the minutes range from the bald to the informative. In addition to these more or less regular uses, this book contains a number of miscellaneous entries, including inventories of the Society's plate and a copy of the petition to the Crown for the grant of the Charter. It was presented to the Public Record Office by Mr. Justice Bargrave Deane, the son of Dr. Deane, in February 1908.

The Minute Book (L.P.L., DC2)

This book continues the series of minutes of meetings in the Long Book from 12 July 1828 until the last meeting on 10 July 1865.

The Library Account Book (P.R.O., PRO 30/26/9)

Started in 1736, this book continued in use until 1843. Some of the accounts are very detailed, including the titles of books purchased. It was presented to the Public Record Office by Mr. Justice Phillimore, grandson of Sir Robert Phillimore, in March 1908.

Leases (L.P.L.)
   1. Dean and Chapter to Doctors' Commons, 1720–70 (DC8)
   2. Trinity Hall and Doctors' Commons to members, 1675–1819 (DC9)

Case Papers (L.P.L.)
   1. *Mason* v. *Trinity Hall* (1656) (DC3)
   2. *Bettesworth* v. *Dean and Chapter of St. Paul's* (1720) (DC4)
   3. *Bettesworth* v. *Dean and Chapter of St. Paul's and Trinity Hall* (1765) (DC5)

Miscellaneous Estate Papers (L.P.L.)
   1. Poor rate etc., 18th and 19th centuries (DC6)
   2. Building repairs etc., 18th and 19th centuries (DC10, DC11)

Treasurer's Accounts (L.P.L)
   1. 1679–1730 (DC13)
   2. 1767–1838 (DC14)
   3. 1839–65 (DC15)
These are highly summarized accounts of payments.

Judges' and Advocates' Term Fees Books (L.P.L.)

   1. 1768–87 (DC16)   3. 1809–42 (DC18)

   2. 1788–1809 (DC17)   4. 1842–64 (DC19)

These books include payments for land tax, fees to servants, and payments for wines and commons.

Proctors' Term Fees Books (L.P.L.)

   1. 1761–1838 (DC20)

   2. 1839–58 (DC21)

These books contain the names of all the proctors practising in the Court of Arches. The fees were their contributions towards the repairs and other expenses of the court-room. They were first charged in 1731,[1] but the records of the earlier payments have not survived.

Rent Book 1787–1830 (L.P.L., DC22)

This book contains the names of the tenants, but not the situation of their houses. Payments for land tax, insurance premiums, and tithe are included from 1810.

Income Book 1730–52 (L.P.L., DC23)

This book is not an account of the Society's income, but a record of the money spent on repairs by each incoming tenant and to be repaid by a succeeding tenant during the next twenty years. There are no 'incomes' entered until 16 December 1735, but they were to begin to run from Michaelmas 1730.

At the other end of the book are resolutions of the Society from 24 January 1759 to 10 June 1760.

Most of the book is blank.

Lee Fund Accounts 1844–65 (L.P.L., DC24)

On 6 August 1844 Dr. John Lee offered to give £500 to form the nucleus of a fund for the benefit of widows, orphans, or relations of members of the College. This was accepted, the money to be designated 'The Lee Fund'[2] The accounts show that no beneficiaries thought to be sufficiently deserving were found, so the whole of the income was invested. Finally the balance was carried to the account of the Trustees of the College at Hoare's Bank, whence it was distributed among the members.

      [1]L.B., f.250ᵛ.   [2]M.B., s.d.

Commons Book 1738–79 (L.P.L., DC25)

This book contains the names of the members in commons and particulars of the quantities of wine drunk.

Vouchers (L.P.L., DC26)

1. 1708–57	4. 1791–1813
2. 1762–81	5. 1813–30
3. 1772–90	6. 1830–41

The vouchers are made up in annual bundles. In some cases the numbers endorsed on the vouchers provide cross-references from the accounts in the Long Book, the baldness of which can be supplemented from the details in the vouchers. The box containing the vouchers for the years 1708–57 also contains a bundle of draft minutes.

Miscellaneous Documents (L.P.L.)

1. Appeals against assessments to Trophy Tax (DC 7)
2. Correspondence and papers relating to chambers, funds, and the Society, 1728–65 (DC 12)

E. Miscellaneous accounts, 1652–1864 (DC 27)

In addition to the Society's records properly so called there is a book entitled 'Thesaury. A Repertory to Books and Writings etc'.[1] This is a compilation of notes and extracts from the records, together with lists of officers of the Society and civilian judges and other memoranda. It was started in 1712 by Sir Nathaniel Lloyd and continued by him until about 1728, after which there are entries in other hands down to 1798, but most of the pages are blank. 'Thesaury' was kept in a trunk in the Treasurer's custody. This trunk (sometimes called 'the Treasurer's Chest') also contained 'The Large Vellum Leav'd Book', i.e. the Subscription Book, 'The Old Long Book', 'The Book of the Treasurer's Accounts of Expenses', and 'several loose papers'.[2]

There are two inventories of the 'loose papers'—one in 'Thesaury', dated 9 July 1726[3] and the other made by Dr. Ducarel on 29 October 1760.[4] Although it is difficult to identify all the

---

[1] L.P.L., MS.2080. It is described as 'Treasurer's Book' in E. G. W. Bill, *Catalogue of Manuscripts in Lambeth Palace Library MSS. 1967–2340* (Oxford, 1976), p. 87. There are references to this book in Dr. Ducarel's own copy of his 'Summary Account' (All Souls Coll. MS.325).

[2] L.P.L., DC13, s.d. 1725.

[3] L.P.L., MS.2080, ff.21–22v.

[4] L.P.L., MS.2216, ff.24–5.

items in these inventories with certainty, most of them appear either to survive in the records preserved at Lambeth or to have been copied into the Subscription Book. One loss which is to be regretted is that of 'Several Plans relating to the Buildings in Drs Commons' included in the 1760 inventory.

On 8 June 1761 there were deposited in the Treasurer's Chest copies of the *London Gazette* for 11–15 and 25–29 November 1760 containing copies of the address of congratulation and condolence presented by the Judges, Advocates, and Proctors of Doctors' Commons to George III at St. James's Palace on 12 November and of the address presented by them to the Princess Dowager of Wales at Leicester House on the same day.[1] In 1807 the affidavit on which Dr. Highmore applied to the Court of King's Bench for a mandamus was left in the Treasurer's Chest.[2] On 23 June 1829 it was resolved that an additional lock should be placed on the box, which was to remain in the Library, and that the Dean of the Arches and the Treasurer should each have a key. On 20 January 1843 it was resolved that a fire-proof iron safe should be obtained in place of the box.[3]

[1] L.B., f.287. Thomas Deeble was paid £6.6s.od. for writing these addresses (ibid., f.286).
[2] Ibid., f.351. For Highmore's case, see p. 42 *ante*.
[3] M.B., s. dd.

APPENDIX II

LIST OF PRESIDENTS

Richard Blodwell, from the foundation; d. by Apr. 1513.
Blodwell's immediate successors in the presidency have not been identified. The next President mentioned in the Society's records was:

Robert Weston, occurs 25 Oct. 1560;[1] res. on or shortly after appointment as Lord Chancellor of Ireland 8 Aug. 1567.

Thomas Yale, apptd. Official Principal 5 Oct. 1567;[2] commission revoked 3 May 1573.[3]

Bartholomew Clerke, apptd. Official Principal 3 May 1573;[4] d. 12 Mar. 1590.

Richard Cosin, apptd. 1590;[5] d. 3 Nov. 1597.

Thomas Byng, succeeded 3 Nov. 1597; res. 1598.

Daniel Dun, apptd. Official Principal 27 May 1598;[6] ktd. 23 July 1603; d. 15 Sept. 1617.

Sir William Bird, occurs 23 June 1618;[7] d. 5 Sept. 1624.

Sir Henry Marten, occurs 27 Nov. 1624[8] and 28 Mar. 1632.[9]

Hugh Barker, occurs 2 May and 24 June 1632;[10] d. 1632.

Sir Henry Marten, occurs 22 June 1633.[11]

Sir John Lamb, occurs 7 Jan. 1634[12] and 15 Feb. 1639[13]

During the suspension of archiepiscopal jurisdiction from 6 September 1646 until the Restoration the *de facto* President was the senior Judge of the Court of Admiralty.

[1] S.B., f.2. Weston was appointed Official Principal on 11 Jan. 1560 and Dean of the Arches the next day (*Registrum Matthei Parker*, i (C. & Y. Soc. xxv, 1928), 334–5).

[2] Churchill, i. 597.

[3] *Reg. Parker*, iii (C. & Y. Soc. xxxix, 1933), 1058.

[4] Ibid.

[5] Cosin was appointed jointly with Thomas Byng to several ecclesiastical judicial offices, but Cosin alone officiated as Official Principal and Dean of the Arches, an arrangement made permanent by an agreement made 13 July 1595, under which the survivor was to enjoy all the offices alone (Inner Temple, MS. Petyt 538/54, f.19; L.B. ff.50–67).

[6] Churchill, i.605.

[7] L.B., f.111.

[8] L.B., f.126.

[9] *C.S.P.D. 1631–3*, p. 296.

[10] S.B., f.79; L.B., f.148.

[11] L.B., f.151.

[12] *C.S.P.D. 1633–4*, p. 232.

[13] L.B., f.170.

William Sammes, d. 13 Oct. 1646.

William Clerke, apptd. 17 Aug. 1647;[1] bur. 3 Aug. 1655.

John Godolphin, succeeded Clerke; re-apptd. 28 Oct. 1658.[2]

Walter Walker, apptd. 12 Mar. 1660; deprived.

Richard Zouche, occurs 13 July 1660;[3]

Giles Sweit, apptd. Dean of the Arches on or shortly after 20 Sept. 1660, when Abp. Juxon's election confirmed; ktd. 1664; d. 3 Sept. 1672.

Sir Robert Wiseman, apptd. 28 Nov. 1672; d. 17 Aug. 1684.

Sir Richard Lloyd, apptd. Sept. 1684; d. 20 June 1686.

Sir Thomas Exton, apptd. June 1686; d. 4 Nov. 1688.

George Oxendon, occurs 23 Oct. 1689;[4] d. 21 Feb. 1703.

Sir John Cooke, apptd. 11 Mar. 1703; d. 31 Mar. 1710.

John Bettesworth, apptd. 19 Apr. 1710; d. 17 Dec. 1751.

George Lee, apptd. Dec. 1751; ktd. 12 Feb. 1752; d. 18 Dec. 1758.

Edward Simpson, apptd. Dec. 1758; ktd. Dec. 1761; d. 20 May 1764.

George Hay, apptd. c. June 1764; ktd. 11 Nov. 1773; d. 6 Oct. 1778.

Peter Calvert, apptd. 17 Oct. 1778; d. 13 Aug. 1788.

Sir William Wynne, apptd. 25 Aug. 1788; res. Jan. 1809.

Sir John Nicholl, apptd. 20 Jan. 1809; res. 1834.

Sir Herbert Jenner (afterwards Jenner-Fust), apptd. 1834; d. 20 Feb. 1852.

Sir John Dodson, apptd. 24 Feb. 1852; d. 27 Apr. 1858.

Stephen Lushington, apptd. 2 July 1858; res. July 1867.

Sir Robert Joseph Phillimore, apptd. 1 Aug. 1867; res. before 20 Oct. 1875. The last member of the College to hold the offices of Official Principal and Dean of the Arches.

[1] 15 L.T.R. 32.
[2] Ibid. 33.
[3] L.B., f.190.
[4] L.B., f.215v.

APPENDIX III

A REGISTER OF MEMBERS

THIS Appendix is 'a Register' and not 'the Register' of members, because it is impossible to state with certainty that it contains the name of every member. The great majority of the names are derived from the signatures in the Subscription Book, but it is clear that the subscriptions do not provide a complete roll of members. The Subscription Book itself contains memoranda concerning members of whom there is no mention in the folios devoted to subscriptions. The names of more such members are to be found in the Long Book during the seventeenth century, while in the early years of the nineteenth century there are some whose membership is attested by a list of the shields of arms on the walls of the court and by entries in the *Law List*.

The names are arranged in the order in which they appear in the Subscription Book. Those who signed the contributor's subscription are indicated by '(C)', and those who also signed the advocate's subscription are indicated by '(A)'.[1] If the date of an advocate's subscription is different from that of his contributor's subscription, it is inserted after '(A)'. If the date of admission as an advocate of the Court of Arches differs by more than a few days from the date of the advocate's subscription, both dates are given. Where there is no subscription by a member his name has been inserted in the place which would have been appropriate if his admission had been on the date of the earliest mention of his name in the records. The names and particulars printed in italics are taken (in translation) from the section of the Subscription Book appropriated to subscriptions.

It has been no part of my design to produce a biographical dictionary of members, for particulars of the majority can be found in the works of Dr. A. B. Emden, Joseph Foster, and J. and J. A. Venn, while many also have biographies in the *Dictionary of National Biography* and the *Dictionary of Welsh Biography*. I have, however, tried to make good the lack of an admission register by

---

[1]There are a few cases in which an advocate did not sign the contributor's subscription.

adding to the names particulars where discoverable of parentage, place of origin, school, college, degree, and age at admission to Doctors' Commons. In order further to indicate the sort of men who became members, particulars are given of any significant office held at the time of admission.[1] There has also been added the date of death or, in the cases in which it is known, earlier cessation of membership by resignation or expulsion. In addition, in order to facilitate identification, changes in style or title during membership have been stated. There have also been added particulars of offices held in the Society. Since the Judge of the Court of Admiralty and the King's Advocate had precedence in the Society next after the President (usually the Dean of the Arches), these appointments have also been included. Although it did not carry with it any precedence in the Society, the Mastership of Trinity Hall, Cambridge, has been included from 1567 to 1768, since the Master had special chambers assigned to him after the move to Mountjoy House until the freehold was acquired.[2]

In many cases the exact date of birth has not been found, so that the age at admission has had to be calculated from the age stated on some other occasion, such as admission to school or college or at death. These calculated ages are indicated by '*c*'. In the cases of some Oxford men the place of origin is the birth-place, which may not have been the residence of the father.[3] Where the date of death has not been found, an approximation can be obtained from the probate of the will, which was usually granted within a few weeks, or in some cases days, after the death.

The names are printed as stated in the subscriptions. Considerable variations are included in the index. If a man was known by alternative names which were completely different (e.g. Hugh Sawnders or Breakspear), both names are given, the name in the subscription being placed first.

In the Subscription Book degrees are designated in a variety of ways. It has seemed better to introduce some uniformity into the

---

[1] In the cases of men who were already members in 1511 and whose date of admission is not stated in the Subscription Book the offices are those held in that year.

[2] See p. 61 *ante*.

[3] e.g. Timothy Baldwin was matriculated at Oxford in 1635 as a son of Charles Baldwin of Burwarton, co. Salop, but his father lived at Elswich, co. Salop, Burwarton being the residence of his maternal grandfather (*Knights*, pp. 238–9).

matter. In the designation of pre-Reformation degrees I have followed the system employed by Dr. Emden.[1] Degrees in canon law are indicated by the contraction 'Cn.L.', and degrees in both laws by 'Cn. & C.L.'. For the few graduates in theology I have used the contraction 'Th.' for those who took their degrees before the Reformation, since 'D.' would be anachronistic. Post-Reformation degrees in civil law conferred at Oxford are indicated by the initials 'C.L.', and those conferred at Cambridge by the initials 'LL.', in accordance with current usage. It should, however, be borne in mind that this usage only became finally settled during the nineteenth century: previously Oxford doctors of civil law were often styled 'LL.D.' and those of Cambridge 'D.C.L.' indifferently.[2]

The marginal dates are those of the earliest references to members in the Subscription Book. In most cases they are the subscriptions as contributors, those forming what Dr. Coote described as 'the first list'. A casual glance at the Subscription Book gives the impression that every member signed the contributor's subscription, and that the members who were advocates signed the advocate's subscription as well. This was indeed the normal practice, but a closer inspection reveals that there were numerous irregularities in the keeping of the record. Some advocate members signed only once, omitting either the contributor's or the advocate's subscription. There were also irregularities in the cases of some of the advocates who signed both subscriptions. Normally an advocate signed both on the same day, but during the sixteenth century there were cases in which the two subscriptions were signed on different days. Sometimes this was because a man became a contributor before he was an advocate, but there seems to be no apparent reason why an advocate should have delayed signing his contributor's subscription, sometimes for several months, or even omitted to do so. Where there was an interval between the dates of an advocate's two subscriptions, the later date is given in the body of the entry.

Some subscriptions have later annotations. The note that Roger Elys, who was admitted in 1529, was the paternal uncle of Thomas

---

[1] *B.R.U.O.* i, p. xlii; *B.R.U.C.*, p. xxviii.
[2] e.g. the bookplates of 'Thos. Bever, LL.D.' and 'Andrew Coltee Ducarel, LL.D. Doctor's Commons' (B.M., Franks Collection of Bookplates, Nos. 2451, 9174). Both Bever and Ducarel were Oxford men.

Yale and his generous benefactor ('*Maecenas*') cannot have been added until after Yale's admission thirty years later, and neither William Pierpont (admitted 1546) nor Robert Oking (admitted 1548) is likely to have been described as 'a married priest' before the death of Edward VI in 1553. On the other hand, some of the additions are less obviously anachronistic. Thus, William Medilton did not become a canon of Lichfield until 1529, but he appears to have been so described when the entry relating to him was made in 1511.

BEFORE 1505

n.d. *Richard Blodwell, D.C.L.*, Oxford, '*huius Collegij primus presidens*'; (C); b. St. Asaph diocese; d. by 12 Apr. 1513.[1]
William Shragger, M.A. Magdalen Coll., Oxford; probably a proctor; d. by 30 July 1519.[2]
Thomas Hede, D.C.L., Oxford; probably an advocate;[3] (C); d. by 21 Jan. 1521.[4]
Edward Lane, D. Cn. & *C.L.*, Cambridge; d. by 13 Dec. 1510.[5]
William Haryngton, D.C.L., Bologna,[6] Prebendary of St. Paul's; probably an advocate;[7] (C); s. William H., of Eastrington, co. York, gent.; d. by 25 Nov. 1523;[8] *D.N.B.*
Walter Stone, D.C.L. (by 1496–7), All Souls Coll., Oxford; probably an advocate;[9] (C); d. by Apr. 1519; left to 'the Honourable Company of the Doctors of the arches' a 'swagyd' cup of silver parcel gilt with a cover.[10]
William Horsey, D.Cn.L. (by 1501), Oxford, Archdeacon of London; probably an advocate;[11] (C); yr.s. Thomas H.,

[1]Will P.C.C. 17 Fetiplace as 'Bladwell'. Blodwell is described as Dean of the Arches in Malden, *Trinity Hall*, p. 104, Senior, *Doctors' Commons*, pp. 72–3, and Holdsworth, *H.E.L.* iv (1924), 235, but there seems to be no evidence that he ever held this office, it apparently having been assumed that he must have done so because he was President of Doctors' Commons.
[2]Will P.C.C. 20 Ayloffe.
[3]Official of vacant see (Churchill, ii. 265).
[4]Le Neve, v. 49.
[5]Will P.C.C. 37 Bennett.
[6]51 *E.H.R.* 285.
[7]Churchill, ii. 249.
[8]Le Neve, v. 45; M.I. Old St. Paul's (*St. Paul's*, p. 55).
[9]Commissary of P.C.C. (Churchill, ii. 237).
[10]Will P.C.C. 28 Ayloffe.
[11]Official of the Bishop of London.

BEFORE 1505

n.d. of Clifton Maybank, co. Dorset, esq.;[1] d. by 10 Apr. 1543.[2]

Christopher Yorke, D.C.L.; (C).

Richard Rawson, D.C.L. (1489), Bologna[3] D.Cn.L. (1500), Ferrara;[4] probably an advocate;[5] 4 s. Richard R., of London, merchant;[6] d. by 29 Oct. 1543.[7]

Robert Bonde, D.Cn.L.

Robert Bryght, D.C.L., King's Coll., Cambridge; (C); d. by 25 Feb. 1534.[8]

John Tayler, D.Cn.L., Prebendary of Bath and Wells; probably an advocate;[9] (C); d. by 12 Mar. 1533;[10] *D.N.B.*

James Denton, D.Cn. & C. L., Valentia and King's Coll., Cambridge, from Eton Coll., Prebendary of Salisbury; d. 23 Feb. 1533;[11] *D.N.B.*

Robert Davell, D.Cn. & C.L., possibly Oxford; (C); b. Durham diocese;[12] d. by 28 Apr. 1558.[13]

Richard Collett, D.C.L.; (C).

Walter Perys, D.C.L., Oxford; (C); d. by 4 Feb. 1540.[14]

Philip Agard, D.Cn.L. (1498), Oxford, Prebendary of Coventry and Lichfield; probably an advocate;[15] d. by 12 Feb. 1517.[16]

Roger Sondeforthe, D.Cn.L., Broadgates Hall, Oxford, Prebendary of Exeter; (C); practised in the Court of Arches;[17] d. by 23 Oct. 1514.[18]

---

[1]J. Hutchins, *History —— of the County of Dorset* (3rd ed., Westminster, 1861–70), iv. 427; will of Dr. Horsey (P.C.C. 25 Spert).
[2]Le Neve, ix. 62.
[3]51 *E.H.R.* 279, 287.
[4]R. J. Mitchell, *Italian Studies*, i (1937), 80.
[5]Master in Chancery.   [6]*B.R.U.C.* p. 473.
[7]Le Neve, v. 11.   [8]Newcourt, ii. 394.
[9]Master in Chancery.
[10]Le Neve, x. 36.
[11]Le Neve, x. 7.
[12]*B.R.U.O.* iv. 674.
[13]Le Neve, vi. 115.
[14]Will P.C.C. 2 Alenger.
[15]Churchill, ii. 255, 258, 269.
[16]Le Neve, x. 51.
[17]*B.R.U.O.* iii. 1638, but no authority cited.
[18]Will P.C.C. 1 Holder. Christopher Middylton, proctor (q.v.) an executor.

BEFORE 1505

n.d. *Thomas Sewell, D.Cn.L.*, Pembroke Hall, Cambridge, Prebendary of St. Paul's; b. Carlisle diocese; d. by 3 Apr. 1527.[1]

—— *Grixon, B.Th.* Perhaps Edward Gregson, B.Th., Jesus Coll., Cambridge, Canon of St. John's, Chester and Rector of Fladbury, co. Worcester; d. by 1 July 1540.[2]

—— *Molens.* Perhaps Simon Molens, D.Th., Merton Coll., Oxford; d. by 28 Jan. 1507.[3]

Robert Pele.

Christopher Midylton, B.C.L., Oxford, *proctor*; D.C.L. by 1521; d. by 20 Apr. 1531.[4]

William Falke, proctor.

John Copland alias Johnson,[5] *proctor*; b. Lincoln diocese.

'Dominus' Robert Portland, proctor; Rector of St. Nicholas Acon, London; (C); d. by 21 Aug. 1531.[6]

Richard Spencer, proctor; Register of the Court of Arches, *c.* 1489;[7] b. Lincoln diocese.[8]

William Goldsmyth, proctor.

1505?

12 May *John Smyth* alias Harrys,[9] *D.M.*, Prebendary of St. Paul's; (C); d. 26 Dec. 1539.[10]

n.d. *William Throkmorton, D.C.L.* of a foreign university;[11] 3 s. Sir Thomas T., of Coughton, co. Warwick, kt.;[12] d. 12 Jan. 1536.[13]

William Bolton, O.S.A., Prior of St. Bartholomew, Smithfield d. by 8 Apr. 1532;[14] *D.N.B.*

[1]Le Neve, v. 55.
[2]Will P.C.C. 8 Alenger.
[3]Will P.C.C. 17 Adeane.
[4]Will P.C.C. 4 Thower. Mentions his 'son' Dr. John Tregonwell (q.v.), perhaps his stepson, but the expression 'son' is more likely to have been used because Tregonwell was Midylton's protégé when a proctor.
[5]*Register of Bishop King* (Somerset Rec. Soc. liv, 1939), p. 126.
[6]Newcourt, i. 505.
[7]Churchill, ii. 242.
[8]*Cal. Papal Registers*, xiv. 15.
[9]Will P.C.C. 19 Alenger.
[10]M.I. Old St. Paul's (*St. Paul's*, p. 127).
[11]*B.R.U.O.* iv. 566.
[12]*Vis. Warwick*, p. 87.
[13]M.I. Shottesbrooke, co. Berks.
[14]Le Neve, ii. 16.

1505?

n.d. *John Jennyn, D.C.L.* (by 1499), Oxford; advocate;[1] (C); b. Bath and Wells diocese; d. by 30 Sept. 1523.[2]

Richard Ghylberd, D.Cn.L., Prebendary of Bath and Wells;[3] (C).

John Wesey alias Harman, *D.C.L.*, Magdalen Coll., Oxford, Dean of Exeter; *c*.58; e.s. William Harman, of Moor Hall in Sutton Coldfield, co. Warwick;[4] Bishop of Exeter 1519–51; d. 28 Oct. 1554; *D.N.B.*

Ralph Colynwod, D.Th., Queens' Coll., Cambridge, Archdeacon of Coventry; yr. s. Robert C., of Wark, co. Northumberland;[5] d. 22 Nov. 1521.[6]

William Robynson, D.Cn.L., Cambridge; b. York diocese.

Hugh Sawnders alias Breakspear, *D.Th.*, Merton Coll., Oxford, Prebendary of St. Paul's; b. Worcester diocese; d. by 3 Nov. 1537.[7]

John Colett, D.Th., Oxford, Dean of St. Paul's; (C); 1 s. Sir Henry C., kt.; d. 16 Sept. 1519;[8] *D.N.B.*

Thomas Hare, D.C.L., All Souls Coll., Oxford; b. Norwich diocese; d. by 14 May 1521.[9]

John Wardraper, B.Cn. & C.L., Magdalen Coll., Oxford, notary public, Archdeacon of Stafford; d. by 28 July 1515.[10]

Geoffrey Blythe, *Bishop of Coventry and Lichfield*, D.Th., King's Coll., Cambridge, from Eton Coll.; s. William B., of Norton, co. Derby; d. by 1 Mar. 1531;[11] *D.N.B.*

1506?

28 May *William Bond, D.Cn.L.*, Cambridge.

n.d. *William* Hyccheman, O.Cist., *Abbot of Stratford*; d. or res. 1516.[12]

---

[1]*L. & P. Hen. VIII*, i, pt. i. 821.
[2]Weaver, p. 42.
[3]Le Neve, viii. 66.
[4]*Vis. Warwick*, p. 105.
[5]*Visitations of the North* (Surtees Soc. cxlvi, 1932), iv. 97.
[6]Le Neve, x. 7.
[7]Le Neve, v. 21.
[8]Le Neve, vii. 11n.; M.I. Old St. Paul's (*St. Paul's*, pp. 64–5).
[9]Will P.C.C. 8 Maynwaryng.
[10]Will P.C.C. 8 Holder.
[11]Will P.C.C. 14 Thower.
[12]*V.C.H. Essex*, ii. 133.

1506?

n.d. *Cuthbert Tunstall, D.Cn. & C.L.* (by 1505), Padua, from Balliol Coll., Oxford, probably an advocate;[1] (C); *c.*32; b. Hackforth, co. York; probably illegit. s. Thomas T., of Thurland Castle in Cantsfield, co. Lancaster; Bishop of London 1522–30; Bishop of Durham 1530–51, 1554–8; 18 Nov. 1559; *D.N.B.*

James Whystons, D.Cn.L., Bologna,[2] incorp. Cambridge, Canon of St. Stephen's, Westminster; d. by 17 Sept. 1512.[3]

Alexander Lawson, proctor.

Miles Salley, *Bishop of Llandaff*; d. by 22 Jan. 1517.[4]

David ——, *Abbot of Talley.*

William Wynslat; d. by June 1510.[5]

John 'Medensis'. Perhaps John Newport, M.A.[6]

John Hogeson, priest.

Thomas Gotson, proctor.

Richard Gardyner, perhaps M.A., Oxford, Prebendary of Salisbury; (C); d. 1518.[7]

Edward Waughan, D.Cn.L., Cambridge, *Bishop of St. Davids*; b. St. Davids diocese; d. Nov. 1522; *D.N.B.*; *D.W.B.*[8]

Henry Mompesson, D.Cn.L. (1494–5), New Coll. Oxford, from Winchester Coll.; probably an advocate;[9] yr. s. John M., of Bathampton Wylye, co. Wilts, esq.;[10] d. by 29 Nov. 1509.[11]

John Vaughan, D.C.L. (by 1503), All Souls Coll., Oxford, Prebendary of St. Davids, probably an advocate;[12] (C); b. St. Davids diocese; d. by 1 July 1528.[13]

---

[1]Keeper of P.C.C. (Churchill, ii. 236).
[2]Parks, i. 627.
[3]Will P.C.C. 20 Fetiplace.
[4]Will P.C.C. 26 Holder.   [5]*B.R.U.O.* iii. 2059.
[6]*B.R.U.O.* iv. 694.
[7]*B.R.U.O.* ii. 742.
[8]The position of Waughan's name indicates that he was a member before his consecration as Bishop of St. Davids on 22 July 1509.
[9]Official of vacant see (Churchill, ii. 256).
[10]*Vis. Wilts.*, p. 132.
[11]Will P.C.C. 23 Bennett.
[12]Official of vacant see (Churchill, ii. 265).
[13]Will P.C.C. 34 Porch.

1506?

n.d. *Richard More, D.Cn.L.* (by 1499), Oxford, Archdeacon, of Exeter; advocate;[1] b. Exeter diocese; d. Christmas Term 1516–17.[2]

—— *Nance.* Perhaps John Nance, D.Cn. C.L., Bologna;[3] Sub-Dean of Exeter; d. by 26 Sept. 1508.[4]

—— *Brent, D.C.L.* Perhaps Thomas Brent, D.C.L., New Coll. Oxford, from Winchester Coll.; 4 s. Hugh B., of Charing, co. Kent;[5] d. by Apr. 1515.[6]

William Morce, D,C.L., Prebendary of Bath and Wells; probably an advocate;[7A] d. by 30 Nov. 1519.[8]

1508

30 Sept. *Henry Wylcokk, D.C.L.*, Oxford, Prebendary of Lincoln; (C); d. by 2 June 1518.[9]

n.d. Lawrence Champyon O.S.B., *Abbot of Battle, at the time of his confirmation*;[10] d. 1529.[11]

Richard Hylley, B.Cn.L.; *Treasurer of Salisbury* Cathedral; b. Worcester diocese; s. John H.;[12] D.Cn.L., Bologna, 1516; d. 1 Sept. 1533.[13]

Polydore Vergil alias Castellensis, *Papal Collector*;[14] Archdeacon of Wells; d. 18 Apr. 1556;[15] D.N.B.

Robert Haldesworth, D.Cn. & C.L., Lincoln Coll., Oxford; murdered May 1556.[16]

John Dowman, D.C.L., Cambridge, Prebendary of St. Paul's; (C); d. by 11 Nov. 1526.[17]

[1]Churchill, ii. 261.
[2]Le Neve, ix. 12.
[3]Parks, i. 626.
[4]Le Neve, ii. 25.
[5]*Vis. Kent*, p. 211.
[6]*B.R.U.O.* i. 260.
[7]Commissary of the Bishop of London, *c.* 1500.
[8]Le Neve, viii. 24.
[9]Le Neve, iii. 93.
[10]Champyon received the temporalities 8 Dec. 1508.
[11]*V.C.H. Sussex*, ii. 55.
[12]Parks, i. 628.
[13]Le Neve, iii. 21.
[14]The reference to the Pope has been deleted. For the order to erase the Pope's name in 1535, see G. R. Elton, *Policy and Police* (Cambridge, 1972), pp. 236–8, 291, 364.
[15]Le Neve, v. 54.
[16]*B.R.U.O.* ii. 948.
[17]Le Neve, v. 65.

1508

n.d. *William Grocyn*, B.Th., New Coll., Oxford, from Winchester Coll., Prebendary of Lincoln; *c.*60; b. Colerne, co. Wilts.; d. by 20 July 1522;[1] *D.N.B.*

John Yonge, D.Th., New Coll., Oxford, from Winchester Coll.; (C), *Bishop of Callipoli 12 Oct. 1514*; b. Newton Longville, co. Buckingham; d. 28 Mar. 1526;[2] *D.N.B.*

—— *Prior of 'Mortyn'*. Perhaps Christopher Laton, O.S.A., Prior of Marton, co. York.

Robert Woderove, D.Th., King's Coll., Cambridge, from Eton Coll.; (C); *c.*57, b. Chelmsford, co. Essex; d. by 6 Mar. 1516.[3]

John Ashdowne, O.Clun., D.Cn.L., Oxford, *Prior of Lewes*.

——, O.S.A., *Prior of Christ Church, London*. Either Thomas Newton or Thomas Percy.[4]

William Medilton, Canon of Lichfield;[5] d. by 28 Jan. 1538.[6]

Nicholas Stokysley, B.Cn.L., Pembroke Hall, Cambridge, *proctor*; b. York diocese; d. by 26 Sept. 1538.[7]

9 Dec. *Robert Spenser, D.* (amended to) *'Scholar' Cn. & C.L.*, Padua, *Prebendary of Milton in Lincoln Cathedral*;[8] (C).

n.d. *William Fayrhayr, D.Cn.L.* (by 1510), Cambridge; probably an advocate;[9] b. Carlisle diocese; living 1 Oct 1515.[10]

Alexander Hody, D.Cn.L., All Souls Coll., Oxford, and Louvain;[11] Prebendary of Bath and Wells; (C); b. Bath and Wells diocese; d. by Feb. 1519.[12]

Charles Bothe, D.C.L., Bologna; (C); b. Barton in Eccles, co. Lancaster; *Bishop of Hereford 30 Nov. 1516; his arrears*

[1] *Collectanea*, ii (Oxford Hist. Soc. xvi, 1890), pp. 378–80.
[2] M.I., New College Chapel.
[3] Will P.C.C. 15 Holder.
[4] Newton was Prior in 1506, and there seems to be no evidence as to when he was succeeded by Percy who d. 1512.
[5] According to Le Neve, x. 34, Medilton did not become a canon until 1529, but the whole entry appears to have been written at one time.
[6] Le Neve, loc. cit.
[7] Le Neve, x. 66.
[8] His successor installed 23 Dec. 1515 (Le Neve, i. 94).
[9] Official of vacant sees (Churchill, ii. 259, 260).
[10] Ibid., ii. 260.
[11] 37 *E.H.R.* 93.
[12] *B.R.U.O.* ii. 941.

1508

n.d. *paid by William Burghill, his Vicar-General 10 Nov. 1522*;
d. 5 May 1535.

Thomas Wodyngton, D.Cn.L. (by 1492), New Coll.,
Oxford, from Winchester Coll., advocate; b. St. John's,
Bristol; d. by Nov. 1522.

Thomas Walshe, O.S.A., *Prior of Bradenstoke*; d. by 23
July 1526.[1]

Gamaliel Clyfton, D.Cn.L., Turin,[2] B.Cn.L., Cambridge;
Prebendary of York; (C); s. Sir Gervase C., of Clifton,
co. Nottingham; d. by 2 May 1541.[3]

Thomas Cornish, O.S.J.Jer., M.A., Oriel Coll., Oxford,
Bishop of Tenos; d. 3 July 1513.[4]

Hugh Oldham, Bishop of Exeter; d. 25 June 1519; *D.N.B.*

Simon Foderby alias Grene.[5] *D.Th.*, Lincoln Coll.,
Oxford, Prebendary of Lincoln; b. Helpringham, co.
Lincoln; d. 27 Mar. 1536.[6]

Thomas Pert, D.C.L. (1501–2), Cambridge; probably an
advocate;[7] d. by Sept. 1526.[8]

1509

12 July *William Walter, D.Cn. & C.L.*, Bologna,[9] Archdeacon
of Brecon; (C); b. Wales; d. by 8 Apr. 1523.[10]

n.d. *Nicholas West, D.Cn. & C.L.*, King's Coll., Cambridge,
and Bologna, from Eton Coll.; Archdeacon of Derby; *c.*
48; s. John W., of Putney, co. Surrey, baker; Bishop of
Ely 1515; d. 28 Apr. 1533; *D.N.B.*

Roger Churche, D.Cn.L. (by 1493), New Coll., Oxford,
from Winchester Coll.; Prebendary of Bath and Wells;
probably an advocate;[11] (C); *c.*48; b. Eastling, co. Kent;
d. by 17 Oct. 1524.[12]

[1]Le Neve, vi. 59.
[2]Parks, i. 640.
[3]Le Neve, vi. 94.
[4]M.I. Wells Cathedral.
[5]Churchill, ii. 247.
[6]Browne Willis, ii. 86.
[7]Commissary of P.C.C. (Churchill, ii. 236).
[8]*B.R.U.C.*, p. 451.
[9]Parks, i. 625.
[10]Le Neve, xi. 62.
[11]Keeper of P.C.C. (Churchill, ii. 236).
[12]Will P.C.C. 26 Bodfelde.

1509

n.d. *Bernard Oldom*, B.Cn.L.; Archdeacon of Cornwall; bro. of Hugh O., Bishop of Exeter;[1] d. by 26 May 1516.[2]

Dec. 19 *Peter Burnell, D.Cn.L.*, New Coll., Oxford, from Winchester Coll.; (C); *c.*31; s. Henry B., of Poyntington, co. Somerset;[3] d. by 28 Jan. 1529.[4]

n.d. *William Gylbert*, O.S.A., D.Th., Oxford, *Prior (altered to) Abbot of Bruton*;[5] Bishop 'in partibus Majorensis' (locality not identified) May 1519;[6] d. by July 1533.[5]

John Edmonds, B.Cn. & C.L., *Canon Residentiary of Wells*; d. by 19 Sept. 1520.[7]

Thomas Thomyow, D.C.L., Bologna, D.Cn.L.; Archdeacon of Bath; d. by Apr. 1518.[8]

Edward Higgons, D.Cn.L., Oxford; Prebendary of Salisbury; 1 s. Richard H., of All Stretton, co. Salop;[9] d. by 8 Jan. 1538.[10]

William Wylton, D.Cn.L. (1491), Bologna;[11] Chancellor of Salisbury Cathedral; probably an advocate;[12] (C); d. by 14 Feb. 1526.[13]

William Smyth, D.Cn.L., Ferrara, perhaps from Cambridge,[14] *Archdeacon of Lincoln*; s. Richard S. and nephew of William S., Bishop of Lincoln; d. by 22 June 1528.[15]

Thomas Lovell, D.Cn.L., Cambridge; b. York diocese; d. by 9 June 1524.[16]

John Adams, D.Th., Merton Coll., Oxford; Vicar of St. Sepulchre, London; (C); b. Bath and Wells diocese; d. by 21 Mar. 1524.[17]

---

[1]Will P.C.C. 24 Holder.
[2]Le Neve, ix. 61.
[3]*Somerset Medieval Wills* (Somerset Record Soc. xl, 1925), i. 291.
[4]Le Neve, x. 24.
[5]Raised to the rank of abbot 1511.
[6]*Regg. Wolsey etc.,* p. 26.
[7]Le Neve, viii. 71.   [8]Le Neve, ix. 58.
[9]*Vis. Salop,* i. 241.   [10]Le Neve, iii. 74.
[11]Parks, i. 626.
[12]Commissary of P.C.C. (*Sede Vacante Wills* (Kent Archaeological Soc., Records Branch, iii, 1914), p. 99).
[13]Will P.C.C. 4 Porch.
[14]*B.R.U.C.*, p. 538.
[15]Le Neve, i. 8.
[16]*Regg. Wolsey etc.*, pp. 27, 34 .
[17]Le Neve, v. 49.

1509

n.d. *Thomas Dalby*, D.Cn.L., Oxford, *Archdeacon of Richmond*; (C); d. 26 Jan. 1526.[1]

John Clerke, *D.C.L.*, D.Cn.L. Bologna,[2] from Cambridge and possibly Louvain, b. Norwich diocese;[3] (C); *Bishop of Bath and Wells*, 1523; d. 3 Jan. 1541; *D.N.B.*

Robert Caudelyn, D.C.L., Cambridge, Rector of Holy Trinity, Chester; d. 1 Jan. 1513.[4]

John Woode, perhaps student in Cn.L., Louvain; b. York diocese.[5]

Robert Beley, Master of the Hospital of St. Bartholomew, London; d. 1516.[6]

Thomas Sawnt, D.Cn.L., Archdeacon of St. Davids; d. by 6 Feb. 1514.[7]

Leonard Medylton, D.Cn.L., Cambridge, Prebendary of Exeter; d. by 6 May 1519.[8]

Peter Bradshawe, D.Cn.L., Louvain, from Cambridge;[9] d. by 30 May 1541.[10]

William Wytlesey, O.S.B., *Prior of Ely*; living 1516.[11]

Oliver Pole.[12]

1511

10 May *Peter Potkyn*, *D.C.L.* (1510), New Inn Hall, Oxford, advocate; (C); d. 1 May 1520;[13] *the Society received from his brother, William Potkyn, on 5 Apr. 1522 a salt weighting 14 oz., inscribed on the cover EX DONO MRI PETRI POTKYN LEGVM DOCTORIS VNIVS ADVO-CATORVM ALME CVRIE CANTVAR CVIVS ANIME PROPITIETVR DEVS AMEN and on the foot AD VSVM COMMVNITATIS ADVOCA-TORVM EIVSDEM CVRIE.*

[1]Browne Willis, i. 97.   [2]Parks, i. 527.
[3]37 *E.H.R.* 93.
[4]Ormerod, i. 331, n.(f).
[5]37 *E.H.R.* 90.
[6]*V.C.H. London*, i. 524.
[7]Will P.C.C. 30 Fetiplace.
[8]Le Neve, ix. 62.
[9]37 *E.H.R.* 94.
[10]Will P.C.C. 29 Alenger.
[11]*V.C.H. Cambridge*, ii. 209.
[12]Subscription 16 May 1517, see p. 135 *post*.
[13]*Ath. Oxon.* (Fasti), i. 30.

1511

28 May *Pietro Griffo*, D.Cn. & C.L.,[1] *Papal Collector*;[2] (C); *c.*40;
        b. Pisa, Italy; left England on or shortly after 9 June
        1512; Bishop of Forli, 10 Nov. 1512;[3] d. *c.* Nov. 1516.[4]

n.d.   *John Cokkys*, D.C.L., All Souls Coll., Oxford, from
        Winchester Coll; (C); *c.*30; b. Cowley, co. Oxford;
        (A.3 June 1519); d. by 28 Feb. 1546.[5]

20 Oct. *Thomas Porte*, D.C.L., St. Nicholas Hostel, Cambridge
        and Turin;[6] (C); b. Coventry and Lichfield diocese.
        John Alyn alias Carver, *'doctor'*, D.Cn.L. (1494–5),
        Oxford, Archdeacon of Middlesex; advocate;[7] (C); d. by
        Aug. 1515.[8]

1512

11 Feb. *Robert Woodwarde*, *'doctor'*, D.Cn.L., All Souls Coll.,
        Oxford, and Louvain;[9] (C); b. Salisbury diocese; living
        1533.[10]

22 Feb. *Thomas Benet*, D.C.L., Oxford; (A); d. by 11 Sept. 1558.[11]

25 Feb. *William Tayte*, *'doctor'*, D.C.L., Bologna;[12] (C); d. by 28
        Oct. 1540.[13]

23 Mar. *Thomas Alcock*, *'doctor'*, D.Cn. & C.L., Bologna[14] and
        Cambridge, *Archdeacon of Ely*; (C); living 9 Nov. 1527.[15]

23 May *William Fitzherbert*, D.Cn.L., Ferrara,[16] *Residentiary Canon
        of Lincoln*; (C); s. Nicholas F.;[17] d. by 20 Apr. 1514.[18]

21 July John ——, O. Cist., *Abbot of St. Mary of Graces, by Robert
        Davell, his agent*; (C).

6 Nov. Morgan ——, O. Cist., *Abbot of Llantarnam*; (C).

[1]Hay, p. 122.
[2]The reference to the Pope has been deleted, cf. p. 126, n, 14 *ante.*
[3]Hay, p. 125.
[4]P. S. Allen, *Erasmi Epistolae*, i (1906), 488 n.
[5]Churchill, i. 594–5.
[6]Parks, i. 640.
[7]All Souls Coll., MS. 325, unfoliated.
[8]*B.R.U.C.*, p. 125.
[9]37 *E.H.R.*, 93.
[10]Wood, *Colleges and Halls*, p. 269.
[11]Will P.C.C. 45 Noodes.
[12]Parks, i. 628.
[13]Le Neve, vi. 38.
[14]51 *E.H.R.* 270.
[15]Le Neve, iv. 19.
[16]Parks, i. 629.
[17]Ibid.
[18]Le Neve, v. 65.

1512

15 Nov. *Richard Harryson, B.Cn.L.*, Cambridge, *Rector of Milton, co. Cambridge*; (C); b. York diocese; D.Cn.L. 1515–16; d. Nov. 1542.[1]

1513

6 Feb. *Cuthbert Conyers, D.Cn.L.* Cambridge, *Archdeacon of Carlisle*; (C); s. William C., of Marske, co. York, esq.; d. 7 Apr. 1517.

18 Feb. *Richard Skypwith, B.C.L.*, St. John's Coll., Cambridge; b. York diocese; d. by 6 Feb. 1521.[2]

24 Apr. *John Rayne, D.Cn. & C.L.* (1506–7), Cambridge; (C; A); b. York diocese; killed by insurgents 3 Oct. 1536.[3]

18 Dec. *Thomas Key,* perhaps B.C.L.; (C); living 5 July 1525.[4]

1514

2 Jan. *John Grigge,* perhaps D.Cn. & C.L., Cambridge; (C); d. by Dec. 1527.[5]

27 Jan. *John Bryme*; (C); d. by 21 Mar. 1526.[6]

13 Mar. *John Brereton, D.Cn.L.*, Bologna;[7] (C; A); 3 s. Sir Randle B., of Shocklach, and Malpas, co. Chester, kt.;[8] d. by 14 Dec. 1542.[9]

20 Mar. *Richard Sampson, D.C.L.* (1512–13), Trinity Hall, Cambridge, from Perugia, Paris, and Siena; (C; A); Bishop of Chichester 1536; translated to Coventry and Lichfield 1543; d. 25 Sept. 1554; *D.N.B.*

25 June *Thomas Fitzherbert, D.Cn.L.*, King's Coll., Cambridge, from Eton Coll.; Prebendary of Coventry and Lichfield; (C); s. Sir Ralph F., of Norbury, co. Derby, Kt.; d. 20 Nov. 1532.[10]

25 June *Joachim Bretumer, D.Th.*, Turin,[11] Prebendary of Coventry and Lichfield; (C); b. York diocese; d. by 18 July 1523.[12]

---

[1]W. K. Clay, *History of the Parish of Milton* (Cambridge Antiquarian Soc. xi, 1869), p. 89.
[2]P.C.C. 5 Maynwaryng.
[3]Le Neve, i. 117.
[4]*Regg. Wolsey, etc.*, p. 81.
[5]*B.R.U.C.*, p. 269.
[6]Will P.C.C. 5 Porch.
[7]Parks, i. 628.
[8]Ormerod, iii. 687.
[9]Le Neve, v. 42.   [10]Le Neve, x. 8.
[11]Parks, i. 640.   [12]Le Neve, x. 18.

1514

25 July *Henry Machel, D.C.L.,* probably Oxford, Prebendary of York; (C); res. or d. by 5 Aug. 1530.[1]

7 Oct. *William Stynt, D.Cn. & C.L.* (by 1517), Oxford; (C; A); d. by 11 Nov. 1521.[2]

8 Oct. *John Incent, D.C.L.* (1513), All Souls Coll., Oxford; (C; A 14 Oct.); d. by 12 Sept. 1545.[3]

10 Oct. *Richard Wolleman, D.Cn.L.* (1511–12), Corpus Christi Coll., Cambridge; (C; A 31 Oct.); b. Clavering, co. Essex; d. by 19 Sept. 1537.[4]

18 Oct. *William Cradok, D.Cn. & C.L.* (by 1512), probably Oxford, Archdeacon of Lewes; (C; A 4 May 1515); living 6 Dec. 1516.[5]

6 Nov. *Hugh Asheton, B.Cn.L.,* probably Oxford; Archdeacon of Winchester; (C); b. co. Lancaster; d. by 9 Jan. 1523;[6] *his executors paid his arrears 20 Oct. 1523; D.N.B.*

8 Nov. *William Home,* perhaps M.A.; (C); d. by 24 Apr. 1522.[7] *Edmund* Birkhead, O.F.M., D.Th., *Bishop of St. Asaph;* (C); d. by 9 Apr. 1518.[8]

13 Nov. *William Carew, D.C.L.;* (C; A).

1 Dec. *Ralph Snede, D.C.L.* (1511–12), Cambridge (C; A); s. William S., of Bradwell in Wolstanton, co. Stafford; d. by 8 Oct. 1549.[9]

3 Dec. *Thomas More, 'laicus', gent.,* Under-Sheriff of London; (C); *c*.36; s. John M., serjeant-at-law; knighted Spring 1521; Lord Chancellor, 1529; beheaded 6 July 1536; *D.N.B.*
Thomas Marcyall alias Beche,[10] O.S.B., B.Th. Gloucester Hall, Oxford, *Monk, Archdeacon of St. Albans;* (C); D.Th. 1515; Abbot of St. Werburgh's, Chester 1527; Abbot of Colchester 1533; executed 1 Dec. 1539.[11]

---

[1]Le Neve, vi. 70.
[2]Le Neve, ix. 65.
[3]Le Neve 1541–1857, i. 5.
[4]Le Neve, viii. 6.
[5]B.R.U.O. iv. 672.
[6]Le Neve, iv. 19.
[7]Weaver, p. 180.
[8]Le Neve, xi. 39.
[9]Le Neve, x. 24.
[10]R. V. H. Burne, *The Monks of Chester* (London, 1962), p. 154.
[11]*V.C.H. Essex,* ii. 100.

1514

3 Dec. *John Vyntener, O.S.A., Abbot of St. Osyth;* (C); d. 19 Apr.
1533.[1]

William Carew, 'laicus', gent.; (C).

1515

1 July *Edward Redmayn, Rector of Terrington, co. York;* (C).

2 July *Christopher Plumer, B.C.L.,* Prebendary of St. Paul's;[2]
(C); attainted 13 Feb. 1535.[3]

Percival Morgan, proctor; (C); living 5 Mar. 1528.[4]

2 Sept. *Andrea Ammonio, Papal Collector and the King's Latin
Secretary;* (C); b. Lucca, Italy; d. by 23 Sept. 1517;[5]
D.N.B.

3 Sept. *Thomas Larke, Prebendary of St. Stephen's, Westminster;*
(C); d. by 15 Jan. 1534.[6]

10 Oct. *William Jonys, Warden of Swavesey;*[7] (C).

10 Nov. *William Fleschmonger, D.Cn.L.* (1514), New Coll. Oxford,
from Winchester Coll., Prebendary of Chichester; (C);
*c.*26; b. Hambleden, co. Buckingham; d. 26 Nov.
1541.[8]

1516

12 Jan. *Maurice Glynne, D.Cn.L.* (1516), Oxford, Archdeacon of
Bangor; (C; A 21 July 1517); d. by 28 July 1525;[9]
D.W.B.

11 Oct. *John Aschewell, D.Cn.L.,* Oxford, Vicar of Littlebury, co.
Essex; (C); d. by 23 Aug. 1541;[10] *D.N.B.*

Nicholas Harpisfield, D.Cn.L. (1505), Bologna,[11] from
New Coll., Oxford, and Winchester Coll.; (C; A); *c.*42;
b. Great Wishford, co. Wilts., d. by Mar. 1550.

20 Oct. *Peter Lygham, D.Cn.L.* (1516), Oxford; (C. A); b.
Exeter diocese; d. by 7 Sept. 1538.[12]

[1] Newcourt, ii. 456.
[2] His right to his stall contested by John Salvago (Le Neve, v. 25).
[3] Le Neve, vii. 43.
[4] Will of Christopher Midylton (q.v.).
[5] Le Neve, iii. 53.
[6] Will P.C.C. 9 Hogen.
[7] Presumably Warden of the twelve poor young clerks maintained at Swavesey by
the Priory of St. Anne, Coventry: see *V.C.H. Cambridge,* ii. 317.
[8] Le Neve, vii. 5.
[9] Will P.C.C. 36 Bodfelde, Mentions his cousin Edmund Hoorde (q.v.).
[10] Le Neve, v. 36.
[11] Parks, i. 628.
[12] Le Neve, v. 70.

1516

20 Oct. *Thomas Wyse, B.C.L.*, probably Oxford; (C); d. 30 June 1548.[1]

31 Oct. *Roger Tochet, D.Cn.L.*, Rector of St. Nicholas Cole Abbey, London; (C); d. by 30 Mar. 1532.[2]

7 Nov. *Gregory Mawer, D.Cn.L.*, Trinity Hall, Cambridge, subdeacon; (C; A 21 May 1517); b. Norwich diocese.

16 Nov. *Edmund Hoorde*, Carth. *D.Cn.L.*, All Souls Coll., Oxford, proctor;[3] (C); s. John H., of Bridgnorth, co. Salop; Prior of Hinton Charterhouse, co. Somerset, 1529–39.[4]

21 Nov. *John Bell, D.Cn. & C.L.*, of a foreign university; (C; A 23 Nov.); Bishop of Worcester 1539; d. 11 Aug. 1556; *his arrears paid 25 Nov. 1556; D.N.B.*

1517

15 Feb. *John* Buckley,[5] O. Cist., *Abbot of Vale Royal*; (C).

16 May *James Fitzjames*, B.Th., St. Alban Hall, Oxford, Prebendary of St. Paul's; (C); s. John F., barrister; D.Th. by Oct. 1519; d. by 22 March. 1541.[6]

Oliver Pole, B.Cn.L., Neville's Inn, Oxford, Archdeacon of Lewes; (C); d. by Aug. 1534.[7]

18 Sept. *William Salyng, O.S.A., D.Th.*, Oxford, *Prior of Merton*; (C); d. or res. 1520.[8]

30 Oct. *John Moris, D.Cn.L.* (1516), Oxford; (C; A); d. by 28 Nov. 1530.[9]

1518

11 Mar. *Silvestro Dario*, D.Cn.L.,[10] Papal Collector; (C); res. or d. 1528.[11]

Felix Massagrogen. Perhaps Felix Massarozee, Rector of Tredington, co. Worcester, nephew of Silvester Giglis, Bishop of Worcester;[12] (C); d. or res. by 24 June 1541.[13]

[1]Le Neve, ix. 63.
[2]Newcourt, i. 507.
[3]Will of Maurice Glynne (q.v.).
[4]*V.C.H. Somerset*, ii. 123.
[5]Ormerod, ii. 151.
[6]Le Neve, viii. 79.
[7]*B.R.U.O.* iv. 453.
[8]*V.H.C. Surrey*, ii. 102.   [9]Will P.C.C. 23 Jankyn.
[10]Le Neve, i. 29.   [11]Hay, p. 123.
[11]*Letters of Denization and Acts of Naturalization* (Huguenot Soc. viii, 1893), p. 165.
[12]When his successor at Tredington was instituted (T. R. Nash, *Collections for the History or Worcestershire* (London, 1782), ii. 432).

1518

21 Mar. *John Edmunds*, D.Th., Peterhouse, Cambridge; Chancellor of St. Paul's; (C); d. Nov. 1544; *D.N.B.*

25 Apr. *William Breteyn, D.C.L.* (1514–15), Cambridge; (C; A); d. by 29 July 1552.[1]

Richard Bulkley, B.C.L., *Archdeacon of Anglesey*; (C); d. by 6 Apr. 1524.[2]

25 Apr. *John Underhyll*, B.Cn.L., *Dean of Wallingford*; (C); d. by 2 Oct. 1537.[3]

8 Oct. *William Myddleton D.C.L.* (1515), All Souls Coll., Oxford; (C; A 31 July 1518); d. by Nov. 1556.

Ralph Lupton, D.Cn. & C.L., King's Coll., Cambridge, from Eton Coll.; (C; A); *c*.40; b. Sedbergh, co. York; d. by 15 Dec. 1523.[4]

1519

26 Jan *John Heryng, B.C.L., Official of the Bishop of Carlisle*; (C); b. Carlisle diocese.

Sampson Michell, D.C.L. (1516–17), Cambridge; (C; A); b. Chichester diocese; d. by 7 Sept. 1550.[5]

6 Feb. *George Billyngton*, B.Cn.L., Oxford, *Rector of 'Radcliff, diocese of Coventry and Lichfield'*; (C); d. by Nov. 1540.[6]

Richard Willeys, B.Cn. & C.L., New Coll., Oxford, from Winchester Coll., *Warden of Higham Ferrers College*; (C); b. West Hanney, co. Berks; d. by Oct. 1523.[7]

9 Mar. *Robert Price* or Aprhys, *Prebendary of St. Asaph*; (C); living 12 July 1518.[8]

11 Mar. *Robert Honywood, D.C.L.*, All Souls Coll., Oxford, *Archdeacon of Taunton*; (C); *On the day of his admission he gave to the Society a gilt spoon with the effigy of one of the Apostles holding a little ship in his left hand and a book in his right*;[9] d. by 26 Feb. 1523.[10]

---

[1]Will P.C.C. 20 Powell.
[2]Will P.C.C. 35 Bodfelde.
[3]Le Neve, iii. 33.
[4]Will P.C.C. 15 Bodfelde.
[5]Le Neve, vii. 23.
[6]B.R.U.O. iv. 664.
[7]M. I. Higham Ferrers, co. Northampton.
[8]Le Neve, xi. 48.
[9]See p. 81 *ante*.
[10]Will P.C.C. 2 Bodfelde.

1519

7 Apr. *John London, D.C.L.* (1519), New Coll. Oxford, from Winchester Coll.; (C; A); *c.*33; b. Hambleden, co. Buckingham; d. in the Fleet prison by 13 Feb. 1544;[1] *D.N.B.*

3 June *John Aley*; (A).

12 Oct. *John Tynemouth* alias Maynelyn, O.S.F., D.Th., *Bishop of Argos*; (C); d. by 12 Nov. 1524.[2]

20 Oct. *William Vaghane, D.C.L.* (by 1519), probably Oxford, Prebendary of St. Davids; (C; A); b. St. David's diocese; d. by 5 May 1541.[3]

Walter Wolmar, B.Cn.L., Canon of St. Mary's, Warwick; (C).

5 Nov. *John Mors, Canon of Lincoln*; (C); d. *c.* Mar. 1526.[4]

John Burges, B.Th., Magdalen Coll., Oxford, *Treasurer of Lincoln Cathedral*; (C); D.Th. 1520; d. by 29 Mar. 1536.[5]

George Hennege, B.C.L., Cambridge, *Canon of Lincoln*; (C); 2 s. John H., of Hainton, co. Lincoln; d. by 22 Sept. 1549;[6] *D.N.B.*

John Jevan, Treasurer of Llandaff Cathedral; (C); d. by 6 Feb. 1542.[7]

Henry Rawlyns, B.C.L., New Coll., Oxford, from Winchester Coll., *Canon of Salisbury*; (C); b. Wareham, co. Dorset; d. by 1 Oct. 1526.[8]

1520

20 Feb. *Fulke Salusbury, Dean of St. Asaph*; (C); d. by 3 Nov. 1543.[9]

4 May *John Gruffytch*, M.A., probably Oxford, *Treasurer of St. Davids Cathedral*; (C); d. by 2 May 1523.[10]

Edward Fynche, D.M., Oxford, *Canon of Salisbury*; (C); d. by 15 Jan. 1539.[11]

[1] Le Neve, i. 94.
[2] Will P.C.C. 27 Bodfelde.
[3] Will P.C.C. 28 Alenger.
[4] Le Neve, i. 110.
[5] Le Neve, i. 68.
[6] Le Neve, vi. 29.
[7] Will P.C.C. 1 Spert.
[8] Le Neve, i. 61.
[9] Le Neve, xi. 41.
[10] Will P.C.C. 8 Bodfelde.
[11] Le Neve, iii. 14.

1520

4 May *Robert Dykar*, B.Cn. & C.L., Oxford, Prebendary of Bath
and Wells; (C); d. by 24 July 1532.[1]

8 Oct. *Geoffrey Wharton, D.Cn.L.* (1519–20), Cambridge; (C;
A); d. by 30 Oct. 1529.[2]

Rowland Lee, D.Cn.L. (1519–20), St. Nicholas Hostel,
Cambridge; (C; A); s. William L., of Morpeth, co.
Northumberland and cousin of Dr. Thomas Legh
(q.v.);[3] Bishop of Coventry and Lichfield 1534; d. 24
Jan. 1543; *D.N.B.*

8 Oct. *William Burghill, D.Cn.L.* (1516), Oxford, Treasurer of
Hereford Cathedral; (C; A); b. Hereford diocese; d. by
7 Sept. 1526.[4]

William Styllyngton, D.Cn.L. (by 1514), possibly of a
foreign university,[5] Archdeacon of Norwich; (C; A); d.
by 16 Aug. 1528.[6]

John Smythe, D.C.L.; (C; A).

29 Oct. *George Dudley, D.Cn.L.*, probably of a foreign university,
from London Coll., Oxford, deacon; (C; A); b. Here-
ford diocese; d. by 27 Dec. 1562;[7] his executors, John
Marett and Henry Adlam of Aston in the Walls, co.
Northampton, paid all arrears 23 Dec. 1563.[8]

29 Oct. *Edward Basset, D.Cn.L*; (C; A).

19 Dec. *Adam Traves, D.Cn.L.* Broadgates Hall, Oxford, Archdeacon of Exeter; (C); d. 27 Dec. 1555.[9]

1521

19 Feb. *Thomas Jakman, B.C.L.*; (C).

15 May *William Wall*, O.S.A., D.Th., Oxford, *Abbot of Kenilworth*; (C); d. or res. 1537.[10]

26 May *Edward Povel, D.Th.*, Oriel Coll., Oxford, Prebendary of
Lincoln and Salisbury; (C); executed at Smithfield 30
July 1540; *D.N.B.; D.W.B.*

[1]Will P.C.C. 16 Thower.
[2]Le Neve, v. 9.
[3]G. R. Elton, *Star Chamber Stories* (London, 1958), pp. 154–5.
[4]*Registrum Caroli Bothe* (C. & Y. Soc. xxviii, 1931), p. 339.
[5]*B.R.U.O.* iv. 541.
[6]Le Neve, v. 62.
[7]Will P.C.C. 33 Streat.
[8]S.B., f.119.
[9]Le Neve, ix. 15.
[10]*V.C.H. Warwick*, ii. 89.

1521

26 May *Nicholas Maynwaryng*, M.A., probably Oxford, *Prebendary of the Collegiate Church of Chumleigh*, co. Devon; (C); d. 15 Jan. 1537.[1]

12 June *William Benet, D.C.L.*, Prebendary of Bath and Wells; (C; A); b. Salisbury diocese;[2] d. 26 Sept. 1533; *D.N.B.*

25 June *Miles Spenser, D.Cn. & C.L.*, Oxford, Prebendary of York; (C; A); *c.* 42; perhaps b. Brough under Stainmore, co. Westmorland;[3] *His executor John Tomson paid all arrears 17 Mar. 1570.*
Nicholas Samme, D.Cn.L. (1518–19), Cambridge; (C; A); d. 1527.

26 July *Thomas Rowland* alias Rowland Pentecost, O.S.B., B.Th., Oxford, *Abbot of Abingdon*; (C); surrendered the Abbey 9 Feb. 1538; d. by 21 Apr. 1540.[4]

8 Oct. *Richard Benger, D.Cn.L.* (1512), New Coll., Oxford, from Winchester Coll.; (C; A); *c.*37; b. Alton Barnes co. Wilts.; d. by Apr. 1545.

1522

14 Jan. *Alexander 'de Capite Bovis', D.Cn.L.* Bologna;[5] (C; A).

26 Mar. *John Pennand, D.Cn.L.*, Perugia;[6] (C; A); d. by 23 May 1529.[7]

31 July *John Fayter* or Fewter, *D.Cn.L.* (1522), All Souls Coll., Oxford; (C; A); d. by 27 June 1532.[8]

7 Oct. *Robert Cliff, D.C.L.* (1522), Cambridge; (C; A); d. by 21 June 1538.[9]

15 Oct. *William Claibroght, D.Cn. & C.L.* (1522), Cambridge; (C; A); d. by 6 May 1534.[10]

12 Nov. *John Olyver* alias Smythe, *D.C.L.* (1522), Oxford, Prebendary of Hereford; (C; A); d. by 3 June 1552; left 40*s.* to 'the Doctors Comons to make them a dynner withall . . . and for the doctors contributions 10*s.*';[11] *D.N.B.*

---

[1]Le Neve, ix. 64.
[2]*Regg. Wolsey etc.*, p. 86.
[3]Provided in his will for scholars from Brough under Stainmore (P.C.C. 8 Lyon).
[4]Will P.C.C. 5 Alenger.
[5]Coote, p. 18.   [6]Parks, i. 637.
[7]Le Neve, v. 25.
[8]Will P.C.C. 15 Thower.
[9]Will P.C.C. 18 Dyngeley.
[10]Le Neve, i. 83.
[11]Will P.C.C. 17 Powell. He left a dozen silver spoons to Dr. Tregonwell (q.v.).

1522

24 Nov. *Hugh* Cook alias Farringdon, O.S.B., *Abbot of Reading* (C); hanged 15 Nov. 1539.

9 Dec. *John Tregonwell, D.C.L.* (1522), London Coll., Oxford, in minor orders; formerly a proctor; (C; A); b. co. Cornwall; Judge of the Court of Admiralty by 1535; ktd. 1553; d. 13 Jan. 1565;[1] *D.N.B.*

20 Dec. *Henry Style, D.C.L.*, of a foreign university, from New Coll., Oxford, and Winchester Coll.; (C; A 20 Jan. 1523); *c.*37; b. Shutford in Swalcliffe, co. Oxford.

1523

30 Jan. *Richard Arche, B.C.L.*, Principal of Broadgates Hall, Oxford. Prebendary of Salisbury; (C; A); b. Bromyard, co. Hereford;[2] d. 8 Dec. 1558.[3]

n.d. *William Cliff, D.C.L.* (1522), Cambridge; (C; A. 15 Dec. 1522); d. by 13 Dec. 1558;[4] *D.N.B.*

29 Apr. *Thomas Parker, B.Cn.L.* Oxford; b. Hereford diocese; D.Cn.L. by 1528; (C); d. 22 Sept. 1538.[5]
Thomas Lloyd, B.Cn. & C.L., All Souls Coll., Oxford. *Precentor of St. Davids*; (C); b. St. Davids diocese; d. by 14 Dec. 1547.[6]

6 May *John Caravanell, Dean of* St. Mary's *Warwick*; (C); d. or res. 1542.[7]

10 May *John Russell, B.Th.*, King's Coll., Cambridge, from Eton Coll., *Master of Fotheringhay College*; (C); b. Oundle, co. Northampton; d. by 17 Dec. 1547.

1 June *Geoffrey Wrenne*, M.A., Oxford, *Canon of York*; (C); d. 5 Apr. 1527.[8]

6 June *Ralph Whytehede, B.Cn. & C.L.*, King's Hall, Cambridge, *Chancellor of Lichfield Cathedral*; (C); d. by 31 Nov. 1535.[9]

6 June *Roland Jukys, M.A.*, All Souls Coll., Oxford, Rector of St. Margaret Pattens, London; (C); b. Worcester diocese; deprived 26 Mar. 1538.[10]

---

[1] M.I. Milton Abbey, co. Dorset.
[2] *C.P.R. 1548–9*, p. 147.
[3] *B.R.U.O.* iv. 11.
[4] Will P.C.C. 16 Welles.
[5] Le Neve, ii. 9.
[6] Will P.C.C. 51 Alen.
[7] *V.C.H. Warwick*, ii. 129.
[8] Browne Willis, i. 432.
[9] Le Neve, x. 10.
[10] Newcourt, i. 409.

1523

4 Aug. *Henry* Standish, O.F.M., D.Th., *Bishop of St. Asaph*; (C);
d. 9 July 1535;[1] *D.N.B.*

Thomas Shevynton, O.Cist., *Bishop of Bangor*; (C); d. 17
Aug 1533.

William Etherway, O. Cist., *Abbot of Stratford*; (C); d.
or res. 1524.[2]

18 Oct. *Thomas Baret, D.C.L.*; (C).

22 Oct. *Robert Dodson, Rector of 'Littlethorp', dio. London* (perhaps
Thorpe le Soken, co. Essex); (C).

29 Oct. *William Cuffold, D.Cn.L.* (1523), New Coll., Oxford,
from Winchester Coll.; (A); *c.*29; b. Basingstoke, co.
Southampton; living 1556.[3]

1524

19 Apr. *John Wylcoks, B.Th.*; (C).

20 Apr. *Robert Frost, B.Cn.L.*; (C).

2 May *Richard Watkyns, B.C.L.*, probably Oxford, *proctor*; (C);
b. Llandaff diocese; d. *c.* 1539.[4]

28 June *John* Merston, O.S.A., *Abbot of Nutley*; (C); *gave two
hogsheads of wine*; res. 1528.

7 Oct. *Ralph Whiet, B.C.L.*, Oxford, *proctor*; (C); d. by 15 Dec.
1528.[5]

13 Oct. *John Blithe*, B.Cn.L., Oxford, *Archdeacon of Coventry*; (C);
d. by 21 Nov. 1547.[6]

Nicholas Coopar, M.A., Cambridge, *Vicar of Cheshunt*,
co. Hertford; (C); b. by 18 Sept. 1526.[7]

Richard Parkar, B.Cn. & *C.L.*, Oxford, Rector of St.
Swithun, London; (C); d. by 26 Jan. 1534.[8]

15 Dec. *William Leson, D.Cn. & C.L.* (by 1522), probably of a
foreign university,[9] Vicar of Cropredy, co. Oxford;
(C; A); d. by 16 Feb. 1550.[10]

---

[1] Le Neve, xii. 39.
[2] *V.C.H. Essex*, ii. 133.
[3] *B.R.U.O.* iv. 156.
[4] *B.R.U.O.* iv. 708.
[5] Will P.C.C. 42 Porch.
[6] For the suit against his executor, see p. 11 *ante.*
[7] R. Clutterbuck, *History ... of the County of Hertford* (London, 1821), ii. 111.
[8] Le Neve, i. 111.
[9] *B.R.U.O.* iv. 353.
[10] Le Neve, x. 43.

1525

14 Jan. *Anthony Draycot, D.Cn.L.* (1522), Great White Hall, Oxford; (C; A); b. Coventry and Lichfield diocese;[1] d. 20 Jan. 1571;[2] *D.N.B.*

20 Mar. *Thomas Pellis,* O.S.B., *D.C.L.* (1514), Cambridge, monk of Norwich; (C; A); d. *c.* 1537.

11 May *Adam Becanshaw, D.Cn.L.* (C); d. by 26 Dec. 1551.[3]

22 Oct. *John Stokisley, D.Th.,* Magdalen Hall, Oxford, *Archdeacon of Surrey*; (C): Bishop of London 1530; d. 8 Sept. 1539; *D.N.B.*

3 Nov. *John Wilson, D.Cn.L.*; (C; A).

10 Nov. *Richard Foxfoord, D.C.L.* (1526) *and D.Cn.L.,* Oxford; (C; A. 20 Oct. 1526); d. by 20 Aug. 1533.[4]

13 Nov. *Edward Carne, D.C.L.* (1524), Oxford; (C; A); *c.*29; s. Howel C., of Cowbridge, co. Glamorgan; ktd by the Emperor Aug. 1540; d. 18 Jan. 1561; *D.N.B.*; *D.W.B.*

1526

20 Jan. *Robert Chalner, D.Cn. & C.L.* (by 1525), probably of a foreign university, from New Coll., Oxford, and Winchester Coll.; (C; A); *c.*35; b. Buckingham; d. by 14 May 1541.[5]

20 Jan. *Richard Mugge,*[6] *D.Cn.L.* (1525), All Souls Coll., Oxford; (C; A); d. by Dec. 1549.[7]

5 Feb. *Walter Cretyng, D.C.L.* (by 1525), possibly of a foreign university;[8] (C; A;[9]) licensed at the full table to practise in any court or consistory in the City of London, paying 22*s.* when present and 6*s.*8*d.* when absent 4 June 1529;[10] d. by 20 Nov. 1557.[11]

21 Mar. *Thomas* Bale, O.S.A., D.Th., Oxford, *Bishop of Lydda and Prior of the New Hospital of St. Mary outside Bishopsgate,* London; (C); d. by 5 Aug. 1530.[12]

---

[1]Probably at Draycott in the Moors, co. Stafford, to which he ultimately retired: see *B.R.U.O.* iv. 176.

[2]Browne Willis, i. 451.   [3]Newcourt, ii. 608.

[4]Le Neve, iv. 70.   [5]Will P.C.C. 28 Alenger.

[6]Misprinted 'Asrigge' in Coote, p. 21.

[7]*B.R.U.O.* iv. 408.

[8]*B.R.U.O.* iv. 672.

[9]Cretyng signed a further contributor's subscription on 22 Dec. 1528.

[10]S.B., f.33.

[11]Will P.C.C. 49 Wrastley.

[12]Le Neve, v. 42.

1526

16 Apr. *Arthur Bulkeley, D.Cn.L.* (1525), Oxford-(C; A); b. Ang; lesey; kinsman of Sir Richard B., of Beaumaris;[1] Bishop of Bangor 1542; d. by 23 Mar. 1553.[2]

17 Apr. *Robert Ayshecu*; (C).

20 Apr. *Richard Gwent, D.Cn. & C. L.* (1525), All Souls Coll., Oxford; (C; A); b. Wales; d. by 23 July 1543;[3] *D.N.B. D.W.B.*

1 July *Roger Clerk*, M.A., probably Oxford, *Prebendary of the Collegiate Church of St. Mary, Warwick*; (C).

15 Oct. *Edmund Boner, D.C.L.* (1526), Broadgates Hall, Oxford; (C; A); perhaps illeg. s. George Savage, Rector of Davenham, co. Chester;[4] Bishop of Hereford 1538, tr. to London 1539; deprived 1549; restored 1553; re-adm. to Doctors' Commons 14 Jan. 1555.

9 Nov. *John Pilkyngton, B.Cn.L.*, probably Oxford;[5] (C).

John Burton, O.S.A., *D.Cn.L.*, Oxford, *Abbot of Oseney*; (C); d. 1537.

Thomas Chetham, O.S.A., *Bishop of Sidon and Commenda-*

1527 *tory of Leeds Priory*; (C); d. by 6 Oct. 1558.[6]

6 May *Robert Byrche, D.Cn. & C.L.* (by 1527), possibly Padua;[7] (C; A); d. by Feb. 1535.[8]

23 July *William Revet, D.C.L.* (1518–19), Cambridge; (C; A); d. by 8 Feb. 1542.

10 Nov. *Nicholas Hancok*, O.S.A., B.Th., Oxford, *Prior of Christ Church, London*; (C); surrendered the Priory July 1532;[9] d. by 24 Aug. 1560.[10]

1528

20 Jan. *Hugh Aprice, D.Cn.L.* (1526), Oxford; (C; A); *c.*33; s. Rees ap Rees, of Brecon, butcher; d. by 31 Aug. 1574;[11] *D.N.B.*; *D.W.B.*

---

[1]L. Baldwin Smith, *Tudor Prelates and Politics* (Princeton, N.J., 1953), pp. 200–1.
[2]Le Neve, xi. 5.
[3]Le Neve, v. 9.
[4]L. Baldwin Smith, op. cit., pp. 298–300.
[5]*B.R.U.O.* iv. 697.
[6]Le Neve 1541–1857, i. 50.
[7]*B.R.U.O.* iv. 93.
[8]Ibid.
[9]*V.C.H. London*, i. 474.
[10]Will P.C.C. 43 Mellershe.
[11]Will P.C.C. 34 Martyn.

1528

21 Jan. *John Docwray, B.C.L.*, Canon of Salisbury; (C); d. by 9 July 1535.[1]

John Stephyns, M.A., Oriel Coll., Oxford; (C); b. Exeter diocese; d. 24 Mar. 1560.[2]

14 Mar. *John Wetwod, B.Cn.L.*, probably Oxford, *Canon and Prebendary of Lichfield*; (C); d. by Dec. 1541.[3]

George Carew, clerk, probably M.A. of a foreign university;[4] (C); *c.*30; 3 s. Edmund C., of Anthony, co. Cornwall; *12 July 1579 paid to Henry Scott, Steward £6.13s.4d. in full satisfaction of his contributions to date*; d. 1 June 1583; *27 Aug. 1583 26s.8d. paid to Mr. Dr. Mowse,[5] Steward in full payment of all arrears*.

7 Oct. *Richard Warham, D.C.L.*, Orleans, from Louvain, incorp. Oxford (1527), Prebendary of Chichester; (C; A); s. Hugh W., of Halling, co. Kent, and of Malshanger in Church Oakley, co. Southampton; d. by 3 Dec. 1545.[6]

Thomas Bagarde, D.C.L. (1528), Cardinal Coll., Oxford; (C; A); b. Hereford diocese; d. by Jan. 1544;[7] *D.N.B.*

27 Oct. *Henry Morgan, D.C.L.* (1525), London Coll., Oxford; (C; A); b. Dewsland, co. Pembroke; Bishop of St. Davids 1554; d. 23 Dec. 1559; *D.N.B., D.W.B.*

Anthony Bellyeys, D.Cn. & C.L.; (C; A); yr. s. Thomas B., of Henknowle, co. Durham; Archdeacon of Colchester 1543; d. by 15 Sept. 1552;[8] *D.N.B.*

28 Oct. *Henry Carbott, D.Cn. & C.L.*; (A); *6s.8d. paid by William Robinson*.[9]

30 Nov. *Nicholas Haukyns, D.C.L.*, King's Coll., Cambridge, from Eton Coll., Archdeacon of Ely; (C; A); b. Putney, co. Surrey; licensed at the full table to practise in any court or consistory in the City of London, paying 22s. when

[1] Will P.C.C. 26 Hogen.
[2] Le Neve, ix. 65.
[3] *B.R.U.O.* iv. 179.
[4] *B.R.U.O.* iv. 102.
[5] 'Mr. Dr.' was commonly used of advocates until the early seventeenth century. cf. Mr. Serjeant X and Mr. Baron [of the Exchequer] Y, which continued until the nineteenth century, and Mr. Justice Z, which is still in use.
[6] Le Neve, vii. 42.
[7] *B.R.U.O.* iv. 20.
[8] Will P.C.C. 24 Powell.
[9] Omitted by Coote.

1528

present and 6*s*.8*d*. when absent 4 June 1529;[1] d. by 24 Jan. 1534;[2] *D.N.B.*

1529

2 July   *Matthew Byll, B.Cn.L.*; (C); probably living 1544.[3]

7 July   *Edmund Stuard, D.C.L.*, Cambridge; (C); *Thomas Hethe, one of the donatories of his goods, paid 40 s. for his arrears 10 June 1560.*
Roger Elys, B.Cn.L., probably Oxford, *Rector of Corwen*, co. Merioneth, *paternal uncle of Thomas Yale, advocate of this Society and his generous benefactor*; (C); d. by 7 June 1547.[4]

31 July   *David Pole, D.Cn.L.* (1528), All Souls Coll., Oxford; (C; A); *Archdeacon of Derby*;[5] Bishop of Peterborough 1557; deprived 1559; d. by 6 July 1568;[6] *D.N.B.*

22 Oct.   *Thomas Stanley, clerk*; (C); perhaps base s. Edward (S), Lord Mounteagle; Bishop of Sodor and Man 1530; (C); d. 1570; *D.N.B.*[7]

24 Oct.   *George Colyer*, M.A., Oxford, *Warden of the Collegiate Church of Manchester*; (C); s. Robert C., a Frenchman who settled at Darlaston, co. Stafford; d. 1557.[8]

25 Nov.   *John Dakyn, D.C.L.* (1528–9), St. Nicholas Hostel, Cambridge; (C; A); d. 9 Nov. 1558.

26 Dec.   *Lewis Griffyth, B.Cn.L.*, Oxford; (C).

1530

14 Jan.   *Thomas Baret, D.C.L.* (1529), New Inn Hall, Oxford; (C; A); b. Winchester diocese; d. by 26 Apr. 1544.[9]
John Veysey, D.Cn.L., Oxford; (C); *his name erased because he accused one of his fellow commoners about words spoken at the common table.*

14 July   *Marmaduke Constable, D.Th.*; (C).

29 Oct.   *Nicholas Wotton, D.Cn. & C.L.*, probably of a foreign university; (C; A); *c.*33; 4 s. Sir Robert W., of Boughton Malherbe, co. Kent, kt.; d. 26 Jan. 1567; *D.N.B.*

[1] S.B., f.33.
[2] Le Neve, ii. 19.
[3] Weaver, p. 51.
[4] Will P.C.C. 38 Alen.
[5] Not in Le Neve's list of archdeacons of Derby.
[6] Will P.C.C. 14 Babington.
[7] *B.R.U.O.* iv. 535.
[8] *B.R.U.O.* iv. 132.
[9] Le Neve, i. 49.

1530

n.d. *Thomas Wynter, Provost of Beverley*; base s. Cardinal Wolsey; (C); living 26 June 1540.[1]

n.d. *John Brereton, Warden of the Chantry or Free Chapel of Elmley under Castle*; co. Worcester; (C); perhaps d. by 14 Dec. 1542.[2]

1531

5 June *Richard Laiton, D.Cn. & C.L.*, possibly Oxford, Prebendary of St. Paul's; (C; A); s. William L., of Dalemain, co. Cumberland; d. by 17 June 1544;[3] *D.N.B.*

7 Oct. *Thomas Legh, D.C.L.* (1531), Cambridge; (C; A); cousin of Dr. Rowland Lee;[4] ktd. 11 May 1544; d. 25 Nov. 1545; *D.N.B.*

n.d. *Robert Bisse, D.Cn. & C.L.* (1507), All Souls Coll., Oxford; (C); d. by 20 Dec. 1546.[5]

1532

27 May *William Lane, D.Cn.L.* (1529–30), Cambridge, from Oxford; (C; A).

n.d. *John Barlo*, M.A., Corpus Christi Coll., Oxford, *Dean of Westbury-on-Trym*; (C); b. Essex; living Aug. 1554.[6]

9 Dec. *John Hughes, D.C.L.* (1528), Merton Coll., Oxford; (C; A); d. by 10 May 1543.[7]

1533

8 Mar. *John Barbar* alias Pryor, *D.C.L.* (1533), All Souls Coll., Oxford; (C; A); d. by 20 July 1549;[8] *D.N.B.*

William Peter, D.C.L. (1533), All Souls Coll., Oxford; (C; A); *c*.28; s. John P., of Torbrian, co. Devon, tanner;[9] ktd. 1543; gave £20 to Doctors' Commons in 1568 'to be employed about the furniture and charges of ye new purchased house lately called Monjoy House for their habitation and commons';[10] d. 13 Jan. 1572; *D.N.B.*

---

[1] Le Neve, xii. 73.

[2] Le Neve 1541–1857, i. 38.

[3] Le Neve, i. 16.

[4] G. R. Elton, *Star Chamber Stories* (London, 1958), pp. 154–5.

[5] Le Neve, iii. 41.

[6] *B.R.U.O.* iv. 26.

[7] Will P.C.C. 20 Spert.

[8] Will P.C.C. 36 Populwell.

[9] Dr. Petre received a grant of arms *c*.1545 (F. G. Emmison, *Tudor Secretary* (London, 1961), p. 302).

[10] Essex Record Office D/DP Z23.

1533

14 Mar. *Griffin Leyson, D.C.L.* (1533), Oxford; (C; A); s. Leyson ap Owen, of Pantowen, co. Carmarthen;[1] d. by 9 Sept. 1555.[2]

29 Apr. *Roger Tonneshend, D.Cn.L.* (1532–3), Cambridge; (C; A); 4 s. Sir Roger T., of East Rainham, co. Norfolk, kt.; d. by 18 Oct. 1538;[3] *D.N.B.*

9 June *Hugh Coren, D.C.L.* (1533), Oxford; (C; A); b. High Knipe in Bampton, co. Westmorland; Archbishop of Dublin 1555; Bishop of Oxford 1567; d. Oct. 1568; *D.N.B.*

14 Oct. *Francis Cave, D.C.L.* (by 1532), Oxford, from Louvain (C; A); 4 s. Richard C., of Stamford, co. Northampton;[4] d. 1583.[4A]

1535

—Feb. *John Vaghan, D.C.L.* (1534), Oxford; (C; A); ktd. 22 Feb. 1547; d. by 1570.[5]

20 Apr. *William Mooke*, B.Cn.L., probably Oxford, Prebendary of York; (C); d. by 20 Apr. 1545.[6]

1536

7 Feb. *Thomas Thyrleby, D.Cn. & C.L.* (1529–30), Trinity Hall, Cambridge, Archdeacon of Ely; (C); Bishop of Westminster 1540; translated to Norwich 1550; and Ely 1554; deprived 1559; d. 26 Aug. 1570; *D.N.B.*

11 Feb. *John Rokeby, D.C.L.* (1532–3), St. Nicholas Hostel, Cambridge; (C; A); 2 s. Ralph R., of Mortham, co. York;[7] d. by 10 Dec. 1573; *D.N.B.*

1537

15 Oct. *William Cooke, D.C.L.* (1537), All Souls Coll., Oxford; (C; A); d. 25 Aug. 1558.[8]

1538

7 Mar. *Richard Lyell, D.C.L.* (1538), All Souls Coll., Oxford; (C; A); living 28 July 1556.[9]

---

[1] 4 Cymmrodorion Rec. Soc. (1903), 177.
[2] P.C.C. 32 More.   [4] Le Neve, iii. 19.
[3] *Vis. Leics.* p. 126.
[4] Will P.C.C. 18 Butts.
[5] *B.R.U.O.* iv. 592.
[6] Le Neve, vi. 84.
[7] 15 *Genealogist*, N.S. (1899), 253.
[8] *Diary of Henry Machyn* (Camden Soc. xlii, 1848), p. 365.
[9] *C.P.R. 1555–7*, p. 275.

1539

n.d. *Rowland Taylor, D.C.L.* (1533-4), Cambridge; (C; A 3
Nov. 1539); b. Rothbury, co. Northumberland; *burned
at Hadleigh*, co. Suffolk for heresy 9 Feb. 1555; *D.N.B.*
Thomas Powell, B.C.L., All Souls Coll., Oxford, Prebendary of Chichester; (C); b. St. Davids diocese; d. by
1 July 1551.[1]
Christopher Neyvynson, D.C.L. (1538), Cambridge; (C; A
1 July 1539); 1 s. Rowland N., of Briggend in Wetheral,
co. Cumberland; d. by 12 Sept. 1551;[2] *D.N.B.*
John Storye, D.C.L. (1538), Principal of Broadgates Hall,
Oxford; (C; A — 1539); *c.*29; s. Nicholas S.; executed
at Tyburn 1 June 1571; *D.N.B.*

9 Nov. *John Butler, B.C.L.*; (C). Perhaps a former Franciscan,
who was dispensed to hold a benefice and change his
habit 31 July 1538.[3]

1540

21 July *Richard Rede, D.C.L.* (1540), New Coll., Oxford, from
Winchester Coll.; (C; A 27 July); b. Nether Wallop, co.
Southampton, ktd. *c.*1545; Lord Chancellor of Ireland
1546-8; m. Anne, d. of Sir John Tregonwell (q.v.); d.
11 July 1575; *D.N.B.*

2 Oct. *John Smyth, D.C.L.* (1540), Oxford; (C; A); d. by Apr.
1564.[4]

n.d. *Henry Cole, D.C.L.* (1540), New Coll., Oxford, from
Winchester Coll. and Padua;[5] Prebendary of Salisbury;
(C; A); *c.*31; b. Godshill, I.O.W.; d. by 15 Jan. 1580;[6]
D.N.B.

n.d. *John Bourchier*; (C).

1541

n.d. *William Geffre, D.C.L.* (1540), Principal of Broadgates
Hall, Oxford; (C; A); d. 1558.

1543

22 May *Richard Standishe, D.C.L.* (1541-2), Cambridge, Chancellor of St. Asaph; (C; A); b. co. Lancaster; d. by 7
Mar. 1553; left 40*s.* to 'the Doctors of the Arches'.[7]

[1]Will P.C.C. 16 Bucke.   [2]Will P.C.C. 4 Powell.
[3]Chambers, p. 145.   [4]*B.R.U.O.* iv. 523.
[5]Parks, i. 836.   [6]Will P.C.C. 2 Arundell.
[7]Will P.C.C. 6 Tashe.

1543

7 Oct. *John Croke, D.C.L.* (1543), New Coll., Oxford, from Winchester Coll.; (C; A); *c.*34; b. Soke of Winchester; perhaps d. 1561.[1]

n.d. *John Cottrell*, B.C.L., New Coll., Oxford, from Winchester Coll.; (C); *c.*35; b. Wootton Rivers, co. Wilts.; D.C.L. 11 July 1545; d. by 25 May 1572.[2]

n.d. *John Worthull, D.Cn.L.*, New Inn Hall, Oxford, Archdeacon of Chichester; (C); b. Exeter diocese; d. by 3 Jan. 1555.[3]

n.d. *John Cooke*, perhaps B.C.L., Oxford, priest; (C) d. 1554.[4]

1544

4 Feb. *Geoffrey Glyn, D.C.L.* (1538–9), Trinity Hall, Cambridge; (C; A); s. John G., of Heneglwys, co. Anglesey; d. July 1557; left 20s. to 'the Doctors Comyns yf I dye at London to make a repast at my buryall'.[5]

n.d. *John Apharry, D.C.L.* (1543), Hinksey Hall, Oxford, from Caen; (C);[6] d. by 1 June 1549.[7]

n.d. *Peter Aysheton*, perhaps M.A., Christ's Coll., Cambridge, Canon of Lincoln, Fellow of the College of Physicians; (C); d. 1548; *D.N.B.*

1546

10 Oct. *John Fuller, D.C.L.* (1546), All Souls Coll., Oxford; b. Worcester diocese; *d. at Cambridge* 30 July 1558; *D.N.B.*

19 Oct. *William Pierpont, D.C.L.*, Orleans, incorp. King's Coll., Cambridge (1540–1), *a married priest*; (C; A); deprived 1554.

n.d. *John Williams, D.C.L.* (1543), Oxford, Prebendary of Gloucester; (C; A 3 Mar. 1550); b. St. Davids diocese; d. Dec. 1558.

1548

20 May *John Mableston*, D.Cn. & C.L., possibly Oxford, Prior of the Hospital of St. John of Jerusalem at Clerkenwell;[8] (C); d. by 14 Mar. 1553.[9]

[1] *B.R.U.O.* iv. 151.   [2] Will P.C.C. 13 Daper.
[3] Le Neve, vii. 13. S.B., f.35ᵛ has 'd. 1558' inserted.
[4] *B.R.U.O.* iv. 126.
[5] Will P.C.C. 25 Wrastley. Left to Dr. Kenall (q.v.) a gown and a great press in 'the upper chamber in the Comyns'.
[6] There is a second subscription by Apharry dated 10 Dec. 1548.
[7] Will P.C.C. 33 Populwell.   [8] Chambers, p. 48.   [9] Will P.C.C. 5 Tashe.

1549

n.d. *John Thornton*, B.C.L., Cambridge, perhaps Vicar of Twickenham, co. Middlesex; (C); deprived 18 Apr. 1562.[1]

10 Dec. *John Griffyth, B.C.L.*; (C).

Robert Oking, LL.D., Trinity Hall, Cambridge, *Archdeacon of Salisbury, a married priest*; (C); d. *c.* 1554; *D.N.B.*

14 June *David Lewes*, D.C.L., All Souls Coll., Oxford; adm. Arches 8 Aug. 1548; (C; A 8 Dec. 1549); *c*.29; 1 s. Lewis Wallis, Vicar of Abergavenny, co. Monmouth; Judge of the Court of Admiralty 1558; Treasurer 1570; d. 27 Apr. 1584; left to 'the Societie of the Doctors of Tharches my bason and Ewer of sylver parcell guilte for a memorie of mee';[2] *D.N.B.; D.W.B.*

n.d. *Thomas Baghe* alias Williams, B.D., *Archdeacon of Surrey*; (C); d. by 7 Feb. 1558.[3]

1550

27 Jan. *Henry Hervie*, LL.D., Trinity Hall, Cambridge; adm. Arches 10 Nov. 1549; (C; A); s. Robert H., of Stradbroke, co. Suffolk; Master of Trinity Hall by Mar. 1559; d. 20 Feb. 1585;[4] left to 'the Company of the Arches keepinge Commons in the Doctors Commons in the Arches' £6.13*s*.4*d*. for a piece of plate;[5] *D.N.B.*

21 Feb. *John Weale*, B.D., Cambridge, from Oxford, Rector of All Hallows the Great, London; (C); d. by 2 July 1569.[6]

1551

14 Jan. *John Gibbon*, D.C.L. (1551), All Souls Coll., Oxford; (C; A); s. Philip G., of Penhebyt in the lordship of St. Fagan, co. Glamorgan;[7] d. June 1581.

---

[1]Newcourt, i.758.

[2]Will P.C.C. 10 Watson. Left to Dr. Griffith Lloyd (q.v.) 'preferment' of the lease of his lodgings for 100 marks.

[3]Le Neve, v. 18.

[4]*Warren's Book*, p. 260. Hervie has frequently been described as Dean of the Arches, but there seems to be no evidence that he ever held that office. The error appears to have been originated by Sir George Buc, who so described Hervie in his *Third Vniuersitie*, p. 1078, which is surprising, since Buc stated that he knew Hervie when he was 'a young Scholler'.

[5]Will P.C.C. 10 Brudenell.

[6]Le Neve, i. 27.

[7]*Vis. London 1568*, p. 79. The family was formerly named Payn. Dr. Gibbon received a grant of a crest 24 Nov. 1570 as 'Payn alias Gybon' (*Grantees*, p. 193).

1552

12 Mar. *Sir John Price, kt.*, Principal Register in Causes Ecclesiastical; (C); d. 15 Oct. 1555; *D.N.B.; D.W.B.*

16 June *Hugh Weston, D.D.*, Rector of Lincoln Coll., Oxford; (C); b. Burton Overy, co. Leicester; d. 8 Dec. 1558; *D.N.B.*

8 Oct. *William Dalby, B.C.L.*, All Souls Coll., Oxford, *proctor*; (C); b. Milcombe, Exeter; living 1560.[1]

14 Oct. *Henry Johns D.C.L.*, All Souls Coll., Oxford; adm. Arches 10 Oct. 1552; (C; A); d. Feb. 1592; left £10 partly to 'amende' the commons on the day of his burial and for some plate for the use of the Company;[2] *D.W.B.*

1553

14 Jan. *Valentine Dale, D.C.L.*, Orleans, from All Souls Coll., Oxford, and King's Sch., Worcester; adm. Arches 6 Jan. 1553; (C; A); Judge of the Court of Admiralty 1585; d. 17 Nov. 1585; *D.N.B.*

4 May *William Ermisted, B.D.*, of a foreign university, incorp. Oxford, *Canon of St. Paul's* and Master of the Temple; (C); d. 31 Oct. 1558.[3]

1554 *Thomas Martyn, D.C.L.*, Bourges, from New Coll.,
15 Jan Oxford, and Winchester Coll., adm. Arches 11 Jan. 1554; (C; A); *c.*32, 1 s. John M., of Cerne, co. Dorset;[4] d. by 7 Aug. 1593.[5]

Nicholas Harpisfeld, Incep. C.L., New Coll., Oxford, from Winchester Coll.; (C; A); *c.*35; b. St. Mary Magdalen Old Fish St., London; s. John H., citizen and draper; D.C.L. 16 July 1554; imprisoned in the Fleet from 25 Aug. 1559; d. 18 Dec. 1575.[6]

17 Jan. *Thomas Abbot, B.D.*, All Souls Coll., Oxford; (C); b. Coventry and Lichfield diocese; d. 1576.[7]

John Kenall, D.C.L. (1553), Oxford; (C; A); d. by 23 June 1591.[8]

[1] *B.R.U.O.* iv. 158.
[2] Will P.C.C. 9 Harrington. Left the lease of his lodging in Doctors' Commons to his cousin Dr. John Lloyd (q.v.) and if he would not have it, to Dr. Styward (q.v.).
[3] *B.R.U.O.* iv. 13.
[4] *Vis. Cambs.*, p. 47. Dr. Martyn received a grant of arms in 1557 (ibid.).
[5] Will P.C.C. 60 Nevell.
[6] *B.R.U.O.* iv. 268–9.
[7] *B.R.U.O.* iv. 1.
[8] *L.B.*, f.57v.

1554

10 Mar. *Edmund West, M.A.*, Pembroke Coll., Cambridge, Prebendary of St. Paul's; (C); d. by 26 Mar. 1554.[1]

Oct. 8 *Thomas Stempe, D.C.L.* (1553), New Coll., Oxford, from Winchester Coll.; (A; C 5 May 1555); *c.*30; b. Soke of Winchester; d. 9 Feb. 1581.

Thomas Huycke, D.C.L. (1554), Merton Coll., Oxford; (A; C 11 May 1555); d. by 10 Oct. 1575; left to 'the Doctour Comons and to the Companye there my dozen of silver spoones and my twoe Double gilt Cupps with a cover'.[2]

1555

14 Jan. *Edmund Bonner, Bishop of London*; (C);[3] deprived May 1559; d. 5 Sept. 1569; *D.N.B.*

Gilbert Bourne, *Bishop of Bath and Wells*; (C); deprived Oct. 1559; d. 10 Sept. 1569; *D.N.B.*

14 Jan. *James* Brooks, *Bishop of Gloucester*; (C); d. in prison Feb. 1560; *D.N.B.*

John Holyman, *Bishop of Bristol*; (C); d. 20 Dec. 1558; *D.N.B.*

5 May *John Warner, D.M.*, All Souls Coll., Oxford, Regius Professor of Medicine, Prebendary of St. Paul's; (C); d. 21 Mar. 1565; *D.N.B.*

Walter Haddon, LL.D. (1549), King's Coll., Cambridge, from Eton Coll.; (C; A); *c.*39; 2 s. William H., of co. Buckingham; bur. Christ Church Newgate, London, 25 Jan. 1573; *D.N.B.*

1556

14 Jan. *William Awbrey, D.C.L.* (1554), All Souls Coll., Oxford, perhaps from Christ's Coll., Brecon; adm. Arches 9 Jan. 1556; (C; A); *c.*27; b. Cantref, co. Brecon; s. Thomas A.; Treasurer 1573; left to the Society a double gilt bowl with a cover;[1] d. 23 July 1595;[2] *D.N.B.*; *D.W.B.*

1 Oct. *Robert Weston, D.C.L.*, All Souls Coll., Oxford; (A; C 7 Oct.); *c.*41; 3 s. John W., of Weeford, co. Stafford;

[1]Le Neve, i. 43.
[2]Will P.C.C. 36 Pyckering.
[3]See p. 143 *ante* for previous subscription.
[4]Will P.C.C. 45 Scott.
[5]M.I. Old St. Paul's (*St. Paul's*, pp. 98–9).

1556

1 Oct. President 11 Jan. 1560; res. on appointment as Lord Chancellor of Ireland 8 Aug. 1567; d. 20 May 1573; *D.N.B.*

27 Oct. *Lawrence Hussey*, D.C.L., Bologna, incorp. Oxford; adm. Arches 26 Oct. 1556 (A; C. 29 Oct.); living *c.*1589.[1]

1557

11 May *Richard Walker*, B.A., Jesus Coll., Cambridge, *Archdeacon of Stafford*; (C); *c.* 56; b. Lichfield, co. Stafford; d. by 11 Nov. 1567.[2]

7 Nov. *William Mowse, LL.D.*, Cambridge; adm. Arches 9 Mar. 1557; (C); d. by 9 Nov. 1588; left to Doctors' Commons the andirons of latten or copper standing in the lower room of his lodgings.[3] *D.N.B.*

2 Dec. *Edward Clere, D.C.L.*; (A); ktd. 22 Aug. 1578; d. by 28 July 1606.[4]

1558

4 Feb. *John Orphinstrange* alias Strange, *LL.D.*, Trinity Coll.; Cambridge, from Padua;[5] adm. Arches 31 Jan. 1558; (C); living 1569.[6]

10 Feb. *Thomas White, D.C.L.*, Warden of New Coll., Oxford, from Winchester Coll.; (C); *c.*44; b. Leckford, co. Southampton; d. 12 June 1588.[7]

9 Nov. *Thomas Powell, D.C.L.*, Oxford; (C; A 1 May 1559); d. by 1586.[8]

10 Nov. *Thomas Yale, LL.D.*, Queens' Coll., Cambridge; adm. Arches 22 Apr. 1559; (C; A 26 Apr. 1559); 3 s. David Lloyd ap Ellis, of Plas-yn-Vale, co. Denbigh; President 5 Oct. 1567 to 3 May 1573; d. Nov. 1577; *D.N.B.; D.W.B.*

1559

28 Jan. *William Jenyns, B.D., Dean of Gloucester*; (C); d. 4 Nov. 1565.

---

[1]'London Subsidy Roll', in *Vis. London 1568*, p. 159.
[2]Will P.C.C. 22 Stonarde.
[3]Will P.C.C. 6 Leicester.
[4]When arrears paid by Dame Agnes Clere, his executrix (L.B., f.84ᵛ.).
[5]I. O. Andrich, *De Natione Anglica et Scota Iuristarum Universitatis Patavinae* (Padua, 1892), p. 131.
[6]L.B., f.6ᵛ. Where he is entered as 'Strange'.
[7]M.I. Salisbury Cathedral.
[8]L.B., f.37ᵛ.

1559

28 Jan   *Matthew Carew*, D. Cn. & C.L., *Archdeacon of Norfolk*; (C); yr. s. Sir Wymond C., of Antony, co. Cornwall; adm. Arches Nov. 1573; (A 1 Dec. 1573); ktd. 23 July 1603; bur. St. Dunstan-in-the-West, London 2 Aug. 1618; *D.N.B.*

1 Feb.   *Maurice Clenoke, B.C.L.*, Oxford, Bishop-elect of Bangor, but never consecrated; (C); b. co. Caernarvon; went to live in Rome 1560; *D.N.B.*

26 Apr.   *Richard Mitche, LL.D.*, Trinity Hall, Cambridge; (C; A); b. co. Essex; living abroad in 1576; *D.N.B.*

25 June   *Richard Catterall, D.M.*; (C); d. May 1584.

21 Oct.   *Æmereus Brethanus from the Duchy of Brabant.* Perhaps Nicholas Aemereus, retained by the City of London and the Merchant Adventurers in their dispute with the Merchants of the Steelyard;[1] (C).

1560

3 Mar.   *Edward Lydes, Lic.C.L.*, Clare Coll., Cambridge, Prebendary of Ely; (C); b. Benenden, co. Kent;[2] 2 s. Walter L., of Canterbury;[3] d. 17 Feb. 1596;[4] *D.N.B.*[5]

10 July   *George Harryson, notary public and proctor*; (adm. proctor Aug. 1551); (C); d. by 25 Aug. 1579.[6]

4 Nov.   *John Gwynne, LL.D.*, St. John's Coll., Cambridge; (C; A); yr s. John Wynn ap Meredydd, of Gwydir in Llanwrst, co. Caernarvon; d. by 22 June 1574;[7] *D.W.B.*

1561

3 Mar.   *Thomas Wilson, LL.D.*, Ferrara, from King's Coll., Cambridge, and Eton Coll.; adm. Arches 28 Feb. 1561; (C; A); *c.*36; s. Thomas W. of Strubby, co. Lincoln; d. June 1581; *D.N.B.*

5 May   *William Drurye, LL.D.*, Trinity Hall, Cambridge; adm. Arches 4 May 1561; (C; A); 3 s. John D., of Rougham, co. Suffolk; d. by 4 Feb. 1590;[8] *D.N.B.*

---

[1] W. J. Jones, *The Elizabethan Court of Chancery* (Oxford, 1967), p. 379.
[2] M.I. Croxton, co. Cambridge.
[3] *Vis. Cambs.*, p. 79.   [4] Browne Willis, i. 405–6.
[5] Where he is mistakenly described as an advocate.
[6] Will P.C.C. 35 Bakon. Left to Anne, his wife, his lease of the mansion house in Paternoster Row called 'the old Comons where the Doctors sometyme dyd dwell or remayne'.
[7] Will P.C.C. 27 Martyn, where Dr. John Lloyd (q.v.) is described as his cousin.
[8] Will P.C.C. 1 Drury.

1561

16 May *James Gervis*,[1] *D.C.L.*, Merton Coll., Oxford; (C; A); d. by 1586.[2]

1562

16 Feb. *John Rous, gent.*; (C); B.C.L., Oxford 9 July 1562; D.C.L., 3 July 1564; bur. St. Gregory, London 25 Dec. 1590.

23 Feb. *George Acworth, LL.D.*, Peterhouse, Cambridge; (C; A 3 Nov); probably s. Thomas A., merchant taylor; d. *c.* 1581; *D.N.B.*

1563

20 Jan. *Robert Forthe, LL.D.*, Trinity Hall, Cambridge; adm. Arches 12 Jan. 1563; (C; A); b. St. Dunstan-in-the-East, London; s. Robert F., Clerk of the Privy Seal, of Streatham, co. Surrey; mar. as his third wife Mary, widow of Dr. William Drury (q.v.); gave two gilt bowls to the Society;[3] d. 3 Oct. 1595.[4]

21 Jan. *William Evans, B.C.L.*, Oxford, *Treasurer of Llandaff Cathedral*; (C); d. 5 Jan. 1590; *D.W.B.*

1564

26 Feb. *John Griffithe, D.C.L.*, All Souls Coll., Oxford, Regius Professor of Civil Law; adm. Arches 17 Feb. 1564; (C; A); probably s. William G., of Plas Mawr, co. Caernarvon, and of Trefarthen in Llanidan, co. Anglesey; living 1587;[5] d. by 24 June 1593;[6] *D.W.B.*

28 Apr. *Edward Biggs, proctor* (adm. 28 Oct. 1552); (C); d. by 21 Jan. 1590.[7]

22 Nov. *John Briggewater, M.A.*, Brasenose Coll., Oxford, Rector of Lincoln Coll.; (C); emigrated to the English College at Douay 1574.

18 Dec. *Geoffrey Morley, M.A.*, St. John's Coll., Cambridge, Prebendary of York; (C); b. Nennington, co. Lancaster; d. by 17 June 1578; left £5 to 'the Company of the Doctors and Advocates of the Arches to buye a pece of plate withall to remaine in theire howse of commons for a memory'.[8]

---

[1]Misprinted as 'Hervie' in Coote, p. 46.   [2]L.B. f.37ᵛ.
[3]See p. 86 *ante*.
[4]Funeral certificate, printed in *Coll. Top. & Gen.* iii (1836), 310.
[5]When Sheriff of Anglesey.   [6]L.B., f.57ᵛ.
[7]Will P.C.C. 3 Drury. Left his office in Doctors' Commons to John Theaker, proctor, sometime his servant.
[8]Will P.C.C. 29 Langley. See pp. 82–3, 84, 86 *ante*.

1565

26 Jan. *Richard Barbar, B.C.L.*, All Souls Coll., Oxford; (C); D.C.L. 5 June 1565; b. co. Stafford; d. 15 Feb. 1590.[1] *Christopher Clerk*, proctor; (C); d. by 9 Aug. 1565.[2]

12 Feb. *Edmund Wyndam, D.Cn. & C.L.*; (C; A); probably illeg. s. Sir Edmund W., of Felbrigg, co. Norfolk, kt.[3]

25 Feb. *Robert Lougher, D.C.L.*, All Souls Coll., Oxford, Archdeacon of Totnes (C); yst. s. Thomas L., alderman of Tenby, co. Pembroke; adm. Arches 1573;[4] d. by 9 June 1585,[5] *D.N.B.; D.W.B.*

8 May *Walter Jones, B.C.L.*, Oxford, *Archdeacon of Brecon*; (C); d. by 18 July 1573.[6]

19 June *John Palley, D.Cn. & C.L.*; adm. Arches 15 May 1565; (C; A).

1566

26 May *Thomas Ithell, LL.D.*, Magdalene Coll., Cambridge; (C; A 11 May 1569); s. Pierce I., of Billesdon, co. Leicester; d. 17 May 1579.

1 July *John Lloyd, D.C.L.*, All Souls Coll., Oxford; adm. Arches 17 June 1566; (C; A); c.32; s. David Ll., of Caunmworth, co. Carnarvon;[7] d. 20 Feb. 1608.[8]

11 July *John Watson, D.M.*, All Souls Coll., Oxford, *Archdeacon of Surrey*; (C); Bishop of Winchester 1580; d. 23 Jan. 1584; *D.N.B.*

8 Dec. *Andrew Oxenbregg, D.Cn. & C.L.*, Trinity Hall, Cambridge;[9] (C); d. 1615.

n.d. — Saxeye, occurs 1566–7.[10] Probably William S., B.Cn. & C.L., Oxford, Treasurer of St. Paul's Cathedral; bur. Swanscombe, co. Kent 1 July 1567.

Peter Osborne, esq., admitted to the privileges and liberties of a contributor between 1566 and 1572;[11]

---

[1]M.I. Yoxall, co. Stafford.   [2]Will P.C.C. 26 Morrison.
[3]H. A. Wyndham, *A Family History 1410–1688* (Oxford, 1939), pp. 122–3.
[4]P.R.O., SP 12/109/39.
[5]Will P.C.C. 29 Brudenell.   [6]Browne Willis, i. 742.
[7]*Vis. Salop*, ii. 329.
[8]M.I. formerly in Chester Cathedral (Ormerod, i. 195).
[9]Coote, p. 47, includes Oxenbregg as an advocate, but there is no subscription by him as such.
[10]L.B., ff.7ᵛ., 9.
[11]L.B., f.376. The date is illegible, but the limiting dates are furnished by internal evidence.

1566

n.d.   probably barr, L.I., Lord Treasurer's Remembrancer of
       the Exchequer; d. 7 June 1592.[1]

1567

4 Oct.   *Nicholas Wendon, D.Cn. & C.L.* of a foreign university,
         from Trinity Coll., Cambridge, Archdeacon of Suffolk;[2]
         (C); emigrated to Louvain *c.*1573.

29 Oct. *Henry Barclay, D.C.L.,* New Coll., Oxford; adm. Arches
         23 Oct. 1567; (C; A); b. Hereford; d. shortly before 16
         May 1587.[3]

7 Dec.   *William Constantine, D.C.L.,* Brasenose Coll., Oxford;
         (C; A 15 May 1568); s. Richard or William C., of
         Bradley in Whitchurch, co. Salop;[4] living 13 Dec.
         1569.[5]

1568

28 Jan. *Francis Newton,* D.D. Michael House, Cambridge, *Dean
         of Winchester*; (C); d. by 18 Nov. 1572;[6] *D.N.B.*

23 Oct. *Richard White, D.Cn. & C.L.* Padua, from New Coll.,
         Oxford, and Winchester Coll.; (C); s. Henry W., of
         Basingstoke, co. Southampton; emigrated to Douay; d.
         1611.

1569

7 May   *James Ellys, LL.D.,* Queens' Coll., Cambridge; (C; A 21
         Jan. 1572); d. by 25 May 1596.[7]

11 May   *John Hammonde, LL.D.,* Trinity Hall, Cambridge; adm.
         Arches 10 May 1569; (C; A); *c.*27; b. Whalley, co.
         Lancaster; d. Dec. 1589; *D.N.B.*

20 May   *John Belley, D.C.L.,* Provost of Oriel Coll., Oxford; (C;
         A); 2 s. John B., of Haselbury Plucknett, co. Somerset,[8],
         non-armigerous;[9] d. by 30 Oct. 1609.[10]

---

[1]*St. Paul's,* p. 126.

[2]Coote, p. 47, includes Wendon as an advocate, but there is no subscription by him
as such.

[3]Coote, p. 48, inserts 'Henry Caroley' on 29 Oct. 1567, a mistaken duplication of
Barclay.

[4]*Vis. Salop,* i. 132, 248.

[5]S.B., f.103.

[6]Browne Willis, i.155.

[7]Will P.C.C. 28 Drake, in which he mentions as his kinsmen Drs. Awbrey, Jones,
Lloyd, and David Yale (qq.v.).

[8]*Visitation of the County of Huntingdon* (Camden Soc. xliii, 1849), p. 122.

[9]Dr. Belley received a grant of arms 23 Oct. 1602 (*Grantees,* p. 20).

[10]Will P.C.C. 95 Dorset.

1569

n.d. 'Dr. Cawdewell', a member by 2 July 1569.[1] Probably Richard Caldwell, D.M., Christ Church, Oxford; President of the College of Physicians 1570; d. 1584; *D.N.B.*

27 June *John Parker, gent*; (C); 1 s. Matthew P., Archbishop of Canterbury; ktd. 23 July 1603.
Matthew Parker, gent; (C); 2 s. Matthew P., Archbishop of Canterbury; d. 1574.

5 Nov. *John Lewys, proctor of the Court of Arches* (adm. 24 Feb. 1548); (C); d. by Feb. 1586.[1]

1570

7 Oct. *Robert Bysshop, LL.D.*, Corpus Christi Coll., Cambridge; ad., Arches 5 May 1570; (C; A); d. 17 Jan. 1590.

1571

11 Apr. *Edward Threlkeld, LL.D.*, King's Coll., Cambridge, from Eton Coll., Archdeacon of Carlisle; (C); *c.*45; b. Burgh-by-Sands, co. Cumberland; d. by 16 Nov. 1588.[3]

11 June *William Maister, LL.D.*, King's Coll., Cambridge, from Eton Coll.; adm. Arches 10 June 1570; (C; A); *c.*39; b. Willington, co. Bedford; his father non-armigerous;[4] d. 2 Feb. 1590.

20 June *Robert Horne, Bishop of Winchester and Prelate of the Order of the Garter*; (C); d. 1 June 1580; *D.N.B.*

1572

21 Apr. *Thomas Byng, LL.D.*, Peterhouse, Cambridge; adm. Arches 20 Apr. 1572; (C; A); 2 s. John B., of Wrotham, co. Kent; President 3 Nov. 1597; res. by 27 May 1598; bur. Hackney, co. Middlesex 23 Dec. 1599; *D.N.B.*

7 June *William Lewen, M.A.*, Christ's Coll., Cambridge; (C); LL.D. 1576; adm. Arches 3 May 1576; (A. 7 May 1576); s. Edmund L., of Cuffley, co. Hertford, non-armigerous;[5]

---

[1] L.B., f.6ᵛ.

[2] L.B., f.37ᵛ. There is also an entry in S.B., f.103 of the payment of Lewys's admission fee to Thomas Byfield, Steward, in the presence of Drs. Lewes, Huick, Jones, Awbrey, and Constantine on 13 Dec. 1569. The presence of this entry among the advocates' subscriptions led Coote to include Lewys in his work (p. 49).

[3] Will P.C.C. 9 Leicester.

[4] Dr. Maister received a grant of arms 17 Nov. 1587 (*Grantees*, p. 142).

[5] William Lewen received a grant of arms in 1575 (*Grantees*, p. 159).

1572
7 June d. 15 Apr. 1598; left a legacy to the advocates and proc-
        tors of the Arches for a dinner and a piece of plate;[1]
        D.N.B.
12 June *John Gibson, LL.D.*, Trinity Coll., Cambridge; (C; A);
        s. Thomas G. of Ireby, co. Lancaster,[2] non-armigerous;[3]
        ktd. 23 July 1603; d. 28 Feb. 1613.
7 Oct. *Richard Sotwell, D.C.L.*, New Coll., Oxford, from
        Winchester Coll.; adm. Arches 2 Oct. 1572; (C; A);
        *c.*32 1 s. William S., of Chute, co. Wilts., gent.[4] d. by 10
        Apr. 1590.[5]
1573
14 Jan. *Bartholomew Clerke, LL.D.*, Paris, from King's Coll.,
        Cambridge, and Eton Coll.; adm. Arches 17 Dec. 1572;
        (C; A); *c* 35; s. John C., of Wells, co. Somerset, notary;
        President 3 May 1573; d. 12 Mar. 1590; *D.N.B.*[6]
26 Jan. *John Langforde, D.C.L.*, Hart Hall, Oxford; adm. Arches
        22 Jan. 1573; (C); d. Nov. 1579.
11 Feb. *William Bingham, LL.D.*, Trinity Coll., Cambridge,
        formerly proctor; adm. Arches 10 Feb. 1572; (C; A); d.
        by 8 July 1611.[7]
29 Oct. *William Clerke, LL.D.*, Clare Coll., Cambridge; adm.
        Arches 27 Oct. 1573; (C; A); d. by 7 Mar. 1587.[8]
        Nicholas Styward, Incep. C.L., Trinity Coll., Cambridge;
        adm. Arches 27 Oct. 1573; (C; A); 6 s. Simeon S., of
        Lakenheath, co. Suffolk;[9] LL.D. 1574; allowed to be
        out of commons by reason of his age and want of teeth
        'so that it might not be an example to any other to desire
        the like with the like reasons';[10] d. by 6 June 1633; left
        £10 to Doctors' Commons.[11]

[1]Will P.C.C. 1 Lewyn.
[2]J. Foster (ed.), *Visitation of Yorkshire made . . . 1584/5* (London, 1875), p. 520.
[3]Dr. Gibson received a grant of arms 2 May 1575 (*Grantees*, p. 99).
[4]*Vis. Wilts.*, p. 185.
[5]Will P.C.C. 24 Drury.
[6]Clerke had been admitted to the privileges and liberties of a contributor while
Master of Arts (L.B., f.376).
[7]Will London Consistory Court, cited in Levack, p. 211.
[8]Will P.C.C. 12 Spencer.
[9]*Visitations of Hertfordshire* (Harl. Soc. xxii, 1886), p. 94.
[10]L.B., f.143v.
[11]Will P.C.C. 52 Russell.

1573

29 Oct. *Thomas Creake, LL.D.*, Trinity Hall, Cambridge; (C; A); c.38; 2s. Thomas C., of Kirtling, co. Cambridge, non-armigerous;[1] d. 21 June 1616.[2]

28 Nov. *John Herbert, M.A.*, Christ Church, Oxford, *at the special request of Archbishop Parker*; (C); c.33; 2 s. Matthew H., of Swansea, co. Glamorgan; D.C.L. 1587; ktd. 31 Jan. 1617; d. 9 July 1617; *D.W.B.*[3]

1 Dec. *Matthew Carew, D.Cn. & C.L.*; (A).[4]

1574

29 May Sir *Thomas Smith*, kt., *LL.D.*, Padua, *Queen's Secretary and Chancellor of the Order of the Garter*; (C); d. 12 Aug. 1577; *D.N.B.*

7 Sept. *Felix Lewys, D.C.L.*, Douay, incorp. Oxford, Principal of New Inn Hall, Oxford; (C; A); b. London; 'gen. fil'; d. abroad 1591.[5]
Arthur Bedyll, D.C.L., Oxford; (C); d. c.1580.[6]

21 Nov. *John Rogers, LL.D.*, Magdalene Coll., Cambridge; (C; A); adm. Arches Oct. 1574; (C; A); c.34; b. Wittenberg, Germany; 2 s. John R., Prebendary of St. Paul's; d. after 3 Mar. 1603; *D.N.B.*

1575

26 Apr. *Michael Mashart, D.C.L.*, New Coll., Oxford, from Winchester Coll.; (C; A); c.31; b. St. Thomas, Salisbury, co. Wilts.; d. Dec. 1598.

1576

15 Jan. *Edward Stanhope, LL.D.*, Trinity Coll., Cambridge; (C; A); c.30; 4 s. Sir Michael S., of Shelford, co. Nottingham, kt.; Treasurer 1588-9; ktd. 25 July 1603; d. 16 Mar. 1609;[7] *D.N.B.*

---

[1]Dr. Creake received a grant of arms 24 Dec. 1613 (*Vis. Cambs.*, p. 57).

[2]M.I. Old St. Paul's (*St. Paul's*, p. 53). He is described as a proctor in *Al. Cant.* The error springs from the mistranslation of his M.I. in P. Fisher, *The Tombs, Monuments, &c. visible in St. Paul's Cathedral* (London 1684, repr. 1885), p. 49.

[3]Coote, p. 51 n., states that Herbert is mentioned in the 'Treasurer's Book' (i.e. L.B.) as an advocate, but I have been unable to find any such reference, though he appears frequently in the lists of extraordinary contributors in L.B.

[4]For subscription as contributor, see p. 154 *ante*.

[5]*Ath. Oxon.* (Fasti), i. 190.

[6]L.B., ff.28, 30.

[7]M.I. Old St. Paul's (*St. Paul's*, p. 56).

1576

11 May *John Chippingdale, D.C.L.*, All Souls Coll., Oxford; (C; A); 1 s. George C., of Craven, co. York, non-armigerous;[1] d. by 24 June 1629.[1]

3 Nov. *John Becon,[3] LL.D.*, St. John's Coll., Cambridge; (C; A); b. co. Suffolk; bur. St. Giles Cripplegate, London 4 Sept. 1587; *D.N.B.*

12 Nov. *Griffin Lloyde, D.C.L.*, Principal of Jesus Coll., Oxford; (C; A); s. Hugh Llewellin Ll., of Llanlhyr, co. Cardigan; d. 26 Nov. 1586.[4]

1577

22 Apr. *Henry Worley, LL.D.*, Jesus Coll., Cambridge; (C); 1 s. James W., of Doddington, co. Kent;[5] d. by 27 Apr. 1586.[6]

4 May *William Smythe, D.C.L.*, New Coll., Oxford, from Winchester Coll.; adm. Arches 5 Mar. 1577; (C; A); *c.*35; b. Worlaby, co. Lincoln; d. *c.*1626.[7]

1578

7 June *Hugh Lloyd, B.C.L.*, New Coll., Oxford, from Winchester Coll.; (C); *c.*30; b. Bangor, co. Caernarvon; D.C.L. 1588; d. 17 Oct. 1601; *D.N.B.; D.W.B.*

1579

15 June *William Goldingham, LL.D.*, Trinity Hall, Cambridge; adm. Arches 15 June 1579; (C; A); living 1589.[8]

1582

22 Jan. *Daniel Dun, D.C.L.*, All Souls Coll., Oxford; adm. Arches 13 Oct. 1582 (*sic*); (C; A); 1 s. Robert D., of London, non-armigerous;[9] mar. Joan d. Dr. William Awbrey (q.v.); President 27 May 1598; ktd. 23 July 1603; d. 15 Sept. 1617; *D.N.B.*

John Deye, LL.D., Jesus Coll., Cambridge; adm. Arches 28 Nov. 1579; (C; A); d. by 19 Aug. 1612.[10]

[1]Dr. Chippingdale received a grant of arms 16 May 1594 (*Vis. Leics.*, p. 157). The grant is attributed to 'Shippingdale' in *Grantees*, p. 228.
[2]Leicestershiri County Record Office, Inventory.
[3]Misprinted as 'Beron' in Coote, p. 53.
[4]M.I. (E. Hatton, *New View of London* (1708), i. 155).
[5]*Vis. Kent*, p. 42.
[6]P.C.C. 21 Windsor. Coote, p. 53, includes Worley as an advocate, but there is no subscription by him as such.
[7]L.B., ff. 130, 133.   [8]L.B., f.43. Not mentioned in 1590 (ibid., f.46).
[9]Dr. Dun received a grant of arms 8 Aug. 1588 (*Grantees*, p. 78).
[10]P.C.C. 74 Fenner.

1582

27 Jan. *William Farrand, LL.D.*, Trinity Coll., Cambridge; adm. Arches 7 Oct. 1580; (C; A); s. Richard F; bur. Mitcham, co. Surrey 1 July 1615.

3 Feb. *David Yale, LL.D.*, Queens' Coll., Cambridge; adm. Arches 19 Oct. 1579; (C; A); base s. John Wyn or Y., of Plas-yn-Yale, co. Denbigh, and nephew of Dr. Thomas Y. (q.v.); mar. Frances, d. Dr. John Lloyd (q.v.); d. by 13 June 1626;[1] *D.W.B.*

25 Apr. *Simon Smyth, LL.D.* Trinity Hall, Cambridge, Archdeacon of Hereford; adm. Arches 16 Feb. 1580; (C; A); 7 s. Thomas S., of Credenhill, co. Hereford;[2] d. by 10 Nov. 1606.[3]

1 May *Matthew Sutcliffe, LL.D.* (1580), Trinity Coll., Cambridge; (C; A); *c.*32; 2 s. John S., of Melroyd in Halifax, co. York, gent.;[4] d. by 24 Nov. 1629;[5] *D.N.B.*

2 May *Richard Bridgewater, 'doctor', LL.D.*, King's Coll., Cambridge, from Eton Coll.; adm. Arches 3 June 1580; (C; A); b. Dedham, co. Essex; d. 15 Feb. 1588.

5 May *Thomas Skeffington, LL.D.*, Trinity Coll., Cambridge; adm. Arches 19 Oct. 1579; (C; A); 5 s. William S., of Fisherwick, co. Stafford; d. by 25 Oct. 1592; left money to provide a dinner or supper in Doctors' Commons for the 'Doctors of my profession' attending his funeral and directed his executors to cause to be made a 'white bowl of silver' worth £3 with his name and arms engraved on it to be given to the Society.[6]

1583

26 Jan. *John Hunt, LL.D.*, Trinity Coll., Cambridge; adm. Arches 31 Oct. 1581; (C; A); d. by 12 June 1630.[7]

2 Feb. *William Griffith, D.C.L.*; adm. Arches 14 Feb. 1581; (C; A). Probably s. William G. of Plas Mawr, co. Caernarvon, and of Trefarthen in Llanidan, co. Anglesey, and bro. Dr. John G. (q.v.); *D.W.B.*

---

[1]Cheshire C.R.O., Will.
[2]*Visitation of Herefordshire made . . . in 1569* (Exeter, 1886), p. 96.
[3]Will P.C.C. 86 Stafford. Left the lease of his chambers in Doctors' Commons to Dr. Creake (q.v.).
[4]J. W. Clay (ed.), *Familiae Minorum Gentium* (Harl. Soc., xxxviii, 1895), ii. 541.
[5]Will P.C.C. 94 Ridley.
[6]Will P.C.C. 75 Harrington.   [8]Will P.C.C. 56 Scroope.

1585

14 Oct. *Richard Cosin, LL.D.*, Trinity Coll., Cambridge, from Skipton Sch.; adm. Arches 9 Feb. 1581; (C; A); s. John C., of Newhall, co. Durham; President 1590; d. 30 Nov. 1597; *D.N.B.*

17 Oct. *Gilbert Bourne, LL.D.*, Orleans; adm. Arches 13 Oct. 1565; (C; A); 1 s. Richard B., of Wivilescombe, co. Somerset, and nephew of Gilbert B., Bishop of Bath and Wells (q.v.);[1] d. by 3 Feb. 1596.[2]

1586

22 Jan. *Julius Caesar, D.C.L.*, Paris and Magdalen Hall, Oxford, barr. I.T.; adm. Arches 20 May 1581; Judge of the Court of Admiralty; (C; A); *c*.38; s. Julius Caesar Aldemare, D.M., and gds. Pietro Maria Aldemare, a civilian; ktd. 20 May 1603; d. 17 Apr. 1636; *D.N.B.*

30 Apr. *John Drury D.C.L.* (1585), Lincoln Coll. Oxford; (C; A); s. John[3] or Humphrey D.;[4] d. by 9 June 1614.[5]

17 May *Thomas Preston, M.A.*, Master of Trinity Hall, Cambridge, from King's Coll., Cambridge, and Eton Coll.; (C); *c*.48; b. Simpson, co. Buckingham, of a Lancashire family;[6] LL.D.;[7] adm. Arches 17 June 1591; d. 1 June 1598.[7]

1590

16 May *Thomas Legge, LL.D.*, Master of Gonville and Caius Coll., Cambridge; adm. Arches 3 June 1580; (C; A); *c*.55; 2 s. Stephen L., of Norwich, co. Norfolk; d. 12 July 1607;[9] *D.N.B.*

7 July *John Bettis, LL.D.*, Trinity Hall, Cambridge; adm. Arches 30 April. 1587; (C; A 25 Sept.); d. by 16 Dec. 1598; left £5 to Doctors' Commons.[10]

[1] *Vis. Somerset*, p. 13.
[2] Will P.C.C. 14 Drake.
[3] *Visitation of the County of Buckingham made in 1634* (Harl. Soc. lviii, 1909), p. 159.
[4] *Vis. Sussex*, p. 126.
[5] Will P.C.C. 65 Lawe.
[6] *Warren's Book*, p. 79.
[7] L.B., f.66ᵛ. Perhaps in 1589, when he became Vice-Chancellor.
[8] M.I. Trinity Hall Chapel.
[9] M.I. Caius College Chapel.
[10] Will P.C.C. 99 Lewyn.

1590

10 July *John Hone, LL.D.*, Clare Coll., Cambridge; adm. Arches 9 July 1579; (A; C 3 Oct); 2 s. William H., of London, one of the Judges at Guildhall;[1] d. by 16 Dec. 1616.[2]

3 Oct. *Richard Swale, LL.D.*, Gonville and Caius Coll., Cambridge; adm. Arches 9 Oct. 1587; (C; A 20 Oct); *c.*45; s. Thomas S., of Askham Richard, co. York, esq.; ktd. 23 July 1603; d. 20 May 1608; *D.N.B.*

John Amye, LL.D., Clare Coll., Cambridge; adm. Arches 13 Oct. 1565; (C A); 6 s. John A., of Great Abington, co. Cambridge,[3] non-armigerous.[4] ktd. 9 Nov. 1619; bur. St. Gregory, London 3 June 1621; left £5 to Doctors' Commons.[5]

3 Oct. *John Gardiner, LL.D.*, Trinity Hall, Cambridge; adm. Arches 13 Sept. 1585; (C; A); d. by 18 Apr. 1594.[6]

7 Oct. *William Wode, D.C.L.*, All Souls Coll., Oxford; adm. Arches 27 Apr. 1589; (C; A); *c.*32; s. Hugh W., of Talyllyn, co. Anglesey;[7] d. by 9 May 1605.[8]

9 Oct. *John Cowell, LL.D.*, King's Coll., Cambridge, from Eton Coll.; adm. Arches 26 Apr. 1589; (C; A); *c.*36; b. Ernsborough in Swimbridge, co. Devon; Master of Trinity Hall 3 June 1598; d. 11 Oct. 1611;[9] *D.N.B.*

Henry Whetcroft, LL.D., Trinity Hall, Cambridge; adm. Arches 8 May 1587; (C; A); 1 s. William W., of Ipswich, co. Suffolk, gent; d. by 1 July 1616.[10]

10 Oct. *Thomas Ridley, LL.D.*, King's Coll., Cambridge, from Eton Coll.; adm. Arches 13 Oct. 1585; (C; A); *c.*40; s. Thomas R., of Bouldon, co. Salop; Treasurer 1612; ktd. 24 June 1619; d. 22 Jan. 1629; *D.N.B.*

13 Oct. *Thomas Glaser, D.C.L.*, Rector of Exeter Coll., Oxford; adm. Arches 2 Feb. 1582; (C; A); d. 9 Mar. 1592.

Francis Bevans, D.C.L. (1583), Principal of Jesus Coll., Oxford; (C; A); b. co. Carmarthen; d. by 3 June 1602.[11]

---

[1] *Vis. Essex*, pp. 220, 422–3.
[2] Will P.C.C. 122 Cope.
[3] *Vis. Cambs.*, p. 61.
[4] Dr. Amye received a grant of arms 10 Apr. 1593 (*Grantees*, p. 4).
[5] Will P.C.C. 49 Dale.   [6] Will P.C.C. 32 Dixy.
[7] *Anglesey Ped.*, p. 136.   [8] Will P.C.C. 30 Hayes.
[9] M.I. Trinity Hall Chapel.   [10] Will P.C.C. 76 Cope.
[11] Will P.C.C. 48 Montague.

1590

14 Oct. *William Bird*, D.C.L., All Souls Coll., Oxford; adm. Arches 27 Apr. 1589; (C; A); *c*.29; 2 s. William B., of Saffron Walden, co. Essex;[1] Treasurer 1609–11; ktd. 22 Mar. 1618; President 1618; d. 5 Sept. 1624.

26 Oct. *Francis James*, D.C.L., All Souls Coll., Oxford; adm. Arches 27 Apr. 1589; (C; A); yr. s. John J., of Little Onn, co. Stafford; d. 26 March 1616.[2]

1591

17 Nov. *Richard Fletcher, Bishop of Bristol, Lord High Almoner*; (C); translated to Worcester 1593 and to London 1595; d. 15 June 1596; *D.N.B.*

1595

10 Jan. *William Redman, Bishop-elect of Norwich*; (C); d. 25 Sept. 1602; *D.N.B.*

28 Jan. *Richard Hudson*, LL.D., Peterhouse, Cambridge; adm. Arches 18 Nov. 1586; (C; A); not in L.B. after 1601.

Henry Manninge, D.C.L., All Souls Coll., Oxford; adm. Arches 12 Feb. 1590; (C; A); *c*.36; b. co. Kent; s. Henry M., Marshal of the Royal Household; d. by 9 Oct. 1614.[3]

1 Feb. *George Dale*, D.C.L., St. Mary Hall, Oxford; adm. Arches 9 May 1592; (C; A); *c*.34; 2 s. Henry D., of 'Yelton',[4] co. Somerset;[5] d. 25 Nov. 1625.

Thomas Edwards, D.C.L., All Souls Coll., Oxford; adm. Arches 9 May 1592; (C; A); b. co. Berks.; 'fil. pleb'; Treasurer 1616; d. by 21 Apr. 1619.[6]

14 May *Henry Hickman*, LL.D., St. John's Coll., Cambridge; adm. Arches 17 Oct. 1586; (C; A); 2 s. Anthony H., of London;[7] d. by 4 Sept. 1618.[8]

[1]Dr. Bird received an exemplification of arms 1606 (*Grantees*, p. 24). Perhaps this was really a grant.

[2]M.I. Barrow, co. Somerset.

[3]Will P.C.C. 99 Lawe.

[4]Probably Yeovilton: see J. Collinson, *History of Somerset* (Bath, 1791), iii. 219.

[5]'Pleb.' in *Al. Ox.*; 'gent' in M.T. admission register of his elder son William in 1577.

[6]Will P.C.C. 40 Parker.

[7]*Lincs. Ped.* ii, 493–4. Arms confirmed and crest granted 1 Dec. 1590 (*Grantees*, pp. 123–4).

[8]Will. *Al. Ox.*, followed by *Al. Cant.* and Levack, p. 239, states that Dr. Hickman's will was proved at Peterborough 4 Sept. 1618, but the will is among the muniments of Westminster Abbey.

1596
16 June *Anthony Hickman, LL.D.*, Peterhouse, Cambridge; adm.
Arches 28 June 1595; (C; A); 4 s. Anthony H., of
London;[1] d. Dec. 1597.

16 Oct. *Henry Marten, D.C.L.*, New Coll., Oxford, from Winchester Coll.; adm. Arches 28 June 1595; (C; A); *c.*34;
s. Anthony M., of London, citizen and grocer; ktd. 21
Dec. 1616; Treasurer 1617–20; Judge of the Court of
Admiralty 1617–41; President 1624–32 and 1632–3; d.
26 Sept. 1641; *D.N.B.*

1598
18 Feb. *Richard Trevor, LL.D.*, Trinity Hall, Cambridge; adm.
Arches 28 June 1595; (C; A); s. Edward T., of Trevalyn,
co. Denbigh; mar. Winifred, d. of Sir Daniel Dun.
(q.v.); d. 1614; *D.W.B.*

12 June *Robert Master, D.C.L.*, All Souls Coll., Oxford; adm.
Arches 21 June 1596; (C; A); *c.*33; s. Richard M., of
Cirencester, co. Gloucester, D.M.;[2] d. 19 July 1625.

1599
5 June *Thomas Browne, LL.D.*, Pembroke Coll., Cambridge;
adm. Arches 28 Nov. 1579; (C; A).

17 Oct. *Henry Moston, LL.D.*, Jesus Coll., Cambridge; adm.
Arches 12 Feb. 1590; (C; A); s. Piers M., of Talacre, co.
Flint, esq.; d. 16 Nov. 1616.[3]

1600
14 Apr. *Richard Bancroft, Bishop of London*; (C); Archbishop of
Canterbury 1604; d. 2 Nov. 1610; *D.N.B.*

21 Apr. *Thomas Bilson, Bishop of Winchester*; (C); d. 18 June 1616;
D.N.B.

1601
21 Jan. Charles Fotherby, B.D., Archdeacon of Canterbury;[4] d.
29 Mar. 1619.[5]

15 Oct. *Bartholomew Jesopp, D.C.L.*, Magdalen Coll., Oxford;
adm. Arches 27 Nov. 1599; (C; A); 4 s. Walter J., of
Chilcombe, co. Dorset, gent.; d. 21 July 1620.

---

[1]See p. 165, n. 7 *ante.*
[2]*Vis. Kent*, pp. 10–11; *Visitation of the County of Gloucester taken in . . . 1623* (Harl.
Soc.xxi, 1885), p. 111.
[3]M.I. Llanasa, co. Flint.
[4]S.B., f.91. No subscription.
[5]M.I. Canterbury Cathedral.

1601

25 Oct. *William Sammes, LL.D.*, Trinity Hall, Cambridge; adm.
Arches 27 Nov. 1599; (C; A); Treasurer 1622–3; Judge
of the Court of Admiralty 1643; President 6 Sept. 1646;
bur. 15 Oct. 1646.

28 Oct. *William Prytherghe, D.C.L.*, Oxford; adm. Arches 19
Apr. 1600; (C; A); d. *c.*1627.[1]

29 Oct. *Edmund Pope, D.C.L.*, All Souls Coll., Oxford; adm.
Arches 27 Nov. 1599; (C; A); *c.*34; b. London; 'gen.
fil'; d. 1630.

1604

21 Jan. *Sir John Benet, kt., D.C.L.*, Christ Church, Oxford; adm.
Arches 17 Feb. 1590; (C; A); 2 s. Richard B. of Clapcot,
co. Berks, gent.; d. 15 Feb. 1627; *D.N.B.*

28 Jan. *James Hussey, D.C.L.*, New Coll., Oxford, from Win-
chester Coll.; adm. Arches 2 Jan. 1602; (C; A); *c.*40; 4 s.
Thomas H., of Edmondsham, co. Dorset, esq.[1] ktd. 9
Nov. 1619; d. 11 July 1625; left £10 to Doctors'
Commons.[3]

30 Jan. *George Newman, LL.D.*, Trinity Hall, Cambridge; adm.
Arches 9 May 1598; (C; A); *c.*42; s. Richard N.;[4] ktd.
12 Nov. 1616; paid 40*s.* as a composition for not being
Treasurer 1620;[5] d. 7 June 1627; left £10 to Doctors'
Commons.[6]

1605

29 Mar. *Sir Edward Bruce, kt., Master of the Rolls*; (C); cr.
Lord Bruce of Kinloss 3 May 1608;[7] d. 14 Jan. 1611;
D.N.B.
*Thomas Nevile, D.D., Dean of Canterbury and Master of
Trinity Coll., Cambridge*; (C); d. 2 May 1614; *D.N.B.*

20 Mar. *Sir Christopher Parkins, kt, Master of the Court of
(sic) Requests*; (C);[8] d. Aug. 1622; *D.N.B.*

[1] L.B., ff. 133, 136.
[2] *Vis. Dorset*, pp. 59–60.
[3] Will P.C.C. 20 Hele.
[4] *Visitation of . . . Kent 1663–1668* (Harl. Soc. liv, 1906), p. 119.
[5] L.B., f.116.
[6] Will P.C.C. 65 Skynner.
[7] He had been created Lord Bruce of Kinlosse on 8 July 1604, but the legality of this creation seems to have been regarded as doubtful (G.E.C., *Complete Peerage*, ii (London, 1912), 351).
[8] *Al. Ox.* mistakenly states that Parkins was admitted as an advocate.

1605

25 Apr. *Sir Peter Young à Seton, kt., Almoner of Scotland and King's Councillor*; (C); returned to Scotland 1620 or 1623; *D.N.B.*

Sir Thomas Crompton, kt., D.C.L., Merton Coll., Oxford, *King's Advocate*; adm. Arches 12 Feb. 1590; (C); c.47; 1 s. William C., citizen and mercer of London;[1] bur. St. Gregory, London 5 Feb. 1609.

1607

8 May *George Abbott, D.D., Dean of Winchester*; (C); Bishop of Lichfield and Coventry 1609; translated to London 1610; Archbishop of Canterbury 1611; d. 4 Aug. 1633; *D.N.B.*

9 June *Henry Mowtlow, LL.D.* (?1594), King's Coll. Cambridge, from Eton Coll.; adm. Arches 1596; (C; A); c.52; b. Winchomb, co. Gloucester; bur. Great St. Mary's, Cambridge 17 Oct. 1634.

Hugh Barker, D.C.L., New Coll., Oxford, from Winchester Coll. (founder's kin); adm. Arches 6 Feb. 1606; (C; A); c.49; 2 s. Robert B., of Culworth, co. Northampton, gent.;[2] Treasurer 1624–5; President 1632; d. 1632,[3] left £10 to Doctors' Commons;[4] *D.N.B.*

1608

16 Sept. *Sir Thomas Parr, kt., Chancellor of the Duchy of Lancaster and Privy Councillor*; (C); bur. Westminster Abbey 1 June 1616; *D.N.B.; D.W.B.*

11 Oct. *Thomas Talbot, LL.D.*, Trinity Hall, Cambridge; adm. Arches 12 Feb. 1590; (C; A); s. Thomas T., of Wymondham, co. Norfolk;[5] Treasurer 1627; d. by 16 Feb. 1628.[6]

1609

2 Nov. *Sampson Hussey, D.C.L.*, New Coll., Oxford, from Winchester Coll.; adm. Arches 26 Feb. 1605; (C; A); c.44; 3 s. Thomas H., of Edmondsham, co. Dorset, esq., and bro. of Dr. James H. (q.v.).[7]

[1]Sir Thomas Crompton received a confirmation of arms (perhaps really a grant) in 1595 (*Grantees*, p. 66). Marchant, p. 249, following *Al. Ox.*, states that he was s. Sir Thomas C., but this was based on a mistaken reading of *Students admitted to the Inner Temple 1547–1660* (n.p., 1877), p. 48. The true parentage is stated in his confirmation of arms.

[2]*Visitations of Northamptonshire made in 1564 and 1618–19* (1887), p. 164.
[3]M.I. New College Chapel.   [4]L.B., f.152.
[5]*Vis. Norfolk*, pp. 213–14.   [6]Will P.C.C. 15 Barrington.
[7]*Vis. Dorset*, pp. 59–60.

1609

22 Nov. *Oliver Lloyd, D.C.L.*, All Souls Coll., Oxford; adm.
Arches 15 Feb. 1603; (C; A); *c*.37; b. co. Montgomery;
'arm; fil.'; d. by 23 Nov. 1625; left £10 to Doctors'
Commons;[1] *D.W.B.*

1610

26 Jan. *Thomas Gwynne, D.C.L.*, All Souls Coll., Oxford; adm.
Arches 24 Nov. 1608; (C; A); b. co. Anglesey; Treasurer
1628; d. by Apr. 1646.[2]

21 Nov. Martin Fotherby, D.D., Prebendary of Canterbury; adm.
without entrance fee;[3] Bishop of Salisbury 1618; d. 11
Mar. 1620; *D.N.B.*

1611

26 Oct. *Thomas Ryves, D.C.L.*, New Coll., Oxford, from Winchester Coll.[4] adm. Arches 16 Oct. 1610; (C; A); *c*.32;
8 s. John R., of Damory Court in Blandford Forum, co.
Dorset;[5] King's Advocate 1620; Treasurer 1621; ktd.
19 Mar. 1644; d. 2 Jan. 1652; *D.N.B.*

24 Nov. *William Aubrey, D.C.L.*, Christ Church, Oxford; adm.
Arches 27 Nov. 1599; (C; A); *c*.40; b. co. Brecon; 'pleb.
fil'; d. between 20 June 1640 and 22 June 1641.[6]

1612

9 May *Clement Corbet, LL.D.*, Master of Trinity Hall, Cambridge; adm. Arches 5 June 1606; (C; A); s. Sir
Myles C., of Sprowston, co. Norfolk, kt.; d. 28 May
1652.

18 May *John* King, *Bishop of London*; (C); d. 30 Mar. 1621; *D.N.B.*
Lancelot Andrewes, *Bishop of Ely*; (C); translated to
Winchester 1619; d. 26 Sept. 1626; *D.N.B.*
James Montague, *Bishop of Bath and Wells*; (C); translated
to Winchester 1616; d. 20 July 1618; *D.N.B.*
Richard Neile, *Bishop of Coventry and Lichfield*; (C);
translated to Lincoln 1614; Durham 1617; Winchester
1628; Archbishop of York 1631; d. 31 Oct. 1640; *D.N.B.*

---

[1] Will P.C.C. 128 Clark.
[2] *P.C.C. Administrations 1649–54* (British Record Soc. lxviii, 1944), p. 157.
[3] S.B., f.92ᵛ.
[4] Studied law in 'the best universities of France' (*Cal. S.P. Ireland 1618–25*, pp.
105–7).
[5] *Vis. Dorset*, p. 80.   [6] L.B., f. 181.

1612

18 May *John* Buckeridge, *Bishop of Rochester*; (C); translated to Ely 1628; d. 23 May 1631; *D.N.B.*

Robert Abbott, D.D., Master of Balliol Coll., Oxford; (C); Bishop of Salisbury 1615; d. 2 Mar. 1618; *D.N.B.*

1613

26 Jan. *Charles Caesar, D.C.L.*, All Souls Coll., Oxford, student I.T.; adm. Arches 20 Jan. 1613; (C; A 25 June 1623); *c.*22; 3 s. Sir Julius C. (q.v.); ktd. Oct. 1613; Treasurer 1636; d. 6 Dec. 1642, *D.N.B.*

5 Feb. *Barnabas Goche, LL.D.*, Master of Magdalene Coll., Cambridge; adm. Arches 16 June 1604; (C; A); 4 s. Barnabas G., of Alvingham, co. Lincoln;[1] d. by 6 May 1616;[2] *D.N.B.*

1614

23 Jan. *Basil Wood, D.C.L.*, All Souls Coll., Oxford; adm. Arches 21 Oct. 1612; (C; A); 2 s. Alexander W., of Shinewood in Sheinton, co. Salop;[3] Treasurer 1629–30; bur. St. Michael, Oxford 30 Nov. 1644.

25 Jan. *Arthur Ducke, D.C.L.*, All Souls Coll., Oxford; adm. Arches 1 Sept. 1612; (C; A); *c.*34; 2 s. Richard D., of Heavitree, co. Devon, 'pleb.';[4] Treasurer 1631; d. 16 Dec. 1648; *D.N.B.*[5]

1615

4 Nov. *Thomas Eden, LL.D.*, Trinity Hall, Cambridge, from Sudbury Sch.; adm. Arches 17 Oct. 1614; (C; A); yr. s. Richard E., of South Hanningfield, co. Essex;[6] Master of Trinity Hall 4 Sept. 1626; Treasurer 1634; d. 18 July 1645;[7] *D.N.B.*

1616

9 May Sir *Henry Savile*, kt., Warden of Merton Coll., Oxford, Provost of Eton Coll.; (C); d. 19 Feb. 1622; *D.N.B.*

5 Aug. *John Hayward, LL.D.*, Pembroke Coll. Cambridge; (C; A); *c.*42; b. at or near Felixstowe, co. Suffolk; ktd. 9 Nov. 1619; d. 27 June 1627; *D.N.B.*

[1]*Lincs. Ped.* ii. 408.   [2]Will P.C.C. 71 Hele.   [3]*Vis. Salop*, ii. 510.
[4]Arms granted to Dr. Ducke's elder brother in 1602 (*Misc. Gen. & Her.*, N.S.i (1874), 317).
[5]Dr. Ducke is credited with a knighthood in *D.N.B.*, but there appears to be no evidence to support this.
[6]*Vis.Esses*, i. 390–1.   [7]M.I. Trinity Hall Chapel.

1617

12 Feb. *Arthur* Lake, *Bishop of Bath and Wells*; (C); d. 4 May 1626; *D.N.B.*

William Goodwin, Dean of Christ Church; (C); d. 11 June 1620; *D.N.B.*

1 Nov. *Robert Aylett, LL.D.,* Trinity Hall, Cambridge; adm. Arches 4 Feb. 1617; (C; A); *c.*34; 2 s. Leonard A., of Rivenhall, co. Essex;[1] Treasurer 1635; d. by 22 Mar. 1655;[2] *D.N.B.*

1618

30 Jan. *Richard Zouche, B.C.L.,* New Coll., Oxford, from Winchester Coll.; (C; A); *c.*28; s. Franciz Z., of Anstey, co. Wilts.; D.C.L. 8 Apr. 1619; adm. Arches 30 Apr. 1619; Treasurer 1627–8; Judge of the Court of Admiralty 1641–3; President 1660; mar. Sarah, d. of John Hart, of London, proctor, and sister of Richard H. (q.v.); d. 1 Mar. 1661;[3] *D.N.B.*

24 Oct. *John Pope, LL.D.,* Clare Coll., Cambridge; adm. Arches 14 May 1591; (C; A); 3 s. Nicholas P., of Hendall in Buxted, co. Sussex, gent.;[4] bur. 10 May 1630.

1619

30 Jan. *Charles Twysden, D.C.L.,* Principal of New Inn Hall, Oxford; adm. Arches 13 Nov. 1618; (C; A); *c.*43; 3 s. Roger T., of East Peckham, co. Kent, esq.;[4] d. by 3 Feb. 1647.[6]

?1619– 21[7]

n.d. Sir John Lambe, kt., LL.D. (1616), St. John's Coll., Cambridge, adm. a proctor 2 Nov. 1599; s. John L., of Rivenhall, co. Essex; ktd. 26 July 1621; a member by 23 July 1623;[8] President by 7 Jan. 1634 until archiepiscopal jurisdiction abolished 6 Sept. 1646; d. by 8 Dec. 1646;[9] *D.N.B.*

---

[1] *Vis. Essex,* i. 339.   [2] Will P.C.C. 236 Aylett.
[3] *Vis. London, 1633,* i. 357.
[4] *Vis. Sussex,* p. 99.
[5] *Vis. Kent,* p. 136.
[6] Will P.C.C. 14 Fines.
[7] There are no subscriptions between 30 Jan. 1619 and 4 Feb. 1622, so it is probable that Lambe, Wyvell, Wodhowse, and Clarke joined the Society during this period, *pace Al. Cant.,* which states that Lambe was admitted advocate 1602.
[8] L.B., f.121[v].
[9] *Cal. Committee for Compounding,* ii. 1514.

? 1619–21

n.d. Christopher Wyvell, LL.D., Trinity Hall, Cambridge; 1 s. Sampson W., of Walworth, co. Durham, gent; adm. Arches 8 May 1615; a member by 2 Dec. 1622,[1] bur. Saffron Walden, co. Essex 12 Oct. 1632.

Henry Wodhowse, LL.D., Trinity Hall, Cambridge; probably yr. s. Sir Roger W., of Kimberley, co. Norfolk, kt.;[2] adm. Arches 21 June 1596; a member by 2 Dec. 1622.[3]

Richard Clarke, D.C.L., New Coll., Oxford; adm. Arches 15 Jan. 1619; a member by 2 Dec. 1622;[4] b. *c.*1573 co. Berks.; 'fil pleb.'; bur. 28 May 1623.

1622

4 Feb. *William Stede, D.C.L.*, All Souls Coll., Oxford; adm. Arches 31 Jan. 1622; (C; A); *c.*28; s. Sir William S., of Harrietsham, co. Kent, kt.;[5] Treasurer 1641.

Martin Aylworth, D.C.L., All Souls Coll., Oxford; adm. Arches 31 Jan. 1622; (C; A); *c.*30; s. Anthony A., D.M., physician to the Queen; d. 11 Jan. 1658.[6]

12 July *Samuel* Harsnet, *Bishop of Norwich*; (C); Archbishop of York 1629; d. 25 May 1631; *D.N.B.*

1623

18 Jan. *Clere Talbot, LL.D.*, Trinity Hall, Cambridge; adm. Arches 13 Oct. 1620; (C; A); 3 s Thomas T., LL.D. (q.v.);[7] Treasurer jointly with his father 1627; d. by 18 May 1654.[8]

1624

27 Jan. *Nicholas* Felton, *Bishop of Ely*; (C); d. 6 Oct. 1626; *D.N.B.*

n.d. William Easdall, LL.D., Trinity Hall, Cambridge; adm. Arches 23 Oct. 1623; a member by 18 June 1624;[8] living 1639.[10]

[1] L.B., f.120ᵛ.
[2] *Visitation of Norfolk . . . 1563 . . . and 1613* (Harl. Soc. xxxii, 1891), pp. 71, 322.
[3] L.B., f.120ᵛ.
[4] L.B., f.120.ᵛ.
[5] *Vis. Kent*, p. 72.
[6] Wood, *Colleges and Halls*, i. 303.
[7] *Vis. Norfolk*, ii. 214.
[8] Will P.C.C. 253 Alchin.
[9] L.B., f.123.
[10] Borthwick Inst. MS. R.VII PR. 108.

1626

28 Jan. *Thomas Benet, D.C.L.*, All Souls Coll., Oxford, member
G.I.; adm. Arches 25 Oct. 1624; (C; A); *c.*34; 2 s. Sir
John B., D.C.L. (q.v.); ktd 21 Aug. 1661; d. 27 June
1670; *D.N.B.*

1627

29 Jan. *William Byrde, D.C.L.*, All Souls Coll., Oxford; adm.
Arches 19 Oct. 1622; (C; A); 2 s. Thomas B., of Little-
bury, co. Essex, 'pleb.', and nephew of Sir William B.,
D.C.L. (q.v.);[1] d. 28 Nov. 1639.

1628

2 Feb. *William Mericke, D.C.L.*, New Coll., Oxford, from
Winchester Coll.; adm. Arches 8 Nov. 1627; (C; A);
*c.*32; b. West Meon, co. Southampton, s. Maurice M., of
Bodeon, co. Anglesey,[2] Steward of New Coll. and
Registrar of Oxford University; ktd. 8 Nov. 1661; bur.
11 Feb. 1669; *D.N.B.*

3 May *William Griffith, D.C.L.*, New Coll., Oxford, from
Winchester Coll., stud. G.I.; adm. Arches 8 Nov. 1627;
(C; A); *c.* 32; 1 s. Robert G., of Carreglywd in Llan-
faethlu, co. Anglesey; d. 17 Oct. 1648.[3]

10 May *Marmaduke Lynne, LL.D.*, Trinity Hall, Cambridge;
adm. Arches 17 Apr. 1619; (C; A); 5 s. John L., of
Bassingbourne, co. Cambridge;[4] d. by 1 Sept. 1640.[5]

3 Nov. *Charles Tooker, D.C.L.*, Oriel Coll., Oxford, stud.L.I.;
adm. Arches 20 June 1628; (C; A); 2 s. Charles T., of
Abingdon, co. Berks, gent.;[6] d. by 1661/2.[7]

George Parry, LL.D., Magdalene Coll., Cambridge, from
Merton Coll., Oxford, stud. I.T.; adm. Arches 22 Oct.
1628; (C; A); *c.*27; 3 s. Henry P., Bishop of Worcester;
mar. Mary, d. of Dr. Sweit (q.v.); ktd. 12 May 1644; d.
by 16 Nov. 1670.[8]

[1]Richard, Lord Braybrooke, *History of Audley End* (London, 1836), pp. 291–2.
[2]*Vis. London 1633*, ii. 97.
[3]*Anglesey Ped.*, p. 26.
[4]*Vis. Cambs.*, p. 104.
[5]Will P.C.C. 118 Coventry.
[6]*Vis. Berks.*, i.294.
[7]When Mrs. Tooker, his administratrix, paid his arrears (L.B., f.196).
[8]Admon P.C.C.

1629

3 Feb. *Robert Mason, LL.D.* (1628), St. John's Coll., Cambridge; (C; A); o.s. George M., of New Windsor, co. Berks.;[1] ktd. 9 Apr. 1661; bur. Bath, co. Somerset 27 June 1662; *D.N.B.*

14 Oct. *Richard Hart, D.C.L.*, St. Alban Hall, Oxford; adm. Arches 22 Sept. 1628; (C; A); 1 s. John H., of London, proctor;[2] discommoned as a popish recusant 2 May 1632; reinstated 6 May 1633;[3] living 7 Dec. 1639;[4] probably d. by 2 July 1642.[5]

23 Oct. *Francis Baber, D.C.L.* (1628), Trinity Coll., Oxford; (C; A); *c.*40; 2 s. Francis B., of Chew Magna, co. Somerset, esq.;[6] d. 17 June 1669.

William Clerk, LL.D. (1629), Trinity Hall, Cambridge; (C; A); President 17 Aug. 1647; bur. 3 Aug. 1655; *D.N.B.*

n.d. 'Dr. Skinner', adm. between 24 June 1629 and 18 June 1630.[7] Probably William Skinner, D.C.L. (1625), Brasenose Coll., Oxford; s. Edward S., of Ledbury, co. Hereford, 'pleb.'; d. 1647.

1630

22 Nov. *William Boswell, D.C.L.* (1630), Wadham Coll., Oxford; (C; A); *c.*31; s. William B., of All Saints, Oxford, alderman; d. 5 Apr. 1678.

1631

7 May *Thomas Goad, LL.D.* (1630), King's Coll., Cambridge, from Eton Coll.; (C; A); *c.*35; m. Mary, d. of Edmund Woodhall, Register of P.C.C.; bur. Grantchester, co. Cambridge 11 June 1666; *D.N.B.*

1632

26 Oct. *William Lewin, LL.D.* (1632), Gonville and Caius Coll., Cambridge, from Hardingham Sch.; (C; A); *c.*31; s. Gilbert L., of Ringstead, co. Norfolk, gent; Treasurer 1662–4; d. by Feb. 1667.[8]

---

[1] *Vis. London 1633*, ii. 85.
[2] *Vis. London 1633*, i. 357.
[3] S.B., f.79.
[4] G. D. Squibb, *Heraldic Cases in the Court of Chivalry* (Harl. Soc. cvii, 1956), p. 44.
[5] L.B., f. 182.
[6] *Vis. Somerset*, p. 5.
[7] L.B., f.143.   [8] Admon P.C.C.

1632

12 Nov. *Giles Sweit, D.C.L.* (1632), St. Mary Hall, Oxford; (C; A); *c.*46; s. Giles S., Bailiff of St John's Coll., Oxford; Treasurer 1651; President 1660; ktd. 25 Mar. 1664; d. 13 Sept. 1672.

1634

14 Oct. *Edward Mottershead, D.C.L.* (1632), New Coll., Oxford, from Winchester Coll.; (C; A); *c.*35; b. London; s. Thomas M., Deputy Registrar of the Court of High Commission;[1] bur. 13 June 1665.

William Nevill, D.C.L. (1633), Merton Coll., Oxford; (C; A); *c.*38; s. Sir Henry N., of Billingbeare, co. Berks, kt.; d. by 5 Mar. 1640.[2]

7 Nov. *Joseph Martyn, D.C.L.* (1633), Wadham Coll., Oxford; (C; A); *c.*35; b. co. Devon; probably 2 s. William M., of Exeter, merchant; d. by 4 July 1677.[3]

4 Dec. *William* Laud, *Archbishop of Canterbury, 'on the day of our visitation'*;[4] (C); beheaded 10 Jan. 1645; *D.N.B.*

William Juxon, *Bishop of London*; (C); Archbishop of Canterbury 1660; d. 4 June 1663; *D.N.B.*

Francis White, *Bishop of Ely*; (C); d. Feb. 1638; *D.N.B.*[5]

1636

13 Feb. *John Exton, LL.D.,* Trinity Hall, Cambridge; adm. Arches 31 June 1635; (C; A); Treasurer 1647; Judge of the Court of Admiralty 1661; bur. 22 Oct. 1668; *D.N.B.*

1637

26 Apr. Sir *Nathaniel Brent*, kt., *D.C.L.,* Warden of Merton Coll., Oxford; adm. Arches 23 Oct. 1624; (C; A); *c.*43; s. Anchor B., of Little Wolford, co. Warwick, 'pleb.'; d. 6 Nov. 1652; *D.N.B.*

27 Apr. *Thomas Heath, D.C.L.,* Merton Coll., Oxford, from St. Paul's Sch.; adm. Arches 13 Feb. 1637; (C; A); *c.*39; b. London; 'gen. fil.'; Treasurer 1639–40; became a Roman Catholic and lived at Ghent; d. 2 Feb. 1680.

[1]Marchant, p. 250.

[2]Will P.C.C. 32 Coventry.

[3]Will P.C.C. 78 Hale. He mentioned his sister Susan Wilts, wid., and William in his will (pr. 26 Dec. 1601, P.C.C. 84 Woodhall) mentioned his daughter Susan and three sons (unnamed).

[4]The visitation was of the Archbishop's Courts held in Doctors' Commons, not of the Society (Bodl., MS. Tanner 315, f.54).

[5]The last non-advocate to be admitted.

1637

6 May *John Farmerie, D.C.L.*, Oxford, from St. John's Coll.,
Cambridge; adm. Arches 18 June 1624; (C; A); *c*.47;
1 s. Willliam F., Rector of Springthorpe, co.Lincoln;[1]
d. by 5 Feb. 1648.[2]

1641

2 Dec. *Robert King, LL.D.*, Trinity Hall, Cambridge; adm.
Arches 23 Oct. 1637; (C; A); *c*.41; b. co. Kent; Treasurer
1645–7; Master of Trinity Hall 2 Aug. 1660; d. 5 Nov.
1670;[2] *D.N.B.*
William Turner, D.C.L., Wadham Coll., Oxford; adm.
Arches 23 Oct. 1637; (C; A); *c*.35; b. Burrington, co.
Somerset; 'cler. fil.'; Second Judge of the Court of
Admiralty 12 Mar. 1660; deprived 1660; ktd. 26 Feb.
1664; d. by 18 Oct. 1670.[3]

1645

4 Nov. *Isaac Dorislaus, LL.D.*, Leyden, incorp. Cambridge
(1631); (C; A);[4] *c*.50, 2 s. Isaac D., Minister of Hens-
brock, Holland; Judge of the Court of Admiralty 1648;
murdered 12 May 1649; *D.N.B.*

1647

29 Jan. *William Foorthe, LL.D.* (1646), Trinity Coll., Cambridge,
from Westminster Sch.; (C; A); s. William F. of Nay-
land, co. Suffolk; d. by 31 Jan. 1672.[5]

6 Feb. *Justinian Lewyn, D.C.L.*, Pembroke Coll., Oxford,
member G.I.; adm. Arches 11 Nov. 1637; (C; A); *c*.34;
s. William L., of London, gent., Clerk of the New
River Company, and gds. William L., D.C.L. (q.v.);
mar. the neice and heiress of Thomas Gwynne, D.C.L.
(q.v.);[6] ktd. 12 May 1661; d. 1 Jan. 1673; *D.N.B.*
Tobias Worlich, LL.D. (1639), Trinity Hall, Cambridge;
(C; A); probably s. Thomas W., of Cowling, co. Suffolk, esq.;[7] ktd. 12 May 1661; d. 1664.

---

[1]*Lincs. Ped.* i. 346.   [2]Will P.C.C. 29 Essex.
[3]M.I. Trinity Hall Chapel.   [4]Will P.C.C. 142 Penn.
[5]Dorislaus stated in his subscription that he had been admitted 'in contubernio
Advocatorum' in 1629, but gave no reason for the long delay in the payment of the
admission fee.
[6]Will P.C.C. 76 Duke.
[7]Wood, *Colleges and Halls*, i.575.
[8]*Knights*, p. 142. Levack, p. 281, following Marchant, p. 251, states that Worlich
came from Cooling, co. Kent.

1647

3 Nov. *John Pepys, LL.D.* (1647), Christ's Coll., Cambridge, from Perse Sch., barr. M.T.; (C; A); *c.*29; 2 s. Talbot P., of Impington, co. Cambridge, barrister; ceased to practise by Dec. 1670.[1]

1648

3 June *James Master, D.C.L.*, New Coll., Oxford, from Winchester Coll., advocate;[2] (C; A); *c.*43; 2 s. Edward M., of Ospringe, co. Kent, esq.; Treasurer 1655–61; d. by 20 Feb. 1664.[3]

1 Nov. *William Paske, LL.D.* (1648), Clare Coll., Cambridge; (C; A); bur. 25 Nov. 1656.

1650

3 July *John Mylles, D.C.L.* (1649). Christ Church, Oxford, from Westminster Sch.; (C; A); *c.*46; s. John M., of Southampton, gent; Treasurer 1665; d. by 18 Apr. 1676.[4]

2 Nov. *John Wainewright, D.C.L.* (1650), All Souls Coll., Oxford; (C; A); living 1682.[5]

1652

12 Nov. *John Cruso, LL.D.* (1652), Gonville and Caius Coll., Cambridge; (C; A); *c.*34; s. John C., of Norwich, co. Norfolk, merchant; ceased to practise before Dec. 1670.[6] *D.N.B.*

Tobias Swinburne, D.C.L. (1652), Lincoln Coll., Oxford, member M.T.; (C; A); *c.*39; 1 s. Henry S. of York, esq.

?1655

John Godolphin, D.C.L. (1642 or 1643), Gloucester Hall, Oxford; b. 29 Nov. 1617; 3 s. John G., of the Isles of Scilly, esq.; President by 25 Apr. 1656–12 Mar. 1660;[7] King's Advocate 1660; d. 4 Apr. 1678; *D.N.B.*

1656

1 May *Thomas Hyde, D.C.L.* (1640), New Coll., Oxford; (C; A); *c.*37; 8 s. Sir Lawrence H. of Salisbury, co. Wilts,

---

[1]15 L.T.R. 70; bur. Cottenham, co. Cambridge 19 Aug. 1692.
[2]Warrant for admission 20 Jan. 1640 (P.R.O., SP 16/442/125).
[3]Will P.C.C. 18 Bruce.
[4]Will P.C.C. 40 Bence.
[5]F. Gastrell, *Notitia Cestriensis,* i (Chetham Soc. viii, 1845), 22.
[6]15 L.T.R. 70; d. 1681.
[7]Probably joined the Society and became President on succeeding Dr. William Clerke as the senior Judge of the Court of Admiralty in Aug. 1655. First mentioned in the list of contributors for the year ending 25 Apr. 1656 (L.B., f.188).

1656

1 May   kt; Judge of the Court of Admiralty 1660; Treasurer 1661; bur. Salisbury 20 Oct. 1661.

1657

10 Feb.   *Walter Walker, LL.D.* (1640), Christ's Coll., Cambridge, barr. I.T.; (C; A); *c.*56; s. John W., of Barton-under-Needwood, co. Stafford, 'pleb.';[1] Advocate-General under the Commonwealth; President 13 May 1660; deprived 1660; ktd. 18 Apr. 1661; d. by 16 Apr. 1674.[2]

1660

24 Jan.   *Timothy Baldwin, D.C.L.* (1652), All Souls Coll., Oxford, student I.T.; (C; A); *c.*40; 2 s. Charles B., of Elsich in Diddlebury, co. Salop, gent.[3] Treasurer 1669; ktd. 10 July 1670; d. by 22 Feb. 1697;[4] *D.N.B.*

26 June   *Edward Alderne, D.C.L.*, Exeter Coll., Oxford; student M.T.; warrant for admission as advocate 28 June 1640;[5] (C; A); 1 s. Thomas A., of Hereford, gent; ceased to practise before Dec. 1670.[6]

1661

8 May   *Thomas Reade, D.C.L.*, New Coll., Oxford, from Winchester Coll.; warrant for admission as advocate 28 Jan. 1640;[7] (C; A); *c.*55; 2 s. Robert R., of Linkenholt, co. Southampton; d. Mar. 1669; *D.N.B.*

3 Dec.   *Sir Edmund Peirce, kt. LL.D.*, Trinity Hall, Cambridge, Master in Chancery; warrant for admission as advocate 28 June 1640;[8] (C; A); b. co. Buckingham;[9] bur. Temple Church 10 Aug. 1667.

    John Berkenhead, D.C.L. (1661), All Souls Coll., Oxford; (C; A); *c.*45; s. Randle B., of Northwich, co. Chester, saddler; ktd. 14 Nov. 1662; d. 4 Dec. 1679; *D.N.B.*

1663

14 July   *Sir Robert Wyseman, kt., LL.D.*, Trinity Hall, Cambridge; warrant for admission as advocate 26 Jan. 1640;[10]

[1] Walker received a grant of arms, *c.*1644 (*Grantees*, p. 265).
[2] Will P.C.C. 52 Bunce.
[3] *Knights*, pp. 238–9.
[4] Will P.C.C. 24 Pyne.
[5] P.R.O., SP 16/442/125.
[6] 15 *L.T.R.* 70; d. by 5 June 1671 (Will P.C.C. 72 Duke).
[7] P.R.O., SP 16/442/125.
[8] P.R.O., SP 16/442/125.
[9] Received a grant of arms 20 May 1661 (*Grantees*, p. 195).
[10] P.R.O., SP 16/442/145.

1663

14 July (C; A); *c.53*; 7 s. Sir Thomas W., of Rivenhall, co. Essex, kt.; President 28 Nov. 1672; d. 17 Aug. 1684.[1]

1664

22 June *Thomas Croft, D.C.L.* (1661), Jesus Coll., Oxford; member G.I.; (C; A); *c.48*; s. Alexander C., of Carmarthen, esq.

Thomas Exton, LL.D. (1662), Trinity Hall, Cambridge, from Merchant Taylors' Sch., barr. G.I.; (C; A); *c.33*; s. John E., LL.D. (q.v.); Treasurer 1674–8; ktd. 23 Nov. 1675; Master of Trinity Hall 10 Nov. 1676; King's Advocate 1679; President June 1686; d. 4 Nov. 1688; *D.N.B.*

Edward Master, D.C.L., New Coll., Oxford, from Winchester Coll.; adm. Arches Oct. 1663; (C; A); *c.29*; Richard M., of East Langdon, co. Kent, gent; Treasurer 1684–9; bur. Holton, co. Oxford 4 Oct. 1692.

1 July *John Clark, LL.D.*, Trinity Hall, Cambridge; adm. Arches 9 Nov. 1663; (C; A); b. co. Suffolk; bur. 3 Mar. 1673.

25 Oct. George *Wake, D.C.L.* (1660), Magdalen Coll., Oxford; (C; A); *c* 54; 2 s. Sir John W., of Clevedon, co. Somerset, bt.; ceased to practise before Dec. 1670.[2]

David Budd, D.C.L. (1661), Oxford, from Gonville and Caius Coll., Cambridge, and Torrington Sch.; (C; A); s. David B., of Torrington, co. Devon, hatter; d. by 7 Feb. 1676.[3]

Richard Lloyd, D.C.L., All Souls Coll., Oxford; adm. Arches Oct. 1663; (C; A); *c.30*; 2 s. Andrew Ll., of Aston, co. Salop, esq.;[4] ktd. 16 Jan. 1677; Treasurer 1679–83; President Sept. 1684; d. 28 June 1686; *D.N.B.*

Thomas Bouchier, D.C.L., All Souls Coll., Oxford, from Winchester Coll.; adm. Arches Oct. 1663; (C; A); *c.30*; s. James B., of Culworth, co. Northampton; d. May 1723.[5]

[1]M.I.
[2]15 *L.T.R.* 70.
[3]L.P.L., Arches VB/2, p. 284.
[4]*Knights*, p. 314.
[5]Wood, *Colleges and Halls*, i.658.

1664

29 Oct. *Henry Alworth, D.C.L.* (1660), New Coll., Oxford, from
Winchester Coll.; (C; A); *c.*44; b. Rowde, co. Wilts.; d.
by 18 Jan. 1701.[1]

3 Nov. *Owen Hughes, LL.D.* (1660), Trinity Hall, Cambridge,
from Felsted Sch., member G.I.; (C; A); *c.*36; s. Francis
H., of Cambridge, esquire bedell.

4 Nov. *John Lowen, D.C.L.* (1660), Christ Church, Oxford, from
Westminster Sch., barrister G.I.; (C; A); *c.*50; s.
Daniel L., of Gyrpins in Rainham, co. Essex, esq.[2] ceased
to practise before Dec. 1670.[3]

11 Nov. *Leoline Jenkins, D.C.L.* (1661), Jesus Coll., Oxford,
from Cowbridge Sch.; (C; A); *c.*39; s. Leoline J., of
Llanblethian, co. Glamorgan, 'pleb.'; Judge of the
Court of Admiralty 1668–73; ktd. 7 Jan. 1669; d. Sept.
1685;[4] *D.N.B.; D.W.B.*

1666

3 Apr. *Sir Ellis Leighton, kt., LL.D.*, Cambridge, barrister M.T.;
adm. Arches 24 May 1665 (to be non-exercent for three
years); (C; A); s. Alexander L., physician and divine; d.
9 Jan. 1685; *D.N.B.*

1667

28 Jan. *Sir Richard Chaworth, kt., D.C.L.* (1640), Christ Church,
Oxford; (C; A); *c.*63; 6 s. John C., of Wiverton, co.
Nottingham, esq.;[5] d. 1672.[6]

1668

28 Apr. *William Trumbull, D.C.L.*, All Souls Coll., Oxford, from
Wokingham Sch., student M.T.; adm. Arches 22 Oct.
1667; (C; A); *c.*29; 1 s. William T., of Easthampstead,
co. Berks., Clerk to the Signet;[7] ktd. 21 Nov. 1684; d.
14 Dec. 1716; *D.N.B.*

3 Dec. *John Elliott, D.C.L.*, New Coll., Oxford, from Winchester
Coll.; adm. Arches 1 Dec. 1668; (C; A); d. 1671.

---

[1]Will proved in Court of Arches (L.P.L., Arches Muniment Book F 9).
[2]*Vis. Essex 1664–68* (London, 1888), p. 59.
[3]15 L.T.R. 70; d. by 13 Mar. 1678 (Will P.C.C. 25 Reeve).
[4]M.I. Jesus Coll. Chapel.
[5]*Visitations of the County of Nottingham in the years 1569 and 1614* (Harl. Soc. iv, 1871), p. 128.
[6]M.I. Richmond, co. Surrey.
[7]Received a grant of arms 10 Oct. 1662 (*Grantees*, p. 258).

1669

20 Jan. *Thomas Pynfold, LL.D.*, Trinity Hall, Cambridge, from Merchant Taylors Sch.; adm. Arches 2 Nov. 1668; (C; A); 35; o.s. Nathaniel P., waterman; King's Advocate 1686; ktd. 4 July 1686; Treasurer 1690–1; d. 30 Apr. 1701.[1]

6 May *Edward Lowe, D.C.L.*, New Coll., Oxford, from Winchester Coll.; adm. Arches 22 Oct. 1667; (C; A); c.33; b. Calne, co. Wilts.; 'arm. fil.'; ktd. 21 Jan. 1673; d. May 1684.

1670

20 Jan. *Thomas Briggs, LL.D.*, St. John's Coll., Cambridge, from Stamford Sch.; adm. Arches 1 Dec. 1669; (C; A); c.37; s. Thomas B., Rector of Wyfordby, co. Leicester; d. 1713.

1 Dec. *William Oldys, D.C.L.*, New Coll., Oxford, from Winchester Coll.; adm. Arches 15 Feb. 1670; (C; A); c.34; s. William O., Vicar of Adderbury, co. Oxford, D.D.; Treasurer 1693–8; d. 28 Mar. 1708; *D.N.B.*

1671

26 Jan. *Richard Raines, LL.D.*, St. John's Coll., Cambridge, from Melton Mowbray Sch.; adm. Arches 19 May 1669; (C; A); s. William R., of Melton Mowbray, co. Leicester; ktd. 18 Dec. 1686; Judge of the Court of Admiralty 1686–9; d. 27 Dec. 1710.

4 Feb. *Christopher Meale, LL.D.*, King's Coll., Cambridge, from Eton Coll., stud. I.T.; adm. Arches 14 May 1670; (C; A); c.37; b. Colnbrook, co. Buckingham; d. 25 Apr. 1672.

26 May *Charles Perrott, D.C.L.*, St. John's Coll., Oxford (founder's kin); adm. Arches 25 May 1671; (C; A); c.28; 3 s. James P., of North Leigh, co. Oxford, and gds. George Dale, D.C.L. (q.v.);[2] d. 10 June 1686.[3]

1 Dec. *John Harrison, D.C.L.*, New Coll., Oxford, from Winchester Coll.; adm. Arches 30 Nov. 1671; (C; A); c.30; 2 s. Sir Richard H., of Hurst, co. Berks., kt.[4]

[1] M.I. Walton, co. Buckingham.
[2] *Vis. Berks.* ii. 194.
[3] M.I. Fifield, co. Oxford.
[4] *Al. Ox.* gives Harrison's date of death as 1698, but the entry seems to be a conflation of two men of the same names.

1672

5 Nov. *John Edisbury, D.C.L.,* Brasenose Coll., Oxford, stud. G.I.; adm. Arches 1 Nov. 1672; (C; A); *c.*26; yr. s. John E., of Pentreclawdd, co. Denbigh, esq.; d. 1713; *D.W.B.*

1673

6 Nov. *Joseph Taylor, D.C.L.,* St. John's Coll., Oxford, from Merchant Taylors Sch., stud. I.T.; adm. Arches 22 Oct. 1673; (C; A); 34; 2 s. Francis T., of London, merchant taylor.

2 Dec. *Robert Thompson, LL.D.,* Trinity Hall, Cambridge, formerly clerk to the Vicar-General; adm. proctor 1667; adm. Arches 20 Jan. 1672; (C; A); *c.*32; d. Feb. 1684.[1]

1674

7 Feb. *William Foster, LL.D.,* Clare Coll., Cambridge; adm. Arches 23 Oct. 1672; (C; A); b. co. Bedford; bur. Great Barford, co. Bedford 5 Apr. 1708.

1 July *Henry Fauconberge, LL.D.,* Trinity Hall, Cambridge, stud. G.I.; adm. Arches 2 Nov. 1668; (C; A); *c.*39; s. John F., of Westminster; d. 29 Oct. 1713.

Joseph Hervy, D.C.L., Merton Coll., Oxford, stud. G.I.; adm. Arches 15 Oct. 1673; (C; A); 'gen. fil.'; d. by 20 Feb. 1680, when Joseph Harvy, his nephew and administrator, paid his arrears.[2]

1675

25 Oct. *Charles Hedges, D.C.L.,* Magdalen Hall, Oxford; adm. Arches 20 Oct. 1675; (C; A); *c.*26 s. Henry H., of Wanborough, co. Wilts., gent.; Judge of the Court of Admiralty 1689; ktd. 4 June 1689; m. Eleanor, d. of George Smith, proctor; d. 10 June 1714; *D.N.B.*

20 Nov. *Charles Davenant, LL.D.,* Cambridge, from Balliol Coll., Oxford, and Cheam Sch.; adm. Arches 20 Oct. 1675; (C; A); *c.*19 (*sic*); 1 s. Sir William D., kt., Poet Laureate; d. 6 Nov. 1714; *D.N.B.*

24 Nov. *Stephen Brice, D.C.L.,* Magdalen Coll., Oxford; (C; A); *c.*29; s. Stephen B., of Eynsham, co. Oxford, gent.; d. 4 Feb. 1689.[3]

---

[1] W. Musgrave, *Obituary,* vi (Harl. Soc. xlix, 1901), 83.
[2] L.B., f.216v.
[3] M.I.

1678
4 Feb. *William Howell, LL.D.*, Magdalene Coll., Cambridge; adm. Arches 29 June 1674; (C; A); *c.*45; s. Robert H., of Walkeringham, co. Nottingham; d. 1683; *D.N.B.*

6 Feb. *Robert Pepper, LL.D.* (1664), Christ's Coll., Cambridge; (C; A); *c.*41; s. Sir Cuthbert P., of Farington Hall in Silkstone, co. Durham, kt.; d. 5 Nov. 1700.[1]

23 Oct. *Fisher Littleton, D.C.L.*, All Souls Coll., Oxford; adm. Arches 21 Oct. 1678; (C; A); *c.*30; 3 s. Sir Walter L., of Lichfield, co. Stafford, kt., LL.D.; d. by 5 Mar. 1697.[2]

Henry Newton, D.C.L., Merton Coll., Oxford; adm. Arches 17 Oct. 1678; (C; A); *c.*27; s. Henry N., of London and Highley, co. Essex, gent.; Judge of the Court of Admiralty 1714; ktd. 4 Mar. 1715; d. 29 July 1715; *D.N.B.*

1679
12 July *George Oxindon, LL.D.*, Trinity Hall, Cambridge; adm. Arches 10 July 1679; (C; A); *c.*28; 3 s. Sir Henry O., of Dene in Wingham, co. Kent, bt; Master of Trinity Hall 8 Nov. 1688; President 2 Feb. 1695; d. 21 Feb. 1703; *D.N.B.*

1681
2 Dec. *George Bramston, LL.D.*, Trinity Hall, Cambridge; (C; A); s. Sir Mundeford B., of Great Baddow, co. Essex, kt.; Treasurer 1699–1706; Master of Trinity Hall 27 Feb. 1703; d. 3 June 1710.

1682
4 Nov. *James Fullwood, LL.D.*, Cambridge, from Exeter Coll., Oxford, member G.I.; adm. Arches 1 Nov. 1682; (C; A); s. Francis F., Archdeacon of Totnes.

1685
23 Oct. *Stephen Waller, D.C.L.*, New Coll., Oxford, from Winchester Coll.; (C; A); *c.*30; s. Edmund W., of Beaconsfield, co. Buckingham, esq., poet; d. 22 Feb. 1707.

13 Nov. *Matthew Tindall, D.C.L.*, All Souls Coll., Oxford; adm. Arches 11 Nov. 1685; (C; A); *c.*28; s. John T., of Bere Ferrers, co. Devon, 'minister'; d. 16 Aug. 1733; *D.N.B.*

[1]M.I. Norwich Cathedral.
[2]Will P.C.C. 58 Pyne.

1685

2 Dec. *John Conant*, *D.C.L.*, Merton Coll., Oxford; adm. Arches 30 Nov. 1685; (C; A); *c*.31; s. John C., D.D., Rector of Exeter Coll., Oxford; d. 23 Aug. 1723.

1686

23 Nov. *Thomas Lane*, *D.C.L.*, Merton Coll., Oxford, from Higham Ferrers Sch.; adm. Arches 20 Nov. 1686; (C; A); *c*.28; 3 s. Francis L., of Glendon, co. Northampton, gent.; Treasurer 1707–8; bur. 13 Feb. 1709; *D.N.B.*

1687

4 Nov. *Thomas Burles*, *LL.D.*, Trinity Hall, Cambridge, from Bury St. Edmund's Sch.; adm. Arches 3 Nov. 1687; (C; A); *c*.36; s. Thomas B., of Depden, co. Suffolk;[1] d. 1690.

12 Nov. *Richard Pagitt*, *LL.D.*, Trinity Hall, Cambridge; adm. 3 Nov. 1687; (C; A); s. Richard P., of Westminster, B.C.L., LL.B.; d. 10 Nov. 1726.

22 Nov. *Philip Foster*, *D.C.L.*, Oriel Coll., Oxford, from Merchant Taylors Sch.; adm. Arches 3 Nov. 1687; (C; A); 37; s. William F., of London, gent.; bur. 9 Dec. 1690.[2]

1688

25 Oct. *Brian Walton*, *LL.D.*, Peterhouse, Cambridge, from Chelsea Sch.; adm. Arches 12 Oct. 1688. (C; A); *c*.30; s. Brian W., Bishop of Chester; d. by 23 July 1696.[3]

1689

24 Oct. *John Harwood*, *LL.D.*, Queens' Coll., Cambridge; adm. Arches 18 Oct. 1689; (C; A); *c*.28; s. John H., of Hagbourne, co. Berks.; d. 1 Jan. 1731.

1690

16 June *John Rudston*, *D.C.L.*, St. John's Coll., Oxford, from Merchant Taylors Sch.; adm. Arches 14 June 1690; (C; A); 33; s. James R., of St. Albans, co. Hertford, gent.; d. by 5 Dec. 1691.[4]

1691

31 Oct. *John Brookbank*, *LL.D.*, Trinity Hall, Cambridge; (C; A); *c*.40; b. Liverpool, co. Lancaster; d. 16 Apr. 1724.[5]

---

[1]*Visitation of the County of Suffolk begun A.D. 1664*. (Harl. Soc. lxi, 1910), p. 175.
[2]Died in such poverty that the Society granted £5 towards the expense of his funeral or (if not necessary) for the relief of his aged mother (Coote, p. 103).
[3]Will P.C.C. 129 Bond.
[4]Admon V.C.C. Oxford.
[5]M.I. Cambridge St. Edward.

1691

3 Nov. *William Clements, LL.D.*, Trinity Hall, Cambridge; (C; A); b. London; d. 22 July 1716.

1692

12 Nov. *William King, D.C.L.*, Christ Church, Oxford, from Westminster Sch.; adm. Arches 11 Nov. 1692; (C; A); *c.*29; s. Ezekiel K., of London, gent.; d. 25 Dec. 1712; *D.N.B.*

1694

22 Jan. *Owen Wynne, LL.D.*, St. John's Coll., Cambridge, from Kinnerley Sch.; adm. Arches 16 Jan. 1694; (C; A); s. William O., of Llanvair, co. Denbigh; d. by Jan. 1701.[1]

23 Oct. *John Cooke, D.C.L.*, St. John's Coll., Oxford, from Merchant Taylors' Sch.; adm. Arches 20 Oct. 1694; (C; A); 28; s. John C., of Whitechapel, co. Middlesex, surveyor of customs, and bro. Edward C., proctor;[2] King's Advocate 26 July 1701; ktd. 21 May 1701; President 11 Mar. 1703; d. 31 Mar. 1710; *D.N.B.*

1696

3 Nov. *Thomas Ayloffe, LL.D.*, Trinity Hall, Cambridge; adm. Arches 22 Oct. 1696; (C; A); b. co. Essex; 2 s. James A., of Melbourne, co. Cambridge;[3] d. 18 Mar. 1714.

William Beaw, D.C.L., Magdalen Coll., Oxford; adm. Arches 2 Nov. 1696; (C; A); *c.*30; s. William B., Bishop of Llandaff; imprisoned for debt in the Fleet Prison for 35 years; d. there 6 Jan. 1738.

21 Nov. *Nathaniel Lloyd, D.C.L.*, All Souls Coll., Oxford, from St. Paul's Sch.; adm. Arches 15 Oct. 1696; (C; A); 27; s. Sir Richard Ll., kt., D.C.L. (q.v.); Treasurer 1709–12; ktd. 29 May 1710; Master of Trinity Hall 20 June 1710; King's Advocate 13 Jan. 1715; retired 24 Oct. 1720;[4] d. 30 Mar. 1741; left 100 guineas to buy books for the library of Doctors' Commons;[5] *D.N.B.*[6]

[1]Will Commissary Ct of Dean and Chapter of Westminster.
[2]*Knights*, p. 475.
[3]Wotton, i. 252.
[4]He 'made a Respectful Speech to ye Profession in ye Court of Arches and quitted his practice' (All Souls Coll. MS. 325, unfoliated).
[5]*Warren's Book*, p. 321.
[6]*D.N.B.* states that Lloyd died in 1745.

1697

8 Feb. *John Bridges*, D.C.L., Christ Church, Oxford, from Westminster Sch.; adm. Arches 30 May 1695; (C; A); *c.*32; s. Southcott B., of London, gent.

1698

23 May *John Exton*, LL.D., Trinity Hall, Cambridge, (C; A); s. Thomas E., LL.D., Master of Trinity Hall (q.v.); bur. 26 Apr. 1716.

1701

6 May *Charles Herriott*, LL.D., Utrecht and King's Coll., Cambridge, from Eton Coll.; (C; A); *c.*32; b. London; s. — H., goldsmith; Treasurer 1713–14; d. *c.*1730.[1]

10 July *James Ayloffe*, LL.D., Trinity Hall, Cambridge; (C; A); b. co. Kent; d. 3 Nov. 1732.

23 Oct. *Henry Raynes*, LL.D., Trinity Hall, Cambridge, from Lewisham Sch.; (C; A); s. Sir Richard R., kt., LL.D. (q.v.); Treasurer 1715–17; d. 3 Oct. 1734.

Robert Wood, D.C.L., All Souls Coll., Oxford, from Eton Coll.; (C; A); 31; s. Thomas W., of Littleton, co. Middlesex, gent.; Treasurer 1718–22, d. 8 Sept. 1738.

1703

23 Oct. *Humphrey Henchman*, D.C.L., Christ Church, Oxford, from Eton Coll.; (C; A); *c.*34; s. Thomas H., of Fulham, co. Middlesex, gent.; Judge of the Court of Admiralty 22 June–1 Dec. 1714; Treasurer 1723–4; mar. Anne, sister of Robert Wood, D.C.L. (q.v.); d. 15 Aug. 1739; *D.N.B.*

1704

23 Oct. *George Paul*, LL.D., Trinity Hall, Cambridge; (C; A); *c.*22; Treasurer 1725–7; King's Advocate 1727; d. 1 Mar. 1755.

Charles Pinfold, LL.D., Trinity Hall, Cambridge; (C; A); *c.*27; s. Sir Thomas P., kt., LL.D. (q.v.); Librarian 1706–28; Treasurer 1728–9; d. 29 May 1754.

Thomas Welham, D.C.L., Merton Coll., Oxford, from Winchester Coll.; (C; A); *c.*29; s. Thomas W., Deputy Register of P.C.C.; d. 3 July 1705.

1706

18 June *Henry Penrice*, LL.D., Trinity Hall, Cambridge, from

---

[1] In Miege 1728, but not 1731.

1706

18 June Merchant Taylors Sch., student I.T.; (C; A); 28; s. William P., citizen and merchant taylor of London; Judge of the Court of Admiralty 1715; ktd. 15 May 1715; d. 10 Aug. 1752.[1]

24 Oct. *John Bettesworth*, LL.D., St. John's Coll., Cambridge, from Baddesley Sch.; (C; A); *c.*28, s. Robert B., of Petersfield, co. Southampton, saddler; President 19 Apr. 1710; d. 17 Dec. 1751.

1707

12 July *Robert Mapletoft*, LL.D., Trinity Hall, Cambridge; (C; A); *c.23*; s. John M., D.D., M.D., Vicar of St. Lawrence Jewry, London; unlikely to have had much practice, for he travelled for some years for his health in France, Portugal, and Italy;[2] d. 3 Dec. 1716.[3]

15 July *William Willymott*, LL.D., King's Coll., Cambridge, from Eton Coll.; (C; A); 2 s. Thomas W., of Royston, co. Hertford, proctor; left Doctors' Commons by 1723;[4] *D.N.B.*

24 Oct. *John Corbett*, LL.D., Trinity Coll., Cambridge; adm. Arches 8 July 1707; (C; A);[5] b. co. Salop; d. Apr. 1737.

3 Nov. *Thomas Paske*, LL.D., Clare Hall, Cambridge; (C; A); *c.32*; s. Thomas P., M.A., of Much Hadham, co. Hertford; d. 18 Sept. 1720.

12 Nov. *William Phipps*, D.C.L., Wadham Coll., Oxford; (C; A); *c.31*; perhaps s. William P., of Kenilworth, co Warwick; d. 6 Mar. 1728.

1709

2 Dec. *Charles Curzon*, D.C.L., Trinity Coll., Oxford; (C; A); *c.24*; 5 s. Sir Nathaniel C., of Tyler's Green, co. Buckingham, bt.; d. by 1741.[6]

'Dr. Pearce' is here inserted by Coote (p. 110) as appearing in the 'Treasurer's Book' as an advocate, but this is due to

---

[1]M.I. Offley, co. Hertford.

[2]*Warren's Book*, p. 133.

[3]M.I. Cambridge St. Edward.

[4]Miege, 1723, p. 16. Probably left 1721, on becoming Vice-Provost of King's; ordained deacon 25 Mar. 1730; d. 7 June 1737.

[5]Dr. Corbett was the last member to be admitted more than a few days after his admission as an advocate of the Court of Arches.

[6]Wotton, ii. 247.

1709

2 Dec. a misreading of the name of Dr. Penrice in a list of those
present at a meeting.[1]

1710

14 July *William Strahan*, D.C.L., Balliol Coll., Oxford, from
Edinburgh; (C; A); s. John S., D.D., Professor of
Divinity, Edinburgh; Librarian 1728–30; Treasurer
1730–1; d. 25 May 1748.

1711

15 Feb. *John Audley*, LL.D., Peterhouse, Cambridge, from Eton
Coll.; (C; A); *c.*36; s. Edward A., of Huntingdon;
Register 1729; Librarian 1730–1; Treasurer 1732–5; d.
Mar. 1747.

Edward Kinaston, D.C.L., All Souls Coll., Oxford; (C;
A); *c.*31; s. Edward K., of Oteley, co. Salop, esq.;
Register 1730–1; Librarian 1732–5; Treasurer 1736–9;
bur. St. Gregory, London 17 Apr. 1747.

23 Oct. *Richard Fuller*, LL.D., Gonville and Caius Coll., Cam-
bridge, from Yarmouth Sch., student G.I.; (C; A); s.
Samuel F., of Yarmouth, co. Norfolk, merchant; d. 3
Oct. 1726.

24 Oct. *John Andrew*, LL.D., Trinity Hall, Cambridge, from
Merchant Taylors Sch.; (C; A); 28; b. London; Register
1732–5; Librarian 1736–? 1739; Treasurer ?1740; d.
1 Oct. 1747.[2]

1712

14 May *Edward Wynn*, D.C.L., Jesus Coll., Oxford; (C; A); s.
E — W., of Anglesey, gent.; d. *c.* Apr. 1754.[3]

10 July *Berney Branthwayt*, LL.D., Gonville and Caius Coll., Cambridge, from Norwich and Bradenham Schh.; (C; A);
*c.*30; s. William B., of Hethel, co. Norfolk, esq., d. 2 Oct.
1730.

1 Dec. *Charles Bertie*, D.C.L., All Souls Coll., Oxford; (C; A);
*c.*33; yr. s. James, Earl of Abingdon; Rector of Kenn,
co. Devon 1726; d. Mar. 1747.

James Bouchier, D.C.L., All Souls Coll., Oxford; (C; A);
*c.*29; s. Thomas B., D.C.L. (q.v.); d. 19 Aug. 1736.

[1]L.B., f.238ᵛ.
[2]M.I. Trinity Hall Chapel.
[3]All Souls Coll. MS. 325, f.18.

1714

3 Nov. *Brook Taylor*, LL.D., St. John's Coll., Cambridge, from Secket's private school; (C; A); 29; b. Edmonton, co. Middlesex; s. John T., of Bifrons in Patrixbourne, co. Kent, merchant; retired *c.* 1720;[1] *D.N.B.*

1716

20 Jan. *William King*, D.C.L., Balliol Coll., Oxford, from Salisbury Grammar Sch., barr. G.I.; (C; A); *c.*30; s. Peregrine K., Rector of Rowington, co. Somerset; did not practise as an advocate;[2] *D.N.B.*

1718

4 July *Exton Sayer*, LL.D., Trinity Hall, Cambridge, stud. L.I.; (C; A); 1 s. George S., of Doctors' Commons, proctor, by Mary, d. and co-h. of Everard Exton, of Doctors' Commons, proctor, and nephew of Sir Thomas Exton, LL.D. (q.v.); d. 21 Sept. 1731.

1724

1 Dec. *Edmund Isham*, D.C.L., Magdalen Coll., Oxford, from Rugby Sch.; (C; A); 33; 4 s. Sir Justinian I., of Lamport, co. Northampton, bt.; Register 1736–7; succeeded to baronetcy 5 Mar. 1737; retired by 22 June 1768.[3]

1725

25 June *William Bramston*, LL.D., Queens' Coll., Cambridge; (C; A); s. William B., Rector of Woodham Walter, co. Essex; d. 16 Dec. 1734.

1727

3 Nov. *Stephen Cottrell*, LL.D., Trinity Hall, Cambridge; (C; A); 3 s. Sir Charles Ludowicke C., kt., Master of the Ceremonies; d. 15 May 1738.

1729

23 Oct. *George Lee*, D.C.L., Christ Church, Oxford; (C; A); *c.*28; 4 s. Sir Thomas L., of Hartwell, co. Buckingham, bt.; Register 1738–9; Treasurer ?1741; President Dec. 1751; ktd. 12 Feb. 1752; d. 18 Dec. 1758;[4] *D.N.B.*

1730

21 Nov. *Francis James*, LL.D., Trinity Hall, Cambridge, student

---

[1] All Souls Coll. MS. 325, unfoliated; d. 30 Nov. 1731.
[2] Coote, p. 114; d. 30 Dec. 1763.
[3] d. 15 Dec. 1772.
[4] M.I. Hartwell.

1730
21 Nov. L.I.; (C; A); 3 s. Sir Cane J., of Chrishall, co. Essex, bt.; ordained deacon 27 Dec. 1733; d. by 28 Sept. 1741.[1]

1734
21 Nov. Thomas Walker, LL.D., Queens' Coll., Cambridge, from Charterhouse; (C; A); c.32; s. Thomas W., Master of the Charterhouse; Librarian c. 1740; Treasurer ?1742–3; d. 17 Sept. 1764.

1735
3 Nov. Robert Foulkes, D.C.L., Christ Church, Oxford; (C; A); c.26; s. Peter F., D.D., Canon of Christ Church; d. 15 Dec. 1739.[2]

1736
10 May Edward Simpson, LL.D., Master of Trinity Hall, Cambridge, barr. L.I.; (C; A); c.37; s. Francis S., of Fishlake, co. York, esq.; Register 1740–1; Librarian 1742–3; Treasurer ?1744–7; King's Advocate June–Nov. 1756; President Dec. 1758; ktd. Dec. 1761; d. 20 May 1764.

14 July Charles Pinfold, LL.D., Trinity Hall, Cambridge; (C; A); c.27; s. Charles P., LL.D. (q.v.); Register 1742–3; Librarian 1744–7; Treasurer 1748–9; Governor of Barbados 1756–67.[3]

Henry Edmunds, D.C.L., Oriel Coll., Oxford; (C; A); c.36; s. John E., of Llandegay, co. Caernarvon, gent.; Register 1744–6; d. 10 June 1746.[4]

14 July Robert Chapman, D.C.L., University Coll., Oxford; (C; A); c.32; s. William C., of Croydon, co. Surrey, gent.; Register 1747; Librarian 1748–9; Treasurer 1750–1; d. 3 July 1753.

1737
1 Dec. Arthur Collier, D.C.L., Trinity Coll., Oxford; (C; A); c.30; s. Arthur C., Rector of Steeple Langford, co. Wilts.; d. 23 May 1777.[5]

---

[1]When the baronetcy, to which he would have succeeded if still living, became extinct.
[2]M.I. Christ Church.
[3]d. 24 Nov. 1788 (M.I. Walton, co. Buckingham).
[4]M.I. Oriel College Chapel. Al. Ox. misattributes Edmunds's doctorate to a namesake.
[5]M.I.

1739
10 July *Robert Dale*, LL.D., Trinity Hall, Cambridge; (C; A); b. Whippingham, I.O.W.; Register 1748–9; elected Librarian 1750, but declined the office on account of his necessary absence;[1] retired or d. by 22 June 1768 [2]

1740
23 Oct *Thomas Salusbury*, LL.D., Trinity Hall, Cambridge; (C; A); *c*.29; s. Thomas S., of Bach-y-Craig in Dymeirchion, co. Flint; m. Anna Maria, d. of Sir Henry Penrice, LL.D. (q.v.); Librarian 1750–1; Judge of the Court of Admiralty 1751; ktd. 18 Nov. 1751; Treasurer 1752–3; d. 28 Oct. 1773.[3]

12 Nov. *Joseph Smith*, D.C.L., Queen's Coll., Oxford; (C; A); *c*.30; s. Joseph S., D.D., Provost of Queen's; retired by 22 June 1768.[4]

1 Dec. *William Wall*, D.C.L., Christ Church, Oxford; (C; A); *c*.35; retired Hilary 1774.[5]

1742
15 Feb. *John Taylor* LL.D., St. John's Coll., Cambridge, from Shrewsbury Sch.; (C; A); *c*.37; s. John T., of Shrewsbury, co. Salop, barber-surgeon; ordained 1747;[6] *D.N.B.*

23 Oct. *George Hay*, D.C.L., St. John's Coll., Oxford, from Merchant Taylors' Sch.; (C; A); 28; s. John H., Rector of St. Stephen Coleman Street, London; Register 1750–1; Librarian 1752–3; Treasurer 1754–6; King's Advocate 1755– May 1756, Nov. 1756–64; President 1764; ktd. 11 Nov. 1773; committed suicide 6 Oct. 1778; *D.N.B.*

23 Oct. *Robert Jenner*, D.C.L., Trinity Coll., Oxford; (C; A); *c*.28; s. John J. of Fetcham, co. Surrey, gent; Register 1752–3; d. by 28 July 1767.[7]

1743
3 Nov. *Andrew Coltee Ducarel*, D.C.L., St. John's Coll., Oxford, from Eton Coll.; (C; A); *c*.29; s. James D. of Greenwich, co. Kent, esq.; Librarian 1754–6; Treasurer 1757–60; d. 29 May 1785; *D.N.B.*

[1] L.B., f.268ᵛ.   [3] Not named in Charter.
[2] M.I. Offley, co. Hertford.
[4] d. 15 Oct. 1776.
[5] d. 11 Nov. 1791.
[6] d. 4 Apr. 1766.
[7] Will V.C.C. Oxford.

1745

4 Nov. *Richard Smalbroke*, D.C.L. All Souls Coll., Oxford; (C; A); *c*.29; s. Richard S., Bishop of Lichfield and Coventry; Register 1754–6; Librarian 1757–60; Treasurer 1761–2; retired by 22 June 1768.

1746

3 Nov. *Dennis Clarke*, LL.D., Trinity Hall, Cambridge, from Westminster Sch., stud. M.T. and G.I.; (C; A); *c*.29; s. John C., of Barking, co. Essex, esq.; Register 1757–60; Librarian 1761–2; Treasurer 1763–4; d. 6 Nov. 1776.

1748

4 Feb. *Francis Topham*, LL.D., Sidney Sussex Coll., Cambridge, from Richmond Sch., advocate of the Chancery Court of York; (C; A); *c*.35; s. Edward T., of Cowton Grange, Richmond, co. York; retired by 22 June 1768.[1]

1749

23 Oct. *John Bettesworth*, D.C.L., Christ Church, Oxford; (C; A); *c*.28; s. John B., LL.D. (q.v.); Register 1761–2; Librarian 1763–4; Treasurer 1765–6; d. 26 Sept. 1779.

1750

23 Oct. *George Harris*, D.C.L., Oriel Coll., Oxford, from Westminster Sch.; (C; A); *c* 28; s. John H., Bishop of Llandaff; Register 1763–4; Librarian 1765–6; Treasurer 1767–70, 1781–2; gave £500 to Doctors' Commons; d. 19 Apr. 1796;[2] *D.N.B.*

1754

4 Nov. *William Macham*, D.C.L., *fellow of St. John's Coll., Oxford*, from Merchant Taylors' Sch.; (C; A); 31; o.s. Joseph M., of Collingbourne Kingston, co. Wilts., Surveyor of the King's Warehouse in the Port of London; did not practise.[3] Register 1765–6; Librarian 1767–70; Treasurer 1771–2; d. 26 Aug. 1789.

1757

3 Nov. *Peter Calvert*, LL.D., *fellow of Trinity Hall, Cambridge*; stud. L.I.; (C; A); s. Peter C., of Hunsdon, co. Hertford; Register 1767–70; Librarian 1771–2; Treasurer 1773–4; President 17 Oct. 1778; d. 13 Aug. 1788.

[1] d. 17 Oct. 1770. [2] M.I.
[3] 'The fortune which he inherited rendered the pursuit of professional emolument unnecessary' (Coote, p. 123).

1757

3 Nov. *William Wynne*, LL.D., *fellow of Trinity Hall, Cambridge*; (C; A); *c* 29; s. John W., Bishop of Bath and Wells; Register 1771–2; Librarian 1773–4; Treasurer 1775–8; King's Advocate 1778–88; President 22 Aug. 1788; ktd. 24 Sept. 1788; Master of Trinity Hall 12 Apr. 1803; d. 11 Dec. 1815.[1]

James Marriott, LL.D., *fellow of Trinity Hall, Cambridge*; (C; A); *c*.27; s. Benjamin M., of Hatton Garden, London, attorney; King's Advocate 1764–78; Master of Trinity Hall 10 June 1764; Librarian 1775–8; Judge of the Court of Admiralty 1778–99; Treasurer 1779–80; d. 21 Mar. 1803; *D.N.B.*

1758

3 Nov. *Francis Simpson*, LL.D., *fellow of Trinity Hall, Cambridge*; (C; A); *c*.30; nephew of Sir Edward S., LL.D. (q.v.); Librarian 1781; d. 11 Nov. 1781.

21 Nov. *Thomas Bever*, D.C.L., *fellow of All Souls Coll., Oxford*; (C; A); *c*.32; s. Thomas B., of Stratfield Mortimer, co. Berks., gent.; Librarian 1779–80; d. 8 Nov. 1791; *D.N.B.*

1759

26 June *William Spry*, D.C.L., *Christ Church, Oxford;* (C; A); *c* 29; s. John S., B.D., Archdeacon of Berks; Judge of the Admiralty for the American Colonies;[2] Governor of Barbados 1767.[3]

1760

3 Nov. *William Burrell*, LL.D., *St. John's Coll., Cambridge*, from Westminster Sch.; (C; A); *c*.27, 3 s. Peter B., of Langley Park, Beckenham, co. Kent, esq.; retired Trinity 1774;[4] *D.N.B.*

1763

3 Nov. *Claude Chamption Crespigny*, LL.D., *fellow of Trinity Hall, Cambridge*; (C; A); 30; 1 s. Philip Champion C., of Camberwell, co. Surrey, proctor; retired Hilary 1771.[5]

[1]M.I. His executors were asked to permit the Society 'to attend his remains to the Grave' (L.B., f.360).

[2]Coote, p. 126.

[3]d. 3 Sept. 1772.

[4]Succeeded by special remainder to the baronetcy of his father-in-law, Sir Charles Raymond, 24 Aug. 1788; d. 20 Jan. 1796.

[5]Created a baronet 31 Oct. 1805; d. 28 Jan. 1818.

1763

3 Nov. *William Compton*, LL.D., *fellow of Gonville and Caius Coll.,*
Cambridge, from Cheam Sch., stud. I.T.; (C; A); *c.*30; 1
s. Edward C., of Argyle Buildings, London, esq.;
Librarian 1781–2; Treasurer 1783–4; retired Trinity
1793.[1]

1771

4 Nov. *John Loveday,* D.C.L., *Magdalen Coll., Oxford,* from
Reading Sch.; (C; A); *c.*28; s. John L., of Caversham,
co. Oxford, esq.; ceased to practise on marrying his
ward 1777;[2] *D.N.B.*

1772

12 Nov. *Denham Skeet,* D.C.L., *Balliol Coll., Oxford*; (C; A); *c.*30;
s. Denham S., of Whitechapel, co. Middlesex, gent.;
retired Trinity 1779.

1779

3 Nov. *William Scott,* D.C.L., *fellow of University Coll., Oxford,*
from Royal Grammar Sch., Newcastle upon Tyne, stud.
M.T.; (C; A); *c.*33; 1 s. William S., of Newcastle upon
Tyne, co. Northumberland, coal fitter; Librarian 1783–4;
Treasurer 1785–6; King's Advocate 1788–98; ktd. 24
Sept. 1788; Judge of the Court of Admiralty 26 Oct.
1798–1828; cr. Lord Stowell 19 July 1821;[3] retired 1828;[4]
D.N.B.

12 Nov. *David Stevenson,* LL.D., *fellow of King's Coll., Cambridge,*
from Eton Coll.; (C);[5] *c.*37; s. David S., of Beaconsfield,
co. Buckingham; retired Michaelmas 1791.

1780

12 Nov. *John Fisher,* LL.D., *fellow of Christ's Coll., Cambridge,*
from Ashford (Kent) Sch.; (C; A); *c.*31; s. John F., of
Cambridge, draper; Librarian 1785–6; Treasurer 1787–8;
d. 1814.

1785

3 Nov. *William Battine,* LL.D., *Trinity Hall, Cambridge,* from
Eton Coll., stud. M.T.; (C; A); 29 1 s. William B., of

---

[1]d. 3 July 1824.
[2]d. 4 Mar. 1809.
[3]The only peerage conferred on a member. The Society presented an address to
Lord Stowell on his elevation (L.B., f.366).
[4]d. 28 Jan. 1836.
[5]The space left for his advocate's subscription is unfilled.

1785

East Marden, co. Sussex; Librarian 1787–8; Treasurer 1789–90; retired Hilary 1829;[1] *D.N.B.*
John Nicholl, D.C.L., *fellow of St. John's Coll., Oxford*, from Cowbridge Sch. and Bristol Sch.; (C; A); 26, 2 s. John N., of Llanmaes, co. Glamorgan, gent.; Librarian 1789–90; Treasurer 1791–2; King's Advocate 1798–1809; ktd. 31 Oct 1798 President 1809; res. 1834;[2] *D.N.B., D.W.B.*

1787

3 Nov. *James Henry Arnold*, D.C.L., *Trinity Coll., Oxford*; (C; A); 29; s. Henry A., of Wells, co. Somerset, D.D.; Librarian 1791–2; Treasurer 1793–5; resignation accepted 20 Jan. 1835.[3]

1788

3 Nov. *French Laurence*, D.C.L., *Corpus Christi Coll., Oxford*, from Winchester Coll., stud. M.T.; (C; A); 31; s. Richard L., of Bath, co. Somerset, watchmaker; Librarian 1793–5; Treasurer 1796–7; d. 27 Feb. 1809; *D.N.B.*

1789

3 Nov. *Scrope Bernard*, D.C.L., *Christ Church, Oxford*; (C; A); *c.*31; 3 s. Sir Francis B., of Nether Winchendon and Kimble, co. Buckingham, bt.; retired Michaelmas 1801.[4]
Maurcice Swabey, D.C.L., *Pembroke Coll., Oxford*, from Westminster Sch., formerly a proctor (adm. 1777); (C; A); 36; s. Samuel S., of Langley, co. Buckingham, esq.; Librarian 1796–7; Treasurer 1798–9; d. 10 Feb. 1826.
Charles Coote, D.C.L., *Pembroke Coll., Oxford*, from St. Paul's Sch.; (C; A); *c.*28; s. John C., of Paternoster Row, London, bookseller; Librarian 1798–9; Treasurer 1800–2; d. 19 Nov. 1833.[5]

1790

3 Nov. *Thomas Champion Crespigny*, LL.D., *Trinity Hall, Cambridge*; (C; A); 2 s. Philip C., of Aldeburgh, co. Suffolk, proctor, and nephew of Claude C.C., LL.D. (q.v.); d. 2 Aug. 1799.

[1]Owed 76 terms' Commons at Hilary 1819, paid nothing thereafter; d. 5 Sept. 1836.
[2]d. 26 Aug. 1838.   [3]M.B., s.d., d. 10 Jan. 1836.
[4]Assumed the name of Morland after Bernard by Royal Licence 15 Feb. 1811; succeeded to baronetcy 1 July 1818; d. 18 Apr. 1830.
[5]His son, Henry Charles Coote, adm. a proctor 1838.

1792

3 Nov. *Samuel Pearce* Tregear *Parson, LL.D., Corpus Christi Coll., Cambridge,* from Clapham Sch., stud. M.T.; (C; A); *c.*27; s. John P., of St. James, Clerkenwell, co. Middlesex, M.D.; Librarian 1800–1; Treasurer 1802–3; d. 2 Feb. 1819.

1795

3 Nov. *John Sewell,* D.C.L., *Pembroke Coll., Oxford;* (C; A); *c.*29; s. Joseph S., of Limehouse, co. Middlesex, gent.; Librarian 1802–3; Judge of the Vice-Admiralty Court in Malta 1803; ktd. 25 May 1815; d. 15 Jan. 1833.

1796

3 Nov. *Christopher Robinson,* D.C.L., *Magdalen Coll., Oxford,* from Charterhouse; (C; A); 30; s. Christopher R., D.D., Rector of Albury, co. Oxford; Treasurer 1804–5; King's Advocate 1809–28; ktd. 6 Feb. 1809; Judge of the Court of Admiralty 1828; d. 22 Apr. 1833;[1] *D.N.B.*

6 July *William Territt,* LL.D., *Trinity Hall, Cambridge,* from Hertford Sch., barr. I.T.; (C; A); *c.*28; 1 s. William T., of Kensington, co. Middlesex; Judge of the Vice-Admiralty Court in Bermuda by 1803; retired Trinity 1829.[2]

1797

3 Nov. *Alexander Croke,* D.C.L., *Oriel Coll., Oxford,* from a private school at Burton, co. Buckingham, barr. I.T.; (C; A); 29; o.s. Alexander C., of Studley Priory, co. Buckingham; Judge of the Vice-Admiralty Court at Halifax, Nova Scotia 1801–15; ktd. 5 July 1816; retired Trinity 1829;[3] *D.N.B.*

1799

4 Nov. *William Adams,* LL.D., *Trinity Hall, Cambridge,* from Tonbridge Sch.; (C; A); 27; 5 s. Patience Thomas A., Filacer of the Court of King's Bench; Librarian 1804–5; Treasurer 1806–7; retired owing to ill health; resignation accepted 10 Nov. 1825;[4] *D.N.B.*

George Ogilvie, D.C.L., *St. Mary Hall, Oxford;* (C; A 9

---

[1] M.I.
[2] d. 11 Aug. 1836.
[3] d. 27 Dec. 1842.
[4] L.B., f.369ᵛ.; d. 11 June 1851.

1799
> July 1800); *c.*30; s. Maj.-Gen. George O., of Swanning-
> ton Hall, co. Norfolk;[1] Librarian 1806–7; Treasurer
> 1808–9; retired Michaelmas 1819.

1801
3 Nov. *Sherrard Beaumont Burnaby*, LL.D., *fellow of Pembroke Hall,
Cambridge,* from Charterhouse; (C; A); 26; s. Andrew
B., D.D., Archdeacon of Leicester; Librarian 1808–9;
Treasurer 1810–11; d. 25 Mar. 1849.[2]

1802
3 Nov. *John Stoddart,* D.C.L. *Christ Church, Oxford,* from Salisbury Grammar Sch.; (C; A); 29;s. John S., of Westminster, Lieut. R.N.; King's Advocate in Malta 1803–7;
Librarian 1810–11; Treasurer 1812–13; Judge of the
Vice-Admiralty Court in Malta 1826–40; ktd. 27 July
1826; retired Trinity 1829;[3] *D.N.B.*

1803
6 July *Herbert Jenner,* LL.D., *Trinity Hall, Cambridge,* from
Reading Sch., barr. G.I.; (C; A); 25; 2 s. Robert J., of
Chiselhurst, co. Kent, proctor; Librarian 1812–13;
Treasurer 1814–15; King's Advocate 1828–34; ktd.
28 June (?Feb.) 1828; President 1834; assumed the
surname of Jenner-Fust 18 Feb. 1843; d. 20 Feb. 1852;
D.N.B.

3 Nov. *John Daubeney,* D.C.L., *Merton Coll., Oxford,* from Winchester Coll.; (C; A); 27; 1 s. John D., of Bristol, esq.;
Librarian 1814–15; Treasurer 1816–17; d. 16 Feb. 1847.[4]

1804
3 Nov. *John Woodfield Compton,* D.C.L., *St. Mary Hall, Oxford;*
(C; A); *c.* 31; s. Thomas C., of Clapton, co. Middlesex,
esq.; Judge of the Vice-Admiralty Court in Barbados;
ktd. 5 July 1816; d. 9 July 1821.

21 Nov. *Joseph Phillimore,* D.C.L., *Christ Church, Oxford;* from
Westminster Sch.; (C; A); 29; 1 s. Joseph P., Vicar of
Orton-on-the-Hill, co. Leicester; Librarian 1816–17;
Treasurer 1818–20; d. 24 Feb. 1855; *D.N.B.*

[1]Coote, p. 139, states that Dr. Ogilvie was heir-presumptive to the earldoms of
Finlater and Seafield, but this seems to have been incorrect.
[2]M.I.
[3]d. 16 Feb. 1856.
[4]M.I.

1805

4 Nov. *Thomas Edwards*, LL.D., *Trinity Hall, Cambridge*; (C; A); *c*.30; s. Thomas E., Master of Chelsea Academy; retired Easter 1815;[1] *D.N.B.*

1807

n.d. William Wellwood Moncrieff, D.C.L., Balliol Coll., Oxford; warrant for admission to Arches 12 July 1803, but went abroad immediately;[2] adm. Arches 17 Nov. 1807; arms in Court Room;[3] *c*.31; s. Henry M., of Cavil, co. Fife, soi-distant baronet; d. 5 Sept. 1813.

1808

7 July *Augustus Gostling*, LL.D., *Trinity Hall, Cambridge*; (C; A); *c*.25; s. George G., King's Proctor in the Court of Admiralty; Librarian 1818–20; Treasurer 1821; not intending to return to practice, continued a member at half fees 22 July 1842; d. 12 Mar. 1849.

3 Nov. *Stephen Lushington*, D.C.L., *All Souls Coll.*, Oxford, from Eton Coll., barr. I.T.; (C; A); 26; 2 s. Sir Stephen L., of Marylebone, co. Middlesex, bt., proctor; Librarian 1821; Treasurer 1822–3; Judge of the Court of Admiralty 1838–67; President 1858; res. 1867;[4] *D.N.B.*

Hon. William Herbert, D.C.L., Merton Coll., Oxford; adm. Arches 24 Oct. 1808; arms in Court Room;[5] 30; 3 s. Henry, Earl of Carnarvon; ordained; resignation accepted 24 May 1814;[6] *D.N.B.*

John Dodson, D.C.L., *Oriel Coll., Oxford*, from Merchant Taylors Sch., barr. M.T.; (C; A); 28; s. John D., D.D., Rector of Hurstpierpoint, co. Sussex; Librarian 1822–3; Treasurer 1824–5; King's Advocate 1834–52; ktd. 29 Oct. 1834; President 1852; d. 27 Apr. 1858; *D.N.B.*

1809

n.d. Charles Gostling Townley, D.C.L., Merton Coll., Oxford, stud. L.I.; adm. Arches 27 Oct. 1809; arms in

---

[1] d. 20 Oct. 1845.   [2] L.P.L., Arches VB1/13, p. 163.

[3] Hemp, p. 75. Although the arms were dated 1807, Coote, whose preface is dated 31 Dec. 1803, states (p. 140) that Moncrieff, who had accompanied 'the new judge' (i.e. Dr. Sewell) to Malta, had been 'gratified with the transmission of an order to that island for his solemn adoption into our chartered fraternity'.

[4] d. 19 Jan. 1873.

[5] Hemp, p. 75. Spaces left for his subscriptions between those of Dr. Lushington and Dr. Dodson, both of whom signed on 3 Nov. 1808.

[6] L.B., f.358; d. 28 May 1847.

1809

n.d. Court Room;[1] 28; s. James T., of St. Benet Paul's Wharf, London, proctor; ordained; resigned between 22 Jan. and 24 May 1814.[2]

1810

n.d. Richard Henry Cresswell, D.C.L., Trinity Coll., Oxford, from Winchester Coll., barr. L.I.; adm. Arches 1 July 1810; arms painted for Court Room 9 July 1810;[3] 28; s. Richard Cheslyn C., of London, proctor; bur. 12 Sept. 1818.

1811

4 July *Samuel Rush Meyrick*, D.C.L., *Queen's Coll., Oxford*; (C; A); 27; s. John M., of St. Margaret's, Westminster, esq.; resignation accepted 18 Feb. 1824;[4] *D.N.B., D.W.B.*

3 Nov. *Jesse Addams*, D.C.L., *St. John's Coll., Oxford*, from Merchant Taylors Sch.; (C; A); 28; s. Richard A., of Rotherhithe, co. Surrey, ship-builder; Librarian 1824–5; Treasurer 1826–7; d. 25 May 1871.

1815

n.d. Richard Berens, D.C.L., All Souls Coll., Oxford; adm. Arches 8 June 1815; arms in Court Room;[5] *c.*33: s. Joseph B., of Sutton-at-Hone, co. Kent, esq.; resignation accepted 6 July 1825.[6]

1816

4 Nov. *John Lee*, LL.D., *St. John's Coll., Cambridge*, from Mackworth Sch.; (C; A); 33; 1 s. John Fiott, of London, merchant; changed name to Lee 1815; Librarian 1826–8; Treasurer 1828–9; d. 25 Feb. 1866; *D.N.B.*

1817

3 Nov. *Thomas Blake*, LL.D., *fellow of Trinity Hall, Cambridge*; (C; A); 27; 1 s. Thomas B., of Norwich, co. Norfolk, barrister; Librarian 1829–30; Treasurer 1831–2; d. by 11 June 1871.[7]

[1]Hemp, p. 76. Spaces left for subscriptions in S.B.
[2]L.B., f. 357ᵛ.
[3]MS. Work-book of Thomas Sharp, herald painter, *penes* G. D. Squibb. Spaces left for subscriptions in S.B.
[4]L.B., f.368ᵛ. Ktd. 22 Feb. 1832; d. 2 Apr. 1848.
[5]Hemp, p. 77. Undated and unsigned subscription at S.B., f. 64ᵛ., and space left for subscription at f.126ᵛ.
[6]L.B., f.369ᵛ.; d. 13 June 1849.
[7]When E. A. Beck was adm. fellow of Trinity Hall in his place.

1818

3 Nov. *John Haggard*, LL.D., *fellow of Trinity Hall, Cambridge,* from Westminster Sch., stud. L.I.; (C; A); 24; 3 s. William Henry H., of Knebworth Place, co. Hertford, esq.; Librarian 1831–2; Treasurer 1832–3; d. 31 Oct. 1856; *D.N.B.*

1820

3 Nov. *George Matcham*, LL.D., *St. John's Coll., Cambridge;* (C; A); 31; 1 s. George M., of Ashfold Lodge in Slaugham, co. Sussex, esq.; retired from practice 1830; resignation accepted 20 Jan. 1835;[1] *D.N.B.*

1822

4 Nov. *John Trenchard Pickard*, D.C.L., *New Coll., Oxford,* from Winchester Coll.; (C; A); 30; 3 s. George P., Rector of Warmwell, co. Dorset; retired Michaelmas 1835.[2]

1824

n.d. Henry Vanne Salusbury, LL.D., fellow of Trinity Hall, Cambridge, from Rugby Sch., stud. I.T.; adm. Arches 9 July 1824; arms in Court Room;[3] 27; 3 s. Sir Robert S., of Llanwern, co. Monmouth, bt.; desired to withdraw on account of continued ill health 11 Nov. 1830.[4]

1826

3 Nov. *John Nicholl*, D.C.L., *Christ Church, Oxford,* from Westminster Sch., barr. L.I.; (C; A); 29; s. Sir John N., kt., D.C.L. (q.v.); Librarian 1833–4; Treasurer 1834–5; d. 27 Jan. 1853; *D.W.B.*

James Chapman, D.C.L., *Christ Church Oxford,* stud. L.I.; (C; A); *c.*28; s. James C., of London, esq.; retired Easter 1843. *William Calverley Curteis*, LL.D., *Trinity Hall, Cambridge,* from Shrewsbury Sch.; (C; A); 28; s. Revd. Samuel C., LL.D., Master of Sunbury Sch., co. Middlesex; Librarian 1835; Treasurer 1836–7; retired 1858.[5]

1830

3 Nov. *William Robinson*, D.C.L., *Balliol Coll., Oxford,* from Charterhouse; (C; A); 29; s. Sir Christopher R., kt., D.C.L. (q.v.); Librarian 1836–7; Treasurer 1838–9; d. 11 July 1870.

[1] M.B., s.d.; d. 15 Jan. 1877.
[2] Assumed the name of Trenchard by Royal Licence 1840; d. 19 Dec. 1875.
[3] Hemp, p. 76. Spaces left for subscriptions in S.B.
[4] L.P.L., DC 2; d. 17 Dec. 1830.   [5] d. 4 Oct. 1894.

1833

n.d. Sir Daniel Keyte Sandford, kt., D.C.L., Christ Church, Oxford, from Edinburgh High Sch.[1] *c.*34; 2 s. Daniel S., D.D., Bishop of Edinburgh; d. 4 Feb. 1838; *D.N.B.*

1835

2 Nov. Herbert Jenner, LL.D., *formerly fellow of Trinity Hall, Cambridge*, from Eton Coll., barr. L.I.; (C; A); 29; 1 s. Sir Herbert J., kt., LL.D. (q.v.); Steward 1837; Librarian 1838–9; Treasurer 1840–1; assumed the additional surname of Fust 14 Jan. 1842; d. 30 July 1904; *D.N.B.*

1836

2 Nov. John Elliott Pasley Robertson, D.C.L., *Magdalen Hall, Oxford*; (C; A); *c.*31; 1 s. Robert R., of Greenwich, co. Kent, 'doctor'; Steward 1838–9; Librarian 1840–1; Treasurer 1842–6; d. 27 Feb. 1886.

1837

2 Nov. Frederick Thomas Pratt, D.C.L., *St. John's Coll., Oxford*, stud. G.I.; (C; A); *c.*38; 3 s. John P., of Lambeth, co. Surrey, gent.; Steward 1840–1; Librarian 1842–3; Treasurer 1847–9; d. 13 Apr. 1868.

John Dorney Harding, D.C.L., *Oriel Coll., Oxford*, from Charterhouse, barr. I.T.; (C; A); *c.*28; 1 s. John H., Rector of Coyty, co. Glamorgan; Steward 1842–3; Librarian 1844–6; Queen's Advocate 1852–62; ktd. 24 Mar. 1852; d. 24 Nov. 1868.

1839

2 Nov. *Augustus Frederick Bayford*, LL.D., *Trinity Hall, Cambridge*, from Kensington Grammar Sch., stud. M.T.; (C; A); 30; 2 s. John B., of Doctors' Commons, proctor; Steward 1844–6; Librarian 1848–9; Treasurer 1850; d. 11 May 1874.

Robert Joseph Phillimore, D.C.L., *Christ Church, Oxford*, from Westminster Sch., stud. M.T.; (C; A); 28, 2 s. Joseph P., D.C.L. (q.v.); Steward 1847–9; Librarian 1850, 1853; Treasurer 1851–2; Queen's Advocate 1862–7; ktd. 17 Sept. 1862; President 1 Aug. 1867; res. 1875;[2] *D.N.B.*

James Parker Deane, D.C.L., *St. John's Coll., Oxford*, from

---

[1]Spaces left for subscriptions in S.B.
[2]Created a baronet 21 Dec. 1881; d. 4 Feb. 1885.

1839

2 Nov. Winchester Coll., stud. M.T.; (C; A); 27; 2 s. Henry Boyle D., of Hurst Grove, co. Berks, gent.; Steward 1850; Librarian 1851–2; Treasurer 1853–5; ktd. 1 Aug. 1885; d. 3 Jan. 1902; *D.N.B.*

Howard Elphinstone, D.C.L., *Merton Coll., Oxford*, stud. L.I.; (C; A); 35; 1 s. Sir Howard E., of Stoke Damerel, co. Devon, bt.; succeeded to baronetcy and retired from practice 28 Apr. 1846.[1]

Alfred Waddilove, D.C.L., *Trinity Coll., Oxford*, from Westminster Sch., stud. I.T.; (C; A); 33; 4 s. John W., of Thorpe, co. York, esq.; Steward 1851–6; Treasurer 1856–60; d. 8 July 1890.

1840

2 Nov. *William Frederick White*, D.C.L., *Trinity Coll., Oxford*, from Charterhouse, barr. I.T.; (C; A); *c.*28, o.s. Lt.-Gen. Frederick Courtland W., of Bath, co. Somerset; d. 3 July 1847.

1841

2 Nov. *Travers Twiss*, D.C.L., *fellow of University Coll.*, Oxford, barr. L.I.; (C; A); 32; 1 s. Revd. Robert T., LL.D., of St. George's, London (unbeneficed); Librarian 1854–9; Treasurer 1860–1; Queen's Advocate 1867; ktd. 4 Nov. 1867; resigned his offices and ceased to practise 21 Mar. 1872;[2] *D.N.B.*

Henry Iltyd Nicholl, D.C.L., *St. John's Coll., Oxford*, barr. I.T.; (C; A); *c.*32; 1 s. Iltyd N., of St. Benet Paul's Wharf, London, proctor; d. 24 Nov. 1845.

1846

12 Jan. Hon. *Richard Edward Howard*, D.C.L., *All Souls Coll.*, barr. M.T.; (C; A); 32; 3 s. Thomas, Earl of Suffolk; d. 27 Feb. 1873.

2 Nov. *William Francis Dodson*, LL.D., *Trinity Hall, Cambridge*, from Westminster Sch., stud. I.T.; (C; A); 31; 1 s. William D., Rector of Well-cum-Claxby, co. Lincoln; Steward 1859–60; d. 19 Nov. 1890.

1847

2 Nov. *Fetherston Stonestreet*, LL.D., *St. John's Coll., Cambridge*,

[1] d. 16 Mar. 1893.
[2] d. 14 Jan. 1897.

1847
2 Nov. from Eton Coll., barr. L.I.; (C; A); *c*.28; o.s. George Griffin S., Prebendary of Lincoln; d. 30 Sept. 1901.

1849
2 Nov. *Thomas Spinks*, D.C.L., *St. John's Coll., Oxford*, from Merchant Taylors' Sch.; (C; A); 30; 2 s. William S., of Kennington, co. Surrey, gent.; Librarian 1860–1; Treasurer 1862–3; d. 14 Jan. 1899.
John George Middleton, LL.D., *St. John's Coll., Cambridge*, from Eton Coll.; (C; A); 32; s. Admiral Robert Gambier M.; Steward 1860–78; d. 6 Mar. 1878.

1850
12 Nov. *Maurice Charles Swabey*, D.C.L., *Christ Church, Oxford*, from Westminster Sch., barr. G.I.; (C; A); 29; 1 s. Maurice S., of Bloomsbury, London, police magistrate and gds. Maurice S., D.C.L. (q.v.); mar. Mary Katherine, d. of John Haggard, LL.D. (q.v.); d. 1 Nov. 1883.
George Edward Hughes, D.C.L., *Oriel Coll., Oxford*, stud. L.I.; (C; A); *c.* 8; 1 s. John H., of Uffington, co. Berks., esq.; d. 2 May 1872.

1852
15 Apr. *Samuel Jewkes Wambey*, D.C.L., *St. Mary Hall, Oxford*; (C; A); *c.*31; 1 s. Samuel W., of St. John's, Worcester, gent.; d. 20 May 1867.
2 Nov. *George Webbe Dasent*, D.C.L., *Magdalen Hall, Oxford*, from Westminster Sch., barr. M.T.; (C; A); 35; 3 s. John Roche D., Attorney-General of St. Vincent; ktd. 27 June 1876; d. 11 June 1896; *D.N.B.*

1855
2 Nov. *Thomas Hutchinson Tristram*, D.C.L., *Lincoln Coll., Oxford*, from Durham Sch.; (C; A); 30; 2 s. Henry Baker T., Vicar of Eglingham, co. Northumberland; d. 8 Mar. 1912, the last surviving member of Doctors' Commons.

APPENDIX IV

CIVILIAN JUDGES AND ADVOCATES NOT MENTIONED IN THE RECORDS OF DOCTORS' COMMONS

SINCE there are some advocates who do not appear in the part of the Subscription Book devoted to the subscriptions and whose membership of Doctors' Commons is known only from casual entries elsewhere in the Subscription Book or in the other records of the Society, it is possible that there were other members of whose membership no record has survived. On the other hand, the fact that many advocates joined the Society long after admission to the Court of Arches, makes it probable that there were others who never joined. It is, therefore, likely that most, if not all, of the advocates not mentioned in the records of the Society are not mentioned because they were not members.

John Yonge, D.C.L., Ferrara, from New Coll., Oxford, and Winchester Coll., Judge of P.C.C. 1503, Master of the Rolls 1508; b. *c*.1467, Heyford, co. Oxford; d. 26 Apr. 1516;[1] *D.N.B.*

Richard Salter, D.Cn.L., All Souls Coll., Oxford, probably an advocate;[2] d. by 27 May 1519.[3]

Humphrey Hawarden, D.C.L., Oxford, Official Principal and Dean of the Arches 1504; d. by 7 Dec. 1515.[4]

Adam Facet, D.Cn.L. (*c*.1497), Cambridge, probably an advocate; d. by 29 Apr. 1513.[5]

John Kydwelly, D.C.L., All Souls Coll., Oxford; commissioner to hear an Admiralty appeal with Dr. Peter Potkyn (q.v.) 4 Nov. 1511;[6] d. by 8 Feb. 1514.[7]

---

[1] M.I., Rolls Chapel, London.

[2] Salter and the other men here so described are included in the list of officials of vacant sees in Churchill, ii. 245–72. Many of the doctors of law in that list were members of Doctors' Commons.

[3] Le Neve, x. 8.

[4] Will P.C.C. 9 Holder.

[5] Will P.C.C. 17 Fetiplace.

[6] *L. & P. Hen. VIII*, i. 292.

[7] Le Neve, ii. 40.

Richard Norton, D.Cn. & C.L., Oxford, probably an advocate; d. by 20 Feb. 1524.[1]

Robert Wotton, D.Cn.L., advocate; d. after 1530.[2]

Thomas Darbysshere, D.C.L., Broadgates Hall, Oxford, vicar-general of the Bishop of London, c. 28 July 1556;[3] deprived 23 Oct. 1559;[4] became a Jesuit.

William Coke, D.C.L., All Souls Coll., Oxford, Judge of the Court of High Commission, 1556.[5]

Thomas Lawes, LL.D. (1578), Corpus Christi Coll., Cambridge, Judge of the Court of High Commission, 1573, 1576;[6] b. c.1537; s. Thomas L., of Aylsham, co. Norfolk; d. 9 Aug. 1595.

Stephen Lake or Lakes, LL.D.King's Coll., Cambridge, from Eton Coll., adm. Arches 4 Apr. 1581;[7] 3 s. James L., of Smarden, co. Kent gent;[8] bur. St. Dunstan in the West, London 2 May 1617.

Giles Fletcher, LL.D., King's Coll., Cambridge, from Eton Coll.; adm. Arches 19 Apr. 1583; s. Richard F., Vicar of Bishop's Stortford, co. Hertford; d. 16 Feb. 1611; D.N.B.

William Wilkinson, LL.D., King's Coll., Cambridge; adm. Arches 12 Feb. 1590; b. co. York; d. by 13 Nov. 1613.[9]

John Estmond, D.C.L., New Coll., Oxford, from Winchester Coll.; adm. Arches 12 Feb. 1590; 2 s. Thomas E., of Chardstock, co. Devon; d. 17 Oct. 1604.[10]

William Gager, D.C.L., Christ Church, Oxford, from Westminster Sch.; adm. Arches 12 Feb. 1590; bur. 1 Sept. 1622 Cambridge All Saints; D.N.B.

Robert Redman, LL.D., St. John's Coll., Oxford; adm. Arches 24 May 1590; b. c.1550 Richmondshire, co. York; d. 5 Aug. 1625.[11]

Clement Colmore, D.C.L., Brasenose Coll., Oxford; adm. Arches 23 Nov. 1590; 2 s. William C., of Birmingham, co. Warwick, gent;[12] d. 18 June 1619.

[1]Le Neve, i. 412.
[2]C. L. Kingsford, The Gray Friars of London (British Soc. of Franciscan Studies, vi, 1915), p. 83.
[3]C.P.R. 1555–7, p. 25.   [4]Le Neve 1541–1857, i. 9.
[5]R. G. Usher, The Rise and Fall of the High Commission (Oxford, 1913), p. 348.
[6]Usher, op. cit., p. 354.
[7]This and the following admission dates are from Dr. Ducarel's notes from the registers of the Archbishops of Canterbury (L.P.L., MS. 1351).
[8]Vis London 1633, ii. 41.   [9]Will P.C.C. 110 Capell.
[10]M.I., Gressenhall, co. Norfolk, where he is described as a proctor.
[11]M.I. Heacham, co. Norfolk.   [12]Vis. Durham, p. 79.

Henry Hawkins, LL.D., Peterhouse, Cambridge; adm. Arches 14 May 1591; s. John H., of co. Essex; d. by 22 Jan. 1631.[1]

Arthur Blencowe, D.C.L., Provost of Oriel Coll., Oxford; adm. Arches 11 Nov. 1592; d. Jan. 1618.

Matthew Settell, LL.D., Corpus Christi Coll., Cambridge; adm. Arches 28 June 1595; b. co. York; d. 1597.[2]

Christopher Helme, D.C.L., Merton Coll., Oxford; adm. Arches 20 June 1595; b. co. Wilts., 'fil. pleb'; d. 1628.

Samuel Goodyear, LL.D., St. John's Coll., Cambridge; adm. Arches 21 June 1596; perhaps s. Leonard G. of Colchester, co. Essex; Dean of St. Asaph;[3] d. by 17 May 1625.[4]

John Seaman, LL.D., Queens' Coll., Cambridge, adm. Arches 21 June 1596; b. c.1564; s. John S., of Chelmsford, co. Essex, woollen-draper; d. 29 June 1623.[5]

Robert Newcomen, LL.D., Clare Coll., Cambridge; adm. Arches 27 Nov. 1599; o.s. Thomas N., of Ingoldmells, co. Lincoln;[6] bur. Cambridge St. Botolph 21 Feb. 1621.

John Weston, D.C.L., Christ Church, Oxford; adm. Arches 27 Nov. 1599; o.s. Robert W., D.C.L., Dean of the Arches; d. 20 July 1632.[7]

Evan Morris, D.C.L., All Souls Coll., Oxford; adm. Arches 27 Nov. 1599; b. co. Carmarthen; d. 1605.

Charles Bellasis, LL.D., Jesus Coll., Cambridge, from Newborough Sch.; adm. Arches 27 Nov. 1599; s. Sir William B., of Newborough, co. York, kt.; bur. Houghton-le-Spring, co. Durham 18 Aug. 1601.

Peter Withipoll, LL.D., Trinity Hall, Cambridge; adm. Arches 27 Nov. 1599; 8 s. Edmund W., of Ipswich, co. Suffolk, esq.[8]

Otwell Hill, LL.D., St. John's Coll., Cambridge; adm. Arches 27 Nov. 1599; b. c.1560; d. 19 May 1616.

Francis Covert, LL.D., Leyden (incorp D.C.L., Oxford); adm. Arches 27 Nov. 1599; d. 1609.

---

[1]Will P.C.C. 2 St. John.
[2]Will P.C.C. 29 Cobham.
[3]Not mentioned in Le Neve, but so described in his will.
[4]Will P.C.C. 55 Clarke.
[5]M.I. Painswick, co. Gloucester.
[6]*Lincs. Ped.* ii. 713.
[7]M.I. Christ Church.
[8]*Visitations of Suffolk made . . . 1564 . . . 1577 and . . . 1612* (Exeter, 1882), p. 82.

John Butts, LL.D., Trinity Hall, Cambridge; adm. Arches 27 Nov. 1599; d. by 27 Nov. 1615.[1]

James Bayly, D.C.L., All Souls Coll., Oxford; adm. Arches 27 Nov. 1599; d. by 19 Oct. 1614.[2]

John Burman, LL.D., Trinity Hall, Cambridge; adm. Arches 6 Feb. 1600, d. by 9 Dec. 1623.[3]

William Ingram, LL.D., Magdalene Coll., Cambridge; adm. Arches 16 June 1604; s. Hugh I., of London, merchant; d. 24 July 1623.

John Budden, D.C.L., Magdalen Coll., Oxford; adm. Arches 20 Feb. 1605; d. 11 June 1620.

John Tuer, LL.D., Cambridge, from Christ Church, Oxford, and Westminster Sch.; adm. Arches 2 June 1609; s. John T., of London; d. 18 Dec. 1621.[4]

Geoffrey Swalman, LL.D., Sidney Sussex Coll., Cambridge; adm. Arches 15 Nov. 1614; b. co. Kent; living 3 Sept. 1632.[5]

John Craddock, D.C.L., New Coll., Oxford, from Winchester Coll.; adm. Arches 4 Aug. 1619; b. c. 1573 Romsey, co. Southampton.

Jonathan Browne, D.C.L., Gloucester Hall, Oxford; adm. Arches c.1630; oc. Trinity Term 1639.[6]

John Levit, LL.D., Christ's Coll., Cambridge, from Conisborough and Houghton Schh.; adm. Arches c.1633, oc. Trinity Term 1639;[7] 3 s. Thomas L. of Melton, co. York.

James Littleton, D.C.L., All Souls Coll., Oxford; adm. Arches 23 Oct. 1637; b. c.1596; 3 s. Sir Edward L., of Henley, co. Salop, kt.,[8] d. 1645.

Oliver Lloyd, D.C.L., All Souls Coll., Oxford; adm. Arches 23 Oct. 1637; yr. s. David Ll., of Llanidloes, co. Montgomery; d. 17 Mar. 1662.

William Greene, LL.D., Magdalene Coll., Cambridge; adm. Arches 23 Oct. 1637; d. by 29 Oct. 1655.[9]

[1] Will P.C.C. 102 Rudd. Dr. Butts had a lease of chambers in Mountjoy House dated 20 March 1606 (All Souls Coll., MS. 325, App. G, p. 3).
[2] Will P.C.C. 102 Lawe.
[3] Will P.C.C. 127 Swann.
[4] Will Consistory Court of London, 91 Bellamy.
[5] C.S.P.D.1631–3, p. 410.
[6] Borthwick Inst. MS.R.VII PR. 108.
[7] Ibid.
[8] Wotton, ii. 61.
[9] Will P.C.C. 393 Aylett.

Gwilliams Roane, LL.D., Trinity Hall, Cambridge; adm. Arches 23 Oct. 1637; b. 1608; s. Anthony R., of Wellingborough, co. Northampton, gent.;[1] living *c*.1642.[2]

Samuel Gardner, D.C.L., New Coll., Oxford, from Winchester Coll.; adm. Arches 23 Oct. 1637; b. *c*.1591, Culworth, co. Northampton, 'fil. pleb.'; cousin of Dr. Hugh Barker (q.v.).

John Worsley, D.C.L., Christ Church, Oxford; adm. Arches 1637;[3] probably d. by 1639.[4]

William Childe, D.C.L., All Souls Coll., Oxford; adm. Arches 1637;[5] 3 s. William C., of Northwick, co. Worcester, gent;[6] ktd. 12 May 1661; bur. 6 May 1678.

John Rackster, LL.D., King's Coll., Cambridge; warrant for admission to Arches 24 Jan. 1640;[7] b. *c*. 1602, co. Worcester, 'cler. fil.'.

Matthew Nicholas, D.C.L., New Coll., Oxford, from Winchester Coll.; warrant for admission to Arches 24 Jan. 1640;[8] b. 26 Sept. 1594; 2 s. John N., of Winterbourne Earls, co. Wilts., gent.; d. 14 Aug. 1661;[9] *D.N.B.*

Walter Littleton, LL.D., St. John's Coll., Cambridge; warrant for admission to Arches 24 Jan. 1640;[10] 3 s. Sir Edward L., of Pillaton Hall, co. Stafford, kt;[11] ktd. 23 Feb. 1664; d. Dec. 1670.

John Norton, LL.D., Trinity Hall, Cambridge, from Leyden Univ. and Colchester Sch.; warrant for admission to Arches 24 Jun. 1640;[12] s. John N., of Colchester, co. Essex, esq.

William Stephens, D.C.L., Oxford; barr. M.T.; advocate in the Court of Probate *c*.1653;[13] d. 1658.

—— Jones, LL.D., or D.C.L.; advocate in the Court of Probate *c*.1653. Perhaps Gilbert J., D.C.L. (1628), All Souls Coll., Oxford.

—— Lake, LL.D. or D.C.L., advocate in the Court of Probate *c*.1653.

—— Bird, LL.D. or D.C.L.; advocate in the Court of Probate *c*.1653.

[1]*Middlesex Pedigrees*, p. 51.   [2]*C.S.P.D. 1641-3*, p. 423.
[3]P.R.O. SP 16/442/125.
[4]Name not included in list of advocates of this date (Borthwick Inst., MS. R.VII. Pr 108).
[5]P.R.O. SP 16/442/125.
[6]*Knights*, pp. 139-40; *Visitation of Worcestershire 1634* (Harl. Soc. xc, 1938), p. 21.
[7]P.R.O. SP 16/442/125.   [8]P.R.O., SP 16/442/125.
[9]*Vis. Wilts.*, p. 145.   [10]P.R.O., SP 16/442/125.
[11]Wotton, ii. 68.   [12]P.R.O., SP 16/442/125.
[13]B.L., MS. Hargrave 289, f.4. I am grateful to Dr. C. J. Kitching for this reference.

John Bond, LL.D. (1645–6), Master of Trinity Hall, Cambridge; advocate in the Court of Probate *c*.1653; b. 12 Apr. 1612, 1 s. Denis B., of Lutton in Steeple, co. Dorset, esq.; bur. Steeple 30 July 1676; *D.N.B.*

Thomas Burrell, LL.D., advocate in the Court of Probate, *c*.1653; bur. 16 Dec. 1689.

Herbert Pelham, D.C.L. (1639), Magdalen Coll., Oxford; advocate in the Court of Probate *c*.1653; b. *c*.1601; s. Sir William P., kt.; d. 19 Jan. 1671.

Thomas Jones, D.C.L. (1653), Merton Coll., Oxford; 'went to Doctors' Commons to gain practice in his faculty' *c*.1660, but failed 'because of his distemper',[1] b. *c*.1618, s. Edward J., of Nanteor, co. Glamorgan; d. of the plague in London 1665.

Kenelm Digby, D.C.L., All Souls Coll., Oxford, stud. G.I.; adm. Arches 26 May 1666; d. 5 Nov. 1688.

Robert Mossom. LL.D., Trinity Coll., Dublin, from Peterhouse, Cambridge; Master in Chancery in Ireland; adm. Arches 13 May 1672; probably s. Robert M., D.D., Bishop of Derry; d. 7 Feb. 1680.

John St. John, D.C.L., Lambeth; adm. Arches 25 Jan. 1681; ceased to practise *c*.1684.

Richard Hey, M.A., Sidney Sussex Coll., Cambridge; fiat for admission to Arches 7 Dec. 1778, but warrant not issued and so no admission;[2] b. 22 Aug. 1745; 4 s. Richard H., of Pudsey, co. York; LL.D., *per Lit. Reg.* 1779; d. 7 Dec. 1835; *D.N.B.*[3]

Charles Robert Prinsep, LL.D., St. John's Coll., Cambridge from Tonbridge Sch; adm. Arches 14 Dec. 1824; 2 s. John P., alderman and merchant of London; practised in India; d. 8 June 1864.

[1] *Ath. Oxon.* iii. 707. He had travelled in Italy with George, son of Sir Nathanial Brent, LL.D., Judge of the Commonwealth Court of Probate.

[2] L.P.L., Arches VB/1/11, p. 211.

[3] *Al. Cant.* and *D.N.B.* state that Hey was admitted into Doctors' Commons, but he is not mentioned in the Society's records.

APPENDIX V

THE ROYAL CHARTER

GEORGE THE THIRD, BY THE GRACE OF GOD, of Great Britain, France and Ireland, King, Defender of the Faith, &c. To ALL to whom these presents shall come, greeting; WHEREAS our trusty and well beloved GEORGE HAY, doctor of law, official principal and dean of the court of arches, and judge of the prerogative court of Canterbury: Sir THOMAS SALUSBURY, knight, doctor of law, judge of our high court of admiralty; JAMES MARRIOTT, our advocate general; ARTHUR COLLIER, WILLIAM WALL, ANDREW COLTEE DUCAREL, DENNIS CLARKE, JOHN BETTESWORTH, GEORGE HARRIS, WILLIAM MACHAM, PETER CALVERT, WILLIAM WYNNE, FRANCIS SIMPSON, THOMAS BEVER, WILLIAM BURRELL, CLAUDE CHAMPION CRESPIGNY, and WILLIAM COMPTON, doctors of law of the universities of Oxford or Cambridge, exercent in the ecclesiastical and admiralty courts, inhabiting the tenement late Mountjoy-House, commonly called Doctors Commons, situated in the parish of Saint Bennet Paul's Wharf, in our city of London, have, by their petition, humbly represented unto us, that they have devoted themselves to the study of the civil and canon law, and are either judges in the courts of his grace the Archbishop of Canterbury, or other Ecclesiastical courts, or of our high court of Admiralty, or admitted, by proper authority, to practice as advocates in our abovementioned courts; and that the petitioners have, for centuries past, been formed into a voluntary society, and lived together in one place, by means of which the business of the publick has been more commodiously carried on; and that they, for the better support of the said society, and for securing to themselves a fixed place of residence for the future, are desirous of becoming a body corporate; they therefore most humbly prayed, that we would be graciously pleased, by letters patent under our great seal of Great Britain, to incorporate them and their successors, by the name, stile and title of THE COLLEGE OF DOCTORS OF LAW, EXERCENT IN OUR ECCLESIASTICAL AND ADMI-

RALTY COURTS, agreeably to the heads thereunto annexed, most humbly submitted to us, and with such other powers, privileges, regulations, restrictions and provisions, as to us, in our great wisdom should seem meet; WE having taken the said petition into our royal consideration, and being willing to give all fitting encouragement to the said study, KNOW YE therefore, that we of our especial grace, certain knowledge and mere motion, HAVE granted, constituted, declared and appointed, and by these presents, for us, our heirs and successors, DO grant, constitute, declare and appoint, the said GEORGE HAY, Sir THOMAS SALUSBURY, JAMES MARRIOTT, ARTHUR COLLIER, WILLIAM WALL, ANDREW COLTEE DUCAREL, DENIS CLARKE, JOHN BETTESWORTH, GEORGE HARRIS, WILLIAM MACHAM, PETER CALVERT, WILLIAM WYNNE, FRANCIS SIMPSON, THOMAS BEVER, WILLIAM BURRELL, CLAUDE CHAMPION CRESPIGNY, and WILLIAM COMPTON, and their successors, shall be, and be called one body corporate in deed, and in name, by the name, stile and title of THE COLLEGE OF DOCTORS OF LAW, EXERCENT IN THE ECCLESIASTICAL AND ADMIRALTY COURTS, and them, by the name of THE COLLEGE OF DOCTORS OF LAW EXERCENT IN THE ECCLESIASTICAL AND ADMIRALTY COURTS, we do, for the purpose aforesaid, really and fully, for us, our heirs and successors, make, erect, create, ordain, constitute, establish, confirm and declare by these presents to be one body corporate and politick in deed and in name for ever; AND that the said college shall consist of a PRESIDENT; namely, the dean of the arches for the time being, and of such doctors of law of either of the universities of Oxford or Cambridge, who have been admitted advocates in pursuance of the rescript of the Archbishop of Canterbury, and who have been elected fellows of the said college in the manner hereafter mentioned; and shall by the said name and stile have perpetual succession; AND shall have and use a COMMON SEAL, which they may be at liberty, and are hereby enabled to alter and change as they shall hereafter find occasion, which seal shall be kept by the treasurer, who shall attend with it, or cause it to be attended with, at all meetings, where is shall be required; AND WE do hereby farther grant, that the said body politick and their successors shall, by the said name and stile, be enabled and rendered capable to sue and be sued, plead and be impleaded, answer and be answered unto, defend and be defended, in whatsoever courts and places, and before any judges or justices, or officers of us, our heirs and

15

successors, in all and singular actions, pleas, suits, plaints, matters and demands of what kind or quality soever they shall be, in the same manner and form, and as fully and amply as any of our subjects of this our realm of Great Britain may or can do, sue or be sued, plead or be impleaded, answer or be answered unto, defend or be defended; AND are hereby enabled to raise any sum or sums of money not exceeding *thirty thousand pounds*, and impowered to purchase, hold and enjoy in perpetuity or otherwise, for them and their successors, any books, manuscripts, goods, chattels, or any other thing whatsoever; AND ALSO to purchase, take, hold and enjoy in perpetuity or otherwise, any lands, tenements or hereditaments whatsoever, not exceeding the yearly value of *one thousand pounds* in the whole, to them and their successors, without incurring any of the penalties or forfeitures of the statutes of mortmain, or of any of them. AND that it shall and may be lawful for any body or bodies corporate, person or persons, to give, grant, bargain, demise, sell or convey any lands, tenements or hereditaments whatsoever, not exceeding the said value of *one thousand pounds* a year in the whole, to the said college, for the use and benefit of the said college and their successors, without licence of alienation in mortmain, and that it shall and may be lawful for them and their successors to aliene or raise money upon all or any part of their estates, at their pleasure; AND the said college shall govern themselves and all their proceedings and business according to the statutes, rules, orders and by-laws, to be made as herein after is mentioned; AND that our royal intention may take the better effect for the good government and regulation of the said college, we have nominated, and do hereby nominate, constitute and appoint the said doctor GEORGE HAY, official principal and dean of the court of arches, and judge of the prerogative court of Canterbury, to be the first and modern PRESIDENT of the said college; AND WE do hereby farther nominate and appoint the said Sir THOMAS SALUSBURY, JAMES MARRIOTT, ARTHUR COLLIER, WILLIAM WALL, ANDREW COLTEE DUCAREL, DENNIS CLARKE, JOHN BETTESWORTH, GEORGE HARRIS, WILLIAM MACHAM, PETER CALVERT, WILLIAM WYNNE, FRANCIS SIMPSON, THOMAS BEVER, WILLIAM BURRELL, CLAUDE CHAMPION CRESPIGNY, and WILLIAM COMPTON, to be, together with the said PRESIDENT, the first and modern members or fellows of the said college; AND it is OUR ROYAL WILL AND PLEASURE, that no person shall be qualified to be a candidate for admission as a fellow of this college, unless he shall have regularly taken the degree of doctor of law in one of the universities of Oxford or Cambridge, and also been duly admitted an advocate of the court of arches; and that such candidate shall not be admitted a fellow of the said college, hereby incorporated, unless a majority of the whole college are present, and a majority of those present concur in the election; WE WILL also, that, in the absence of the dean of the arches from any meeting, the doctor, who is the next in the ordinary course of precedence, which has been heretofore usually observed in the society, shall act as Vice-president at that meeting; MOREOVER WE WILL, that, when any doctor shall be admitted into the said college, his name shall be registered in a REGISTER-BOOK to be kept for that purpose, and that he shall remain a fellow as long as he shall continue to be rated to the commons and other annual dues of the said college; AND WE do farther, for us, our heirs and successors, hereby give and grant unto the said president and fellows, and their successors, for ever, full power and authority, from time to time, to make, constitute, ordain and establish such and so many reasonable BY-LAWS, rules, orders, ordinances and constitutions, as they, or the greater part of them, being there present, shall judge proper and necessary for the regulation and management of the possessions and revenues of the said college, and the same, from time to time, as they may see occasion, to vary, alter or revoke, and to make such new orders and regulations in their stead, as they shall to the best of their judgments and discretions think most proper and expedient, so as the same be just, honest and reasonable, and no way repugnant or contrary to the laws of this our realm; AND OUR ROYAL WILL AND PLEASURE is, that a majority of the members of the college shall be present at any meeting when business is to be transacted, and that a majority of those present must concur in any act, which shall be binding upon the college. PROVIDED always, that nothing herein contained shall extend or be construed to extend, to affect any rights of the Archbishop of Canterbury, or his officers, or of the judges of the several courts, or any privileges heretofore enjoyed by the society; AND FARTHER WE do hereby give and grant to the president and fellows of the college of doctors of law, exercent in the Ecclesiastical and Admiralty courts, and their successors, that they shall and may, from time to time, nominate and appoint so many and such persons as they shall think proper to be treasurers, secretaries, clerks and officers of the said college, for the carrying on and transacting their necessary affairs. PROVIDED also that, if any abuses or differences shall, at any time hereafter, arise and happen concerning the government or affairs of the said college, whereby the constitution, progress, improvement and business thereof may suffer or be hindered, in such case, we do hereby, for us, our heirs and successors, assign, constitute, authorize and appoint the most reverend the lord Archbishop of Canterbury, the lord Chancellor or lord Keeper of our great seal of Great Britain, the lord Keeper of our privy seal, and our two principal Secretaries of state, for the time being, to be VISITORS of the said college, with full power and authority to them, or any three or more of them, from time to time, to compose and redress any such differences or abuses. And lastly, we do by these presents, for us, our heirs and successors, grant unto the said corporation hereby established, and their successors, that these our letters patent, or the inrolment or exemplification thereof, shall be in, and by all things, good, firm, valid, sufficient and effectual in the law, according to the true intent and meaning thereof; and shall be taken, construed and adjudged in the most favourable and beneficial sense for the best advantage of the said corporation, as well in all our courts of record as elsewhere, by all and singular judges, justices, officers, ministers, and subjects whatsoever, of us, our heirs and successors, any nonrecital, misrecital, or any other omission, imperfection, defect, matter, cause or thing whatsoever to the contrary thereof in any wife notwithstanding. IN WITNESS whereof, we have caused these our letters to be made patent; WITNESS Ourself, at Westminster, the twenty-second day of June, in the eighth year of our Reign.

By writ of privy seal,

COCKS.

BIBLIOGRAPHY

I. MANUSCRIPTS

1. Public Record Office
Long Book (PRO 30/26/8).
Library Account Book (PRO 30/26/9).
State Papers Domestic, Elizabeth I (SP 12/109/39).
Close Roll (C 54/3547).
Lay Subsidy Roll (E 179/252/23).

2. Lambeth Palace Library
Records of Doctors' Commons (DC 1–27).[1]
MSS. 958; 1351; 1560; 2080; 2216; 2976.

3. Law Society
Ducarel's 'Summary Account of the Society of Doctors' Commons'.

4. Guildhall Library
MSS. 263; 1353.

5. British Library
Add. Charter 15,009.
Add. MSS. 24, 102; 25,040; 25,098; 28,843.

6. College of Arms
Hutton's Church Notes.
Processus in Curia Marescalli.

7. Inner Temple Library
MS. Misc. 56.

8. Cambridge, Trinity Hall
MS. Cupboard No. 5, Parcel No. 2.
Deed 28 May 1650.
MS. Miscell. Papers, vol. iv.

[1]For details, see p. 110 *ante*

9. Oxford, Bodleian Library

MS. Tanner 39.

10. Oxford, All Souls College

MS. 325; 353.

11. Sir Anthony Wagner, K.C.V.O., Garter King of Arms
Additions by James Kennerley Hemp to a copy of W. B. Wilson, *A Plea for the Entire Suppression of Patronage.*

II. PRINTED BOOKS AND ARTICLES
(Works of general reference, books mentioned incidentally, and biographical works referred to in Appendices III and IV are not included. Unless otherwise indicated, books are published in London.)

Ackermann, R., *Microcosm of London.* 1808.

Allen, P. S., *Erasmi Epistolae.* 1906.

Anon., *Thomas Hutchinson Tristram; A Memoir.* 1916.

Bateson, M. (ed.), *Grace Book B.* Cambridge, 1903.

Bell, W. G., *The Great Fire of London.* 3rd ed., 1922.

Buc, G., *The Third Vniuersitie of England,* in J. Stow, *Annales,* 1615.

Calendar of Close Rolls. 1892–.

Calendar of Letters and Papers, Foreign and Domestic, Henry VIII. 1864–1932.

Calendar of State Papers, Domestic. 1856–.

Calendar of Wynn (of Gwydir) Papers. Aberystwyth, Cardiff, and London, 1926.

Catalogue of Sale of Library of College of Advocates. 1861.

Catalogue of the Books in the Library of the College of Advocates in Doctors' Commons. 1818.

Chandler, P. W., 'Doctors Commons', *L.T.R.* 15 (1931), 4.

Cheshire and Lancashire Funeral Certificates. Lancashire and Cheshire Record Society, 1882.

Churchill, I. J., *Canterbury Administration.* 1933.

Coote, C., *Sketches of the Lives and Characters of Eminent English Civilians.* 1804.

Davies, J. Conway, *Catalogue of the Manuscripts in the Library of the Inner Temple.* Oxford, 1972.

Davis, E. Jeffries, 'Doctors' Commons, its Title and Topography', *L.T.R.* 15 (1931), 38.

—— 'Doctors' Commons; The Later History of the Property', ibid. 78.

Dickens, A. G., *The English Reformation*. 1964.

Ducarel, A. C., 'Summary Account of Doctors' Commons', *L.T.R.* 15 (1931), 21.

Dugdale, W., *History of St. Paul's Cathedral*. 1716.

Elton, G. R., *The Tudor Constitution*. 1968.

—— *Policy and Police*. Cambridge, 1972.

Firth, C. H., and Rait, R. S., *Acts and Ordinances of the Interregnum 1642–1660*. 1911.

Foster, G. J., *Doctors' Commons: Its Courts and Registries*. 1871.

Godfrey, W. H., 'Church of St. Benet, Paul's Wharf', *L.T.R.* 15 (1931), 35.

Hemp, W. J., 'Coats of Arms from "Doctors' Commons"', *Antiquaries Journal*, 26 (1946), 74.

Holdsworth, W. S., *A History of English Law*, vol. i, 1924.

Inquisitions post mortem for London. British Record Society, xxxvi, 1908.

Irving, D., *An Introduction to the Study of the Civil Law*. 4th ed, 1837.

Jones, P. E. (ed.), *The Fire Court*. 1966.

Law, J. T., *Forms of Ecclesiastical Law*. 1831.

Levack, R. P., *The Civil Lawyers in England 1603–1641*. Oxford, 1973.

London Inhabitants within the Walls 1695. London Record Society, ii, 1966.

McAlpine, W. H., *Catalogue of the Law Library at Hartwell House*. 1865.

McConica, J. K., *English Humanists and Reformation Politics*. Oxford, 1965.

Malden, H. E., *Trinity Hall*. 1902.

Marsen, K. G. (ed.), *Reports of Cases determined in the High Court of Admiralty*. 1885.

Morgan, S., *The Sphere of Gentry*. 1661.

Nys, N., *Le Droit Romain, le Droit des Gens et le Collège des Docteurs en Droit Civil*. Brussels, 1910.

Oswald, A., 'Fulham Palace', *Country Life*, 76 (1939), 193.

Oughton, T., *Ordo Judiciorum*. 1728.

Pickard, E. A., and Davies, E. Jeffries, 'The Rebuilding of Doctors' Commons', *L.T.R.* 15 (1931), 51.

Reddaway, T. F. *The Rebuilding of London after the Great Fire.* 1940.

Registers of St. Benet and St. Peter, Paul's Wharf, London. Harleian Society, 1909, 1912.

Senior, W., *Doctors' Commons and the Old Court of Admiralty.* 1923.

——, 'The Rise of the College of Advocates', *L.Q.R.* 26 (1931), 195.

Simon, J., *Education and Society in Tudor England.* Cambridge, 1966.

Steer, F. W., *Guide to the Church of St. Benet Paul's Wharf.* Chichester, 1970.

Sturge, C., *Cuthbert Tunstall.* 1938.

Stow, J., *Survey of London* (ed. J. Strype), 1720; (ed. C. L. Kingsford), Oxford, 1908.

Sutherland, A. E., *The Law at Harvard.* Cambridge, Mass., 1967.

Warren's Book. Cambridge, 1911.

Wilson, W. B., *ps.* 'Lynx', *A Plea for the Entire Suppression of Patronage.* 1874.

Wren, C., *Parentalia.* 1750.

INDEX

An asterisk (*) indicates a member of Doctors' Commons.